A JOURNEY OF ONE'S OWN

A Journey of One's Own

Uncommon Advice for the Independent Woman Traveler

THALIA ZEPATOS

The Eighth Mountain Press

Portland ✦ Oregon ✦ 1992

Cover art by Maggie Rudy
Cover and book design by Ruth Gundle

Manufactured in the United States of America
This book is printed on acid-free paper.
First edition 1992
10 9 8 7 6 5 4 3 2

LIBRARY OF CONGRESS CATALOGING-IN-PUBLICATION DATA

Zepatos, Thalia, 1955-
    A journey of one's own: uncommon advice for the
independent woman traveler / Thalia Zepatos.
        p.   cm.
    Includes bibliographical references.
    ISBN 0-933377-21-5. — ISBN 0-933377-20-7 (pbk.)
    1. Travel. 2. Women travelers.
G151.Z46   1992
910'.82—dc20   92-28081

THE EIGHTH MOUNTAIN PRESS
624 Southeast Twenty-ninth Avenue
Portland, Oregon 97214
(503) 233-3936

For my parents, Sophia and Spero,
who taught me how to live.

TABLE OF CONTENTS

Chapter IV ➤ Creating Your Own Journey

Chapter V ➤ Lessons of a Traveler

Chapter VI ➤ Safe Passage

Chapter VII ➤ Traveling Smart and Light

Chapter VIII ➤ Extended Travel

INTRODUCTION

Perched on the windswept ruins of a Spanish castle high above the Mediterranean, a teenage foreign-exchange student on my first trip abroad, I vowed to spend my life traveling. I returned to the United States at summer's end and barely left again for over a decade. Oh, I dreamed about traveling. I studied maps. I read travel books. But, like most women, I waited.

Why do we wait to travel? We wait until the time is right, until the car is paid off, until the kids are grown. We wait for someone else to plan the trip and buy the tickets. We wait to feel secure and confident enough to go alone.

One day I decided to stop waiting and start traveling. As a woman, I had frequently challenged the restrictions others had placed on what I could do. While traveling, I challenged the limits I had placed on myself. I got tired of the way my own fears restrained my ideas of where I could go, with whom and how.

My biggest fear was of traveling alone. Confronting and overcoming that fear opened the door to remarkable adventures. I took an eighteen-month trip around the world and found myself fishing off the west coast of India, traveling by camel across the Thar Desert near Pakistan, living in a tribal village in the Golden Triangle, hitchhiking up the Malaysian peninsula, and trekking the high country of Nepal. Traveling changed my view of the world, and my place in it.

Each time I returned from another journey, I was called upon to give advice and encouragement to other women. They were friends, or friends of friends, planning their own trips. Soon I was not just talking on the phone, I was printing lists and giving them away. Unable to keep up with the requests, I organized a series of workshops called "The Independent Woman Traveler." The workshops were a great success, and before long I was encouraged to write this book.

As part of my research, I interviewed women who had traveled to places I haven't yet been and women with life experiences vastly different from my own. On the telephone, via cassette tapes and in kitchens and cafes, we traded tales, laughed at ourselves, and established common ground, in the tradition of travelers (and women) everywhere. Their "travelers' voices" are sprinkled throughout the book, along with stories of my own.

My conversations with women travelers helped crystallize some important themes of this book:

Traveling independently is a state of mind and a state of being. It has to do with taking charge of your own trip, whether you are traveling alone, with a partner or a group.

Women travelers face particular challenges. Sexual harassment, safety and health concerns, internalized fears, and barriers to being accepted as a traveler in many parts of the world are real components of every woman's travel experience.

Women travel differently than most men. Women actively explore the inner as well as the outer landscapes of our journeys—we don't just take in the sights, we are changed by the things we see and the people we meet. And as part of a global sisterhood of women, we have ready-made opportunities for interaction wherever we go.

Perhaps you're hatching a plan for a traveling adventure. Whether you are an armchair traveler itching to get your feet wet or an experienced traveler wanting to make the next trip more meaningful than the last, this book was written for you, with the hope that it will help ease your concerns and nurture your dreams.

Thalia Zepatos

TO THE READER

Full information for all the books mentioned in the text is given in the "resources" section at the end of the book. Addresses are provided for small presses that may be difficult to locate. Your local bookstore should be able to order any of the books that are in print. For those that are not, check with used-book stores and your public library.

Full contact information for organizations is given in the text and is listed again in the "resources" section for your convenience.

We'd be delighted to receive recommendations for subsequent editions of this book.

I

---

*Traveling Alone
or with Others?*

The Benefits of Traveling Alone

If you've been waiting to find the right person to go along on your trip, look in the mirror and then get out your passport. By traveling alone, you can follow your heart and move in your own rhythms without compromising your plan, your goals, your schedule, your budget, or style of travel.

Here's how Kathleen Serrell describes her decision to travel solo to Japan: "My friends always said, 'The tour was wonderful. Next time I'd like to go by myself.' So, I decided my first trip would be like their next trip."

You Will Meet More People

Kathleen traveled steerage in a boat across the Japan Sea. "I sat on a small raised platform amongst a crowd of people. A young man started practicing his English, an older man joined in, as did a group of blind Japanese children. We passed my dictionary back and forth to keep the conversation going. When the young man didn't know the name of his hobby in English, he looked it up and told me he loved fencing! That dictionary was a better companion than a friend."

Traveling alone multiplies the possibilities of meeting people everywhere you go as you discard the protective shell of common language, culture, and experience that surrounds you when traveling with a companion.

"I think that I was a better focus for conversation because I was alone," Kathleen continued. "They were willing to tackle conversation with one stranger, but maybe they wouldn't have tried with two."

You'll experience an accelerated transition into different cultures and absorb new languages more rapidly while traveling solo. You'll receive invitations from local people who are much more likely to find room for one more. By forfeiting the support of a single companion, you open yourself up to the support of the whole world.

You Can Be Flexible

An unexpected festival, an extra seat on an excursion boat offered at half price, a town so inviting you decide to hop off the train and explore it—you'll enjoy being able to change your plans without discussion.

As a solo traveler, you have the flexibility to join other travelers who are going your way. As long as your interests and plans converge, you travel together. When your spirit leads you in a different direction, it's easy to say good-bye.

You Will Discover New Strengths in Yourself

Traveling alone lets you gain confidence in new situations. You can be as cautious or adventurous as you like. Women who hesitated for years before traveling solo have an almost universal response during their first unaccompanied trip—"Why did I wait so long to do this?"

Almost everyone is hesitant at first. No matter how many times I've traveled alone, I am tweaked with uncertainty before a new trip. But each time I push myself forward, I find my faith well rewarded. Whether you are actively planning a solo trip for next month or musing about the possibility for next year, see Chapter II for specific strategies to help you rise to the challenges.

Partner Travel—Is Your Trip Negotiable?

Perhaps you just don't want to travel alone.

Instead, you convince your friend or lover to join you on that long-awaited trip or seek out someone who has been looking for a travel partner like you. Let's say the two of you agree to tour Europe together next July. Now you sit back on the park bench where you've been talking, each gazing into the distance as you dream of your upcoming trip.

For your friend, the route is clear. She's been planning this journey for years. Finally, she has the time, the money, and someone to travel with.

> *We'll fly directly to London, of course, attend the theater each night, and visit the British Museum and the art galleries by day. Then, take the boat-train to Paris— the Louvre! Notre Dame! the Eiffel Tower! A side trip to Versailles. See Switzerland by train, with a day or two for hiking in the Alps. Then on to Italy! First stop Milan, to see Leonardo's* Last Supper, *then to Florence and Michelangelo's* David. *A day trip to Venice is de rigueur. Ride the train to Rome—so much to see! Spend a morning in Pompeii. On to Brindisi, and the ferry crossing to Greece. Gee, there won't be much time to spend on the islands, just a day or two on the beach before heading to Athens and the Archaeological Museum, the Parthenon, and the flight home.*

Meanwhile, your own plan takes a different form. Southern Europe is the place to escape the midsummer heat—that crystal clear, blue-green Mediterranean....

Let's fly to Rome and get out of the city as quickly as
possible. We'll travel south along the Italian seacoast,
stopping at little towns along the way. Spend long days
at the beach, evenings in the cafes, talking to the locals.
Work our way down to the ferry at Brindisi, and then on
to the Greek islands...Crete, Santorini, Mykonos...
several days on each, returning to Athens just in time to
catch the flight home. A restful vacation away from the
big cities.

Clearly, you each have very different visions for that same "month in Europe." Both bring you into contact with European cultures but in contrasting ways. Neither travel style is right or wrong; each simply reflects divergent interests and will produce different experiences.

Your first reaction may be to start crafting a third itinerary, a compromise plan that combines elements from both your visions.

But should you do it? Is your trip negotiable? Only you can decide. Take the time to explore thoroughly the pros and cons of traveling with a partner. This major decision will affect every aspect of your trip.

Four Good Reasons to Travel with a Partner

Togetherness

The best reason to travel with someone else is a true desire to spend time with her or him. Whether it be your life partner, an old friend, or a new intrigue, joint travel will afford you plenty of time to be together.

Hoping to rebuild a shaky relationship while on vacation? Choose a low-stress travel plan. Removing someone from his or her comfort zone, even on holiday, can create tension. Make sure you are emotionally prepared to deal with problems, or take steps to minimize the strain of difficult traveling.

Economy

Many women seek a travel partner in order to save money. Solo travelers may be burdened with paying the same price as two for a room (the infamous "single supplement"). Since lodging is the primary source of the price differential, research the cost of rooms at your proposed destination. Low-cost lodging in less-developed countries, for example, makes the potential savings less of an issue there.

Safety

Some trips are better pursued with a compatriot. Don't join an all-male sailing crew alone, even if you have to pass up free passage to Tahiti. Most trekking and back-country travel, especially in countries with political turmoil, should be undertaken by two or more travelers. (It is possible to meet travel partners along the way, however, to share those offbeat adventures.)

Comfort

Patriarchal religious and cultural attitudes, as expressed in some countries and regions, can set the stage for constant difficulties for women travelers. Although women do travel solo through countries such as Morocco and Turkey, teaming up with a travel partner can help you cope with intense sexual harassment and will lessen the strain.

There are real advantages to partner travel—it's fun to share new experiences with someone else. Foreign situations can be less intimidating with a friend from home right beside you. Logistics are simplified when handled as a team—one person can watch the luggage while the other buys the tickets.

Traveling with the right partner—someone who shares your interests, pace, itinerary, and budget—can be a delight. A mismatched travel partner, on the other hand, can be more irritating than a blister from your new walking shoes.

A Couple of Not-So-Good Reasons to
Travel with a Partner

Fear of Going Alone

Don't let fear send you on someone else's trip instead of your own. For the added safety and companionship of having another person along, many women trade away independence and self-determination. If your travel goals are non-negotiable, don't set yourself up for disappointment by compromising them away.

We each have our own concept of an "interesting" or "relaxing" trip; sometimes these ideas just don't match with those of a cherished friend or beloved partner. Overcoming your fear of traveling alone may be an exhilarating alternative to constant negotiations which can turn a trip into one long meeting.

Pleasing Someone Else

Desire to please a friend or partner can put you on shaky travel terrain. One woman's sense of adventure can be another's recipe for torture. Do you *really* want to paddle down the Amazon, fighting off leeches and avoiding crocodiles? If the trip seems a bit daunting, you may appreciate some gentle encouragement. But if the idea is truly distasteful, don't get talked into it by yourself or anyone else.

An Element of Risk

Taking a trip with someone you've never traveled with is a gamble. You don't really know how they will react to strange people and situations or how you will react to each other. Even if you've shared some fun times together, you can't anticipate what might happen under the inevitable stress of travel.

A funny quirk of a friend at home can become a source of frustration when traveling. Sure, the way Henrietta vaults to her seat the moment before the movie starts is comical, but when traveling together her constant tardiness can cause *you* to nearly miss every train, plane, or bus connection, too.

"People who are very flexible, and who can handle covering for each other, make good travel partners," says Martha Banyas, who travels for several months each year, both alone and with others. "But some people who seem open and flexible get very rigid when under stress. Someone may seem willing to compromise a lot to get the travel partner; but once on the trip, they find out what is really important to them."

Before you agree to travel with another person, be clear about your own goals for the trip. Martha advises, "You need to talk in depth before you leave, interview each other, discuss as many aspects of the trip as you can possibly think of. People travel for radically different reasons. You've got to be very honest about what you really want, and not just say what the other person wants to hear. If it seems like it's not going to work out, you both have to let go of the idea of traveling together—you should agree at the beginning of the discussions that either of you can call it off without any hard feelings."

Use the questionnaire that follows to clarify your travel goals, or copy it for potential travel partners as a prelude to conversation. Take a short trip to try out your traveling partnership. And seriously explore your options for traveling alone.

If you and your partner already have a joint travel plan, the questionnaire can help you identify problems and concerns of traveling together.

Travel Questionnaire
(What do you really want out of this trip?)

For potential travel partners—use the questionnaire as an outline for a joint discussion, or photocopy it and complete it individually before comparing responses.

For solo travelers—use the questionnaire to help plan your journey. (Skip those marked with a ❖, which relate only to partner travel.)

PURPOSE

◆ Why are you going on this trip?

◆ What do you hope to get out of it?

SCHEDULE

◆ How much time do you have to travel? When?

◆ Is this time frame flexible or not?

BUDGET

◆ How much money do you have for the trip?

◆ What is your projected weekly budget?

◆ Do you have access to more money if you overspend?

ITINERARY AND PLAN

◆ Draft an itinerary for your trip with an estimate of time you'd like to spend in each place. Is this itinerary flexible or fixed?

◆ What activities do you want to pursue in each place you plan to visit?

◆ What's your idea of a good time?

◆ What tourist/travel activities do you least enjoy?

◆ What's your idea of a bad time?

❖ When traveling with another person, how much time do you imagine spending together?

   —Basically all the time together, with few exceptions.

   —Eating meals together, but planning separate activities.

   —Sharing the same itinerary and rooms, but otherwise being independent.

   —Separating occasionally for several days.

❖ Would you accept an invitation (for a two-day sailing trip, for example) if it meant leaving your travel partner behind?

◆ Are you open to the possibility of a romantic involvement during the trip?

◆ Are you open to spontaneously changing your itinerary?

TRAVEL STYLE

◆ Do you have usable language skills for the places you'll be?

❖ Are you comfortable traveling with someone with much greater/ fewer language skills than yours?

◆ What type of accommodations do you imagine staying in most frequently?

> —Luxury hotels with full comforts and services.

> —Moderately priced accommodations with private bathrooms and hot water.

> —Budget accommodations with common bathroom facilities that may lack hot water.

> —Youth hostels.

> —Camping out and carrying your own gear.

❖ Would you share a sleeping room with your travel partner? A bed?

◆ Is it important for you to have reservations booked in advance?

◆ Do you like to "shop around" for restaurants, accommodations, and purchases or would you rather accept the first reasonable option?

◆ Where do you feel most comfortable eating most of your meals?

> —Restaurants located in hotels that cater to foreigners.

> —Restaurants listed in the guidebook with menus written in English.

> —"Out of the way" places frequented by local residents.

> —Inexpensive street-side food vendors.

◆ Are you opposed to or unable to eat any foods? How do you feel about smoking? Drinking?

◆ How adventurous are you about eating? Would you eat an exotic dish if you had no idea what it was?

◆ In a country where bargaining is traditional, do you feel comfortable bargaining for purchases?

◆ Will you need to be in contact with family, job, or friends back home? How often?

PACE AND ROUTINES

◆ What time do you usually wake up in the morning? What time do you go to sleep? How will that change during your trip?

◆ How much daily activity do you anticipate on the trip? Do you like to keep very busy? Do you have any physical limitations that affect your level of activity? Do you need time for a daily siesta?

◆ How quickly do you like to get going in the morning? Do you have a regular exercise or other routine that you follow daily?

❖ Are you a morning or a night person?

◆ Do you find it boring to stay in one place for a long time? Do you find it tiresome to move quickly from place to place without a long stop?

❖ Can you adapt to a travel pace very different from your own?

◆ How long can you walk comfortably? In hot weather?

◆ Do you plan to use mass transit? In what circumstances?

◆ Would you consider renting a car?

❖ Who would drive?

Group Travel

If you enjoy sharing travel experiences with others and don't feel up to planning a trip and traveling on your own, then you should consider group travel. A good tour or adventure travel group will combine the best elements of solo and group travel.

Tour group arrangements have developed far beyond herding forty people into a bus. You can pamper yourself or challenge your limits by selecting the appropriate travel company. Travel styles range from allowing a fair amount of independence to maintaining a busy group schedule.

Women travelers often feel safer in groups. Whether your destination is a large South American city or the summit of Mt. Fuji, it can be wise to travel with a tour operator who knows the local hazards and is prepared to deal with them.

If you have just two or three weeks to travel and want to maximize your activities during that time, you may want to use a travel company that has done the research, can smooth the bumps, and avoid frustrating delays. It would be difficult to set off in a fully loaded kayak just hours after arriving at an airport in Belize if you had to rent the equipment, shop for provisions, get a map, and plan an itinerary on your own.

Even experienced solo travelers find it a relief to relinquish decision-making and problem-solving to the pros. You can take part in group decisions while being assured that the program will move smoothly because someone else is handling the details.

Countries like Tanzania and China gear tourist activities and accommodations towards groups. In those countries, traveling as an individual can feel like swimming upstream, with days consumed by ticket lines and permit applications. Myanmar and Tibet are two places that prohibit travel by individuals; you *must* visit as part of a group.

Choosing the Right Group for You

There are, literally, thousands of tour operators offering myriad travel options. And each company is different—every European tour, photographic safari and white-water rafting trip is unique, reflecting the style of the tour operator.

Research widely, and be prepared to ask lots of questions to find the right group for you. Your list of questions should include:

Does the company itself run the trip? Who are your guides?

Many Western-based companies simply contract with locally based operators to carry out the trip; this can be difficult to ascertain from the company's brochure. Ask if the company is sending their own representative along with the tour group. If they maintain control of the trip, they can more easily deliver what they have promised. If not, they may be selling a faraway product or service that they really don't know much about.

How big is the group?

What is the minimum and maximum size of the group? An ideal size for adventure travel is twelve; urban-based tours may comfortably fit more.

What's the typical pace for the day?

Will you have any alone time? Will you be able to explore on your own as well as with the group? Does the itinerary include daily moves to a new location or do you have some layovers? Most tour companies arrange at least two nights in one place to prevent exhaustion of participants.

What opportunities will you have to really connect with the local people, in a noncontrived way?

Local guides and interpreters, if hired to work alongside their staff, can help facilitate these contacts.

How long have they been operating tours in the area?

A company with three or more years of experience should be able to anticipate most problems and deliver a comfortable trip. A first-time tour should be considered an "exploratory" trip, with clients and guides both prepared for unexpected developments.

What exactly is included in the price of the trip? What isn't?

Costs of meals and side trips vary from company to company; be specific in your questions.

What type of accommodations do they arrange? Where will meals be eaten?

You'll maximize local contacts by staying in locally owned guest houses or lodges. If you're hoping for a lot of amenities, you may prefer large hotels.

Do they have contingency plans designed to handle health and other emergencies?

What are they?

What do their own clients have to say about the trips?

Ask for references; get the name and telephone number of someone in your area who has been on one of their trips and give them a call.

Tours for Women

A growing roster of travel companies offers tours exclusively for women. Participants cite varied reasons for choosing these trips. Many women enjoy the special camaraderie that develops on an all-women trip. And there is welcome relief from the gender-based roles both men and women tend to fall into in a mixed group. (Who's going to steer the boat?) As women, we often feel more comfortable trying out a new skill in the supportive environment of other women. This is especially true of outdoor, adventure-based travel.

In-Country Tours

Flexible decision-making and bargain opportunities await travelers who arrange for tours after they've already arrived in a country. The questions listed above also apply to in-country tours. In addition, you have the ability to inquire about, or even inspect, vehicles that will be used for the tours. Are the vehicles in good condition? Will a qualified mechanic accompany the tour? You may be able to find out more specific information about the other participants on the tour; you will often find a more international mix of travelers on in-country tours.

II

Going Solo

Trying On Solo Travel for Size

When planning my trip to Asia, I was thrilled when a friend and co-worker, Mary Heffernan, agreed to join me. We decided to travel together for three months. After that, she planned to go trekking in Nepal and I would continue alone or return home.

By the end of the second month of our journey, I was certain that I wanted to continue traveling. I was just beginning to unravel the complex wrappings of Southeast Asian religion, culture, and language, and my simple travel style kept my spending well under budget. It made sense for me to go on alone. Yet the idea truly frightened me.

I wondered if I would be safe by myself. Would days or weeks pass without my finding a friend to talk to? Could I not only manage, but actually enjoy, solitary travel? During the final weeks of my travel with Mary I decided to test the feel of solo travel, to try it on for size and see how I fared.

Experiment with these suggestions on a short journey close to home, or keep them in mind for that big trip you've been planning for so long.

One-Half Day to One-Day Solos

When traveling with a friend, it's easy to develop the "we-we" habit:

"What are we going to do today?"

"Where are we going to eat lunch?"

"When are we going back to the hotel?"

Whether planned or not, you can easily spend all your time together, making all decisions jointly. Instead, try spending part of the day alone. If having a specific plan will make you more comfortable, create an itinerary for yourself for the day. Otherwise, grab a map and wander the streets, markets, or shops. Be open to opportunities to meet people. Set a goal of having conversations with two or three strangers, starting with the person next to you on the park bench. If you feel comfortable, invite them to join you for coffee or tea. That evening, meet your travel partner for dinner, and compare notes on the day's developments.

Parallel Travel

When traveling with a partner, use the transition to another city or town as a trial at going solo. Make the trip separately, a day apart from your friend. (If that's too intimidating, just sit in separate sections of the train or bus, as if you don't know each other.)

Parallel travel gives each of you the experience of booking a train or bus ticket (perhaps without a working knowledge of the language), making the trip and finding a place to stay independently. Make a firm plan to meet at a specific time at a known location—a large hotel mentioned in the guidebooks, the main church or cathedral, or in front of the main post office.

Have a contingency plan. In case of delays, the first person there should check back at that same spot every two hours (as previously arranged) or could leave a note at *poste restante* (general delivery at the post office), a hotel desk, or the American Express office, if there is one.

Three-Day to Five-Day Side Trips

When you and your partner's interests diverge, give yourselves permission to take separate side trips. Make a date to meet back at a (temporary) "home city."

For example, you are both in Florence, Italy. She is just dying to see Venice. Yet, the idea of one more cathedral or another tourist-filled piazza is simply more than you can stand. You're ready to escape to the wine country of Tuscany for a few days. Indulge your whims by organizing separate side trips.

Establish a home base: a hotel, pensione, or friends' house where you can leave messages if necessary. (Store some of that excess luggage there, too.) Agree on a reunion date, place, and time, and *stick to it*.

Then you're off! No matter how well you get along with your travel pal, you will find it refreshing to be on your own. You might welcome a change of pace, without that slowpoke or speed queen to cramp your style. Here's a chance to find your own rhythm and do just what you want for a few days.

No matter what adventures present themselves, don't stray from meeting your travel partner at your agreed-upon time and place. While you may think a few hours' detour impossible to pass up, your partner won't appreciate a worrisome delay.

Start Out Together, Separate Later On

Start out a lengthy trip with a friend, especially to places that seem intimidating.

When planning that journey to Southeast Asia and China, I simply couldn't imagine what it would be like there—buying food, finding lodging, making my way in a totally different culture and language. Mary and I learned a lot while traveling together.

By the time we separated, I had the experience and the confidence to go on alone. I knew how to buy a second-class train ticket, how much it would cost, and what kind of food to pack for the train ride. I had seen enough small guest houses to be able to judge quickly where I would or wouldn't stay.

I decided to keep going, all the way around the world. Sure, I was scared. But experimenting with solo travel helped me push my limits. I got accustomed to doing things that, at first, seemed difficult. And you can, too.

As you keep stretching your realm of comfort, your definition of what you're used to doing will continually expand.

One of the best things I ever did was to travel solo for fifteen months. Traveling alone, I had no choice but to be open to the people around me. There's nobody else—there's no safety net in terms of relationship. To have human contact, you have to make it. Traveling alone led to very intense personal experiences with people all over; I'm sure they wouldn't have been the same with someone else along.

Of course, being alone is all relative; you're never really alone. There are travelers moving across the earth everywhere. I connected with other travelers of many other nationalities for two days, two weeks, five days— however long our directions or desires to stay with one another seemed to match. Then we went our separate ways. The quality of those friendships was rare, and the information I got from those contacts was crucial.

For three months I bicycled across Europe. I had the hardest time traveling alone in Italy. I was harassed constantly. There and in Germany some difficult things happened, but I expected some difficult things to happen if I was going to travel for over a year by myself. I never considered stopping.

In Greece the harassment was different—it felt playful. Guys would go by on the street and say "I want to kees your face." If you'd kind of kid back, they'd laugh and you'd laugh, and it felt less dangerous. They seemed to feel, "I'll give it a try, and if it doesn't work, that's okay."

One night in Greece I was walking home in Patras, after eating dinner. I heard people singing in the street. It was dark, and I followed them, listening to their singing. When they'd stop, I'd kind of hide in a doorway until they went on. They figured out that I was following, and they turned around and invited me to go home with them. There were ten men and me all sitting in the kitchen. I listened to them sing, and we talked until two or three in the morning. I had been on the road for five months at that point, so I wasn't nearly as afraid as I had been in the beginning, when I might not have joined them.

I traveled in Iran and Turkey and had absolutely no trouble. It's fine for women to travel alone in Kenya, Tanzania, and Malawi. In places where tourism is very important economically, there's a sense that the penalty will be high if someone bothers a tourist.

One time I was trying to fly out of Calcutta to Burma. The day I was leaving India, there was a huge transportation strike. No mode of transportation moved. So I spent about three days in the Calcutta airport with hundreds of people from all over. We shared the food that was in the airport restaurants and talked and talked. I never did get to Burma, but I made friends with a Malaysian family. So I ended up going to Malaysia and living with them for a couple of weeks. I didn't know anything about Malaysia, I hadn't planned on going there, but I had a wonderful time, and we became good friends. I'm not sure that that would have happened had someone else been traveling with me.

Loneliness

What do you do when you're feeling lonely? Pick up the phone and call a friend? Drop by a local cafe where you're sure to know someone? When I'm low, I find comfort in friends and familiar places. Taking myself thousands of miles from hometown sources of support was one of the most intimidating aspects of solo travel for me.

My eighteen–month trip around the world marked, for me, the transition from being in a long-term relationship to being single once again. That trip was a way to regain my equilibrium. It allowed me to explore how it felt to be on my own and to discover that, yes, I *could* make it. For months at a time, I traveled completely alone.

It was challenging to spend much more time alone than I was accustomed to, but I learned to relax and enjoy my solitude. I learned to be happy by myself, with myself. If you already feel this way, you will not be afraid as a solo traveler. If you feel anxious when alone in new situations, then you can look forward to finding a heightened sense of comfort and self-confidence that unaccompanied travel can bring.

I met many other travelers experiencing transition in their lives. Taking a purposeful break from their career, their hometown, life as it was, they'd hoisted themselves into different circumstances in order to reflect on the life and identity they'd left behind. Don't worry, you won't be the only one out there by yourself.

Unpack

The only constant in travel is change, and constant change can be disconcerting. Whether you are staying a night or a month, make yourself at home in each place of lodging. Unpack a few things, and set up your room; set out some photos on the dresser, light a candle or burn incense, buy flowers—anything that helps make your room a temporary home.

Follow Routines

Establish a morning or evening routine. Carrying the same habits to different places can bring welcome consistency to an otherwise unstructured life. Stretch or do yoga upon arising, listen to a favorite cassette tape before bed, take an evening stroll, or write in your journal. Drink a leisurely cup of coffee each morning, make a daily trip to the market in the afternoons. Work on handicrafts, such as knitting or embroidery. Rituals engender feelings of comfort and safety.

Set Up a Home Base

No matter where you go or how long you plan to stay, create a temporary home base for yourself. Find a local, family-run restaurant or cafe, and start each morning there, or eat dinner there every night. After a short while, the proprietors will come to expect you. If you skip one day, they'll ask where you were. Solicit their advice on where to go in the area and how to get there. Get to know their kids, and let them get to know you.

There's nothing like being greeted as a "regular" in a place 3,000 miles from home. There's a certain reassurance in having your coffee served the way you like it. On a lengthy trip it can be tiresome to eat every meal at a different restaurant and a real relief to find someplace that feels a little bit like home.

In Bangkok I frequented a small seafood restaurant on Khao San Road on a daily basis. The family lived in the back room, with a newborn baby passed from hand to hand. After a few days, I took my turn with the baby, like everyone else. For a week they became my substitute family; they cared what happened to me, and I cared about them.

Ease into Eating Alone

Many travelers find eating alone to be the most difficult and uncomfortable aspect of solo travel. If you're away from your home base, ease the situation by:

•Seeking out other unaccompanied diners. Some informal eating places have common tables or a row of stools for solo diners.

•Bringing a book to read and luxuriating at a table all to yourself. Or using your guidebook or map to plan the next part of your trip.

•Contemplating the day's events by writing them in your journal.

•Sharing your dinner with faraway friends by writing letters. Start the letters with mouth-watering descriptions of the exotic food set before you.

You can avoid restaurant meals by purchasing groceries for a picnic lunch. Or visit marketplaces at mealtimes, where you'll find the local version of fast-food restaurants.

Join Other Travelers

It's surprisingly easy to link up with other travelers for short- or long-term companionship. An intriguing network of travelers' meeting places is located at beach or mountain resorts. Any place glowingly mentioned in the guidebooks will be frequented by travelers using that guidebook. Beaches in Mexico, Central America, Southern Europe, and Asia are crowded with travelers in groups, pairs, and going solo.

Traveler Mary Zinkin observes, "Traveling alone is an oxymoron, because you're really never alone." You're likely to find yourself joining two Australians, someone from Holland, and a Swede for dinner. You'll find so many other single travelers willing to team up temporarily that you'll really have to persist if you want to travel alone. When you are feeling the need for companionship, head to one of these spots, and locate a travel partner going your way.

Just Let Yourself Feel Lonely

Instead of seeking to escape feeling lonely, try experiencing it. Note your feelings, and get used to them. It's really not so bad, and it probably won't get worse. Then you won't have to fear it any more. Remember, you've probably felt lonely at home, too, among your family, friends, and possessions.

Keep a Journal

A bookcase in Kathleen Serrell's house holds a dozen or more of her travel journals. She holds the journal from her recent trip to Japan as she explains how they evolved. "I started out with bound books and then switched to these small three-ring binders. I leave the heavy binder at home and take the prepunched notebook pages with me, along with a pair of scissors and some glue. I usually punch holes in a map and insert it as my opening page. I fill up blank pages with notes, glue in mementos, tour itineraries, photos of people I've met. I buy postcards, make notes on the back, and mark the places where I will punch holes and insert them into the binder. I write notes and advice for others who may be traveling there next."

No matter what format you choose, journal-keeping allows a more active relationship with your inner self. I've used my travel journal as a portable support system, as a repository of lists, and as a place to record notes for memoirs.

On Keeping a Journal

My friend Sarah gave me my first journal, a hardbound book of blank pages with a linen cover the color of a supermarket paper bag. It creaked each time I opened it; its vacant whiteness stared back at me. What to write? How to start? I packed it, still blank, into my suitcase, and approached it again a few days after my arrival in Hong Kong. Twelve days into the trip, I rallied the courage to write neatly on the first page:

> *This is to be a journal of my travels. In it, I will record both the inner and outer journeys of my life over the coming months.*

That journal became my traveling companion and confidante. I learned that one way to handle difficult moments is to record them.

Crossing China by train:
> *Tried to book a hard sleeper (second class as it was called before the Revolution removed the class system even from trains) and ended up in a hard seat. The overhead luggage racks are piled with every imaginable type of box, bundle, and bag. I'd never seen a train so crowded as when we pulled out of Xi'an—since then, we've made a half-dozen local stops, with more people crushing on each time! The aisle is now a solid mass of bodies crunched together, reading newspapers over each other's shoulders. Passengers periodically climb their way over the huddled bodies with a metal cup or pot in hand to fill with tea water from a samovar at the end of the car. They come yelling back down the aisle, I guess warning others not to move lest they get doused with boiling water. It's incredibly hot, yet people keep their Mao jackets on over one or two undershirts. Every single*

*fan is broken. Windows are controlled by those sitting
beside them, who firmly keep them shut. People smoke
cigarettes incessantly. Luckily I have a cold; it keeps the
smoke from making me sneeze. Well, five hours down,
seventeen more to go. Hope I can survive. What happens
when I have to go to the bathroom? There are four people
camped out in there.*

Observations recounted only in conversation are blown away by
the wind, but those you capture in your journal remain a permanent
record of a unique moment in time.

Camel trekking in the Rajasthani desert:

*I've learned to steer Rupa, the camel, and to keep from
being thrown when we get up or down—the hardest
part! Our first night's camp was spectacular, a twinkling
of cookfires among the dunes. Our camels slept circled
around us, wagon-train style, protection from wild dogs
that roam the night desert. I slept soundly, waking only
for brief moments of wide-eyed observation. The stars
were throbbing gobs of light in a velvet sky; the desert
wind whistled a tune through brush and cactus. Just
before dawn, I spotted a camel standing sentinel beside
the camp, silhouetted by the first light of the eastern sky.*

There are no rules in journal writing. Don't feel obligated to make
daily entries, although the practice may become a comforting daily
ritual. Write in it while eating alone or sitting in the park, on a train,
plane, or oxcart—whenever and wherever you have something to
write.

A journal can be more than a record of sights and events. Transcribe
memorable quotes from books or from people you meet.

*But if you travel far enough, one day you will recognize
yourself coming down the road to meet yourself. And you
will say—YES.*

Marion Woodman[1]

Make lists:

What I took trekking in Nepal:

1 pr. heavy cotton pants
1 pr. wool pants
2 pr. wool socks, 2 pr. cotton
1 pr. tights
1 flannel shirt
1 wool sweater
1 thermal undershirt
1 rented down jacket
1 rented sleeping bag
1 pr. running shoes
1 pr. flip-flops
medicines, pocket knife

What else I wish I had taken:

family photos and postcards
a skirt
my sarong
more cotton socks

Record recipes to recreate at home:

Doña Tito's Chile Rellenos

1. Buy 10-12 green chile peppers. Burn on a gas flame till skin is blackened and wrinkled. Put chiles in a plastic bag; close tightly for 10 minutes. Remove and peel.
2. Stuff chiles with crumbly white Mexican cheese, and sausage if desired.
3. Separate 4 eggs; beat whites until stiff, fold in yolks.
4. Put a handful of flour in a small bowl, and mix a teaspoon of flour into the egg-white mixture. Sprinkle flour on outside of each chile (it doesn't have to be completely covered).
5. Heat 1/2 inch oil in a skillet; coat each chile with the egg mixture, slide into pan and bathe with oil.

As you leave a town, list the people you met and what you did there. Map the locations of favorite places to eat, stay, rent bicycles, go fishing. Jot down new vocabulary words learned. These details may loom large in the moment, but will fade quickly with time.

Playa El Sesteo:

Very small, very quiet beach town north of San Blas.

Hotel El Sesteo—only place to stay in town, very basic: cold water, broken sink, 25,000 pesos/night; ocean view from 2nd floor.

Santiago works there; likes to be entertained by guests (and we were the only guests!)

Three palapa *restaurants on beach, all have same food:* shrimp empanadas *(800/each) and* pescado dorado *(22,000/kilo).*

We made friends with Silvia and her brother Manuel; send them a photo.

Good starting place for day trip to Mezcaltitan, Aztec-style island with canals instead of streets. Multi-generations crowded into houses—no place to grow.

Take ferry from La Batanga (5,000 RT per person); lots of herons there.

Neat hotel on Mezcaltitan; we didn't know about it and didn't bring overnight stuff; a great place to stay for a few days.

Make your traveler's journal into a scrapbook. Affix a postage stamp to the top of a page, or use a glue stick for ticket stubs, fallen leaves, matchbook covers, or dried flowers. Use your pocketknife, or an artist's X-acto knife, to make collages from gathered mementos. Draw pictures with colored pencils.

A journal can be a private venue to explore issues—a place to examine pain, express fears and hopes, and negotiate with yourself a new way of being in the world. My travel journals of 1985 to 1986 chronicle a trembling inner journey— my struggle to regain equilibrium after a divorce.

May 1985

I've looked forward to this trip for a long time. In some ways, it's what I have wanted to do my whole life. And, after the crushing pain of my divorce from Kevin, this trip has become a way for me to regain control of my life, to move into the future.

October 1985

It all comes down to "What do I want?" The whole world is open to me now, it's up to me to decide my next move. Maybe it's still a new experience for me to decide what I want—me, myself, I, and no one else. It is scary to think of going to India alone, but I must do it. Life is full of excitement, the world full of wonder.

December 1985

I have walked through the fear I had about being alone to find myself safe and whole on the other side. I've realized a lot of things about that fear. It took me on a road away from other people. But I had to travel that road alone in order to find out that I could make it. And that is a good feeling.

May 1986

My thirtieth year has ended. An entire year spent traveling. And I've come a long, long way. Physically traversed thousands of miles, walking, hiking, traveling by train, bus, bicycle, donkey, and horse cart, boat, truck, you name it. Emotionally, I've passed many milestones. Giving up the pain of the past, learning how to be happy by myself. Sharing a lot of myself with other people, many of whom can't imagine the life I left behind. Making mistakes and suffering the consequences. Getting sick and taking care to get well. Circling the globe, just me and my backpack. Now only one question remains. How will I know when it's time to go home?

It took over a year for me to fill that first journal, words gushing out in barely legible script to chronicle my life and lessons as a traveler. Now, it sits mutely at the back of a file cabinet, its corners rounded from wear, the binding broken, white webbing visible at the spine. Keepsakes are tucked inside the covers—a sticker proclaiming, "Nepal, the top of the world"; an unsmiling portrait of Halinka from Warsaw; a Greek museum entrance ticket, detailing a thirteenth century woman's head *en fresco*; feathers gathered from the streets of Pushkar, India, where wild peacocks roamed.

Other wonder-filled journals have accompanied me since then—a red composition notebook with blue-grid-lined pages purchased in Holland and a large flat ledger bound in green leather. They work better, these other journals. They lie flat, with wide pages that are easier to write on. But none compares to that original brown journal, my first.

IN THE LADIES' COMPARTMENT

A mango moon ripened as the day's heat drifted into the South Indian night. I fidgeted on the noisy train platform at Ernakulum Junction, alongside the north-bound express that was to carry me on the overnight journey up the west coast of the subcontinent to Bombay. Under the watchful eyes of a six-year-old vendor, I drained the last of the *chai*, the pungent cardamom-spiced tea that punctuates the Indian day at regular intervals, and returned the glass to his waiting hands.

The platform buzzed with now-familiar railway station life. Indian travelers lugging parcels of all shapes and sizes picked their way between sleeping figures huddled under shawls. Wealthier travelers paraded before their hired coolies, who calmly balanced metal suitcases and trunks on their red turbans as they followed in single file. Men and women lined up at water stands, washing away the heat and dust of the day. *Chai* and coffee *wallahs* bellowed their wares, each toting a huge aluminum kettle in one hand, a bucket of repeatedly rinsed glasses in the other. Food vendors chanted their way alongside the train, exchanging fruit and chili-laced snacks for one- and two-rupee notes pushed between the metal bars that crossed each window of the ancient train cars.

I'd traveled over 5,000 kilometers by train during six months of wandering India. The second-class trains were always hot, the seats often crowded, the air dusty. Riding down the east coast and up the west, I bounced babies in my lap, practiced new words in Telegu, Malayalam, and Kokkani, and traded fruit for homemade meals. Tiny villages ringed by rice paddies and banana plantations passed outside the window in an unending panorama of rural Indian life.

Trains in the south provided an unusual treat—a small "ladies' compartment" at the end of each car, designed to carry six or eight women traveling without the protection of a male. They seemed unneeded for these strong Indian women who dealt matter-of-factly with numbing adversity. I was thankful, however, that the Indian Railway system had provided me an exclusive place to meet Indian women without hovering husbands, fathers, and brothers edging in to control the conversation. My previous journeys in the "ladies' compartments" had been the scene of some of my most delightful and instructive encounters.

On one twelve-hour ride across the shimmering heat of the Thar desert to the fortress city of Jaiselmeer, I was surrounded by fierce looking, bejeweled, Rajasthani women. They frankly reviewed my foreign looks and dress, their black eyes wandering slowly from my wavy brown hair to my ringless toes.

I returned the interest, pointing to their red and blue patterned skirts and the scores of ivory bracelets that climbed past their elbows and under the sleeves of their tight-fitting bodices. With shy smiles, they admired my silver ankle bracelets and, one by one, displayed theirs. They removed their necklaces and earrings with girlish giggles and adorned me like a doll. Riotous laughter met my polite refusal of a tattooed matron's offer to pierce my nose. Heads shook with approval as a young woman with high cheekbones and a lustrous smile combed and oiled my hair. As we approached Jaiselmeer, we scrambled to return jewelry and sandals to their owners.

Days later as I wandered through the walled town, these same women drew me into their houses, painting elaborate designs on my palms and feet with henna that lasted for weeks.

A shrill whistle from the steam locomotive jolted me and urged me inside for the long trip to Bombay. This "ladies' compartment" was crowded, with eight or nine women sharing seats for six. We smiled and nodded greetings in Hindi; no one offered a word of English. As a wiry young woman in a tattered green sari closed the door that separated the compartment from the rest of the train, I glanced around and wondered what new play would unfold during this night's ride.

While the train pulled out of the station, I was preoccupied with the necessity to transfer in Mangalore in the middle of the night. With sign language and a few words, I indicated that I was headed for Bombay. A confident, middle-aged woman with silver streaks highlighting her thick black braid alternately pointed her finger at my chest and hers, repeating "Bombay" with each movement. Yes, yes, we both had the same destination. She then started the process anew, this time saying "Mangalore" while using sign language to pantomime that we would get down and change trains there. I hoisted my pack and followed it up to the overhead bunk. I folded myself into sleep, hoping to keep her in sight during the late-night transfer.

Dozens of jangling bangle bracelets sounded a tinny alarm as a brown hand shook me repeatedly. It was 3 A.M. and I struggled awake as the slowing of the train's momentum signaled the approach of Mangalore station. My protector picked up her own small bag, pulled my backpack from the overhead rack, grabbed my hand and hauled me down from my berth. It seemed that keeping her in sight would not be difficult .

We wandered up and down the platform in a zigzag pattern to avoid sleeping travelers. Carrying her cloth bag without trouble, she headed straight for the corner where the red-shirted coolies were dozing and negotiated with one until he accepted her offer. He then led us along an empty track until we came to a spot that looked to me like any other. His fee paid, he floated away as she triumphantly smiled and pulled me down to squat beside her. She indicated that we would wait in that spot for the Bombay train.

I decided to put my faith in her, discarding the notion of finding a railway employee for official verification, and settled down to wait. Other travelers emerged from the night and spread their bundles to claim sections of the platform. Their low murmurs were silenced by the deep rumbling of the approaching train. As the steam-belching locomotive screeched into the station, people and luggage multiplied around us. Suddenly we were at the head of a pulsating crowd. Madame, as I thought of her, firmly stood her ground and barked at anyone who tried to usurp my spot. I knew that none of us transferring from other trains would have reserved seats; now I realized that many might not even make it onto the train.

The air brakes hissed and we bounded up the steps of the car still lumbering slowly before us. I stopped short as we entered the corridor; every spot was already filled, there was simply nowhere to go. Madame propelled me forward as I struggled to keep my pack from battering other passengers. The first compartment we passed had twelve or fourteen women sardined into a space designed for six. As we pushed our way forward I realized that *every* compartment was a ladies' compartment. The entire train car was packed with hundreds of Indian women—matrons, teenagers, and tiny grandmothers shushing girl and boy children. The ultimate Ladies' Compartment.

My advocate moved ahead of me, regally examined the two benches that faced each other in the next section and parted the women on one bench with a sweep of her mighty arm. She parked me firmly between those on one bench and inserted herself opposite me. A howl went up from women on both sides. Color rose to my face, and I started to relinquish my place, but Madame pushed me back down and answered each argument with a quick retort. A quiet woman wrapped in a blue sari edged in gold brocade murmured in clipped English, "She is informing everyone that you are a visitor to our country and we must show you hospitality." Grateful for a translator, I implored, "Please apologize for me and explain that I will sit in the corridor."

As the argument proceeded, a growing faction seemed to be urging acceptance. To make more room, some of the children were sent to join the luggage in the upper berth. The train moved out of the station, and everyone became resigned to our presence. Arms and parcels were adjusted for the most comfortable fit; several women lifted the ends of their saris over their faces as they prepared for sleep. I tipped my head to get a better view down the corridor; it looked like a refugee train, a scene from a movie where all the men were gone and only women and children remained.

Then a single masculine figure began working his way toward us from the opposite end of the car. A grizzled old man dressed for colder climes in a green wool army-surplus coat, he lumbered down the aisle, a vintage musket resting in the crook of his arm. Stopping before each compartment, he peered nearsightedly at the faces crowded inside and then moved on. As he inspected our section, I questioned the English-speaking woman again, "Who is he?"

"A guard hired to protect the women."

Incredible, I thought, and smiled at him. He stared. Perhaps he didn't encounter too many foreigners in the second-class train.

Then he said something urgent, lifted the gun, and pointed it straight at me. The women around me all started chattering at once, with Madame trying to yell louder than the rest. My translator tilted her head to one side as she listened, and then said in a low voice, "He thinks you are a man and has ordered you out of this car." A moment later, she added, "The others are arguing whether you are a man or a woman."

I laughed briefly at this turn of events, until he jerked the gun at my insolence. I wore neither the long braid, nor the sari or knee-length tunic over trousers of the other women on the train. My close-cropped hair, baggy pants, and collarless white cotton Indian man's shirt were chosen for comfort, ease of travel, and to help me avoid harassment. I stood and rocked unsteadily among the jumbled feet and discarded sandals of my travel-mates in the narrow space between the two facing benches. Momentarily turning my back to the old fellow, I pulled the baggy shirt taut under both arms and showed the women the outline of my chest. They roared in laughter and approval, and pushed the old man and his gun away.

As dawn approached, food and hot *chai* were produced from among the folds of bags and parcels. The story of the guard and the foreigner passed in waves up and down the train, the punch line always enacted amid gales of laughter. Madame seemed especially proud of me as women and girls craned their necks or shyly walked over to see me in person.

When we reached Bombay, Madame was reluctant to turn me loose. She walked me to the front of the station and negotiated fiercely with the autorick driver for my fare to the General Post Office. Then, she gave me a long lecture in rapid dialect. Her accompanying gestures advised me to be careful of men driving rickshaws, on the streets, in buses, or just about anywhere. Despite the language difference, her message was clear. She seemed to be saying that if I got scared or had a problem, I should always rely on women for help.

III

---

*Traveling with a
Partner*

How to Make Partner Travel Work

The keys to successful travel with a partner (as with any important relationship) are the four C's: commitment, communication, creative problem solving, and compromise.

Commitment

After comparing your responses to the Travel Questionnaire, you should have a better idea of whether you are ready to commit to traveling together. Can both of you get what you want during the trip? Are your travel styles compatible? Are you both willing to work out solutions to differences? This is a moment of truth—it's better to say no to the trip than to go along with a plan you won't enjoy.

Despite anything that may happen, are you committed to leaving and returning together? If not, under what conditions would you separate?

Communication

Whether the issue is money, the terrible restaurant *you* chose last night, or how *she* lost your umbrella, small resentments are likely to surface during your journey. If you pack resentments into your bag and carry them with you from town to town, you'll find the burden can get quite heavy. Unless you are booked on an organized tour where virtually all decisions have been made for you, constant decision-making during your travels provides many opportunities for conflict.

Use your pretrip planning to establish a pattern of communication, negotiation, and compromise that will continue throughout your travels together. Take the time to talk things through. Try not to get stuck at polar opposites. Search for common ground that will allow both of you to be satisfied. Remember that for your trip to work, you both have to be honest and open.

A handy tool for tuning up communication between travel partners is a regular "check-in" session. For a trip of up to three weeks, plan to schedule some time every few days. For three weeks or longer, make it a weekly session. This need not be a formal meeting; it can occur during breakfast, an evening walk, or whenever you choose. Let it be a regular time to discuss your trip and plan changes for the future.

Try to end each check-in session with specific agreements for the future. For example, "We're going to slow down our pace and try to spend less." Don't forget the positive feedback; it helps put those small conflicts into perspective.

Outline for Check-In Session

Our pace of travel is: ...too quick.
    ...about right.
    ...too slow.

I'm spending: ...too much money.
    ...about what I planned.
    ...less than I expected.

What I liked *best* about last week/the last few days was...

What I liked *least* about last week was...

Something different I'd like to try is...

The one thing that really gets on my nerves is...

Something I really appreciate about you is...

Experienced traveler Martha Banyas points out that, "One nice thing about traveling together is that when one person gets really frazzled and fried, the other one can sort of take over. By checking in with the other person, you start to figure out that what pushes her buttons doesn't necessarily push yours. So when one of you is feeling a bit of strain from traveling, she can take it easy, while the other one takes over responsibility to be the buffer with the world."

Creative Problem-Solving

Don't be passive about getting what you want out of your trip. You might have to sit down and explain that you had no intention of going shopping everyday; you want to see archaeological sites, or sit and do watercolors, or just relax and read for a while.

When divergent goals emerge, take some time to brainstorm creative solutions to the dilemma. See if you can *both* get what you want without either of you needing to compromise.

Here, two Bali-bound travelers are discussing their first stop. One wants to stay at lively Kuta Beach, while the second prefers the more remote and placid Candi Dasa Beach. It seems like a direct conflict, until they explore the reasons behind their preferences:

> *"The reason I want to go to Candi Dasa Beach is that I've heard it was really quiet there. It's important for me to be in a peaceful place away from traffic, loud noise, and disco music."*
>
> *"It's true there's a lot of activity at Kuta Beach...that's one reason I'd like to go. But how about if we found a quiet place on the edge of town, far away from all the noise? We can keep looking for a place until we find one that seems right to you, and then I can walk into town when I want to."*
>
> *"Okay, that sounds fine. I think we can both be happy here."*

Compromise

Even creative problem-solving can't resolve all dilemmas. Regular check-in sessions and effective two-way communication will establish a firm basis for negotiations when compromise is necessary. Apply the following ground rules for working out a compromise:

•Explain your proposal and why you think it will work. Offer trade-offs if you are asking your companion to give something up. Weigh long-term harmony against short-term victories.

•Stick to the facts when discussing your options; maintain a positive attitude and sense of humor.

•Set a time limit for reaching a compromise; consider creating new options to break an impasse.

•Honor your agreements; don't continually renegotiate.

Travel for Two: The Art of Compromise by Margot Biestman offers practical techniques and real-life examples to help explode the myth that vacations can be or should be without conflict, and assists travelers in coping with disagreements and difficulties that might arise while away from home.

Finding a Travel Partner

If you want a travel partner, and your network of friends and family hasn't already turned up a prospect, search out a partner by checking these sources:

•Bulletin boards of community colleges, travel bookstores, and feminist bookstores—look for notices or place your own.

•**Travel Companion Exchange** bills itself as "North America's most successful match-up service for travel-minded singles seeking good friends, travel companions and/or partners." It maintains a large file of traveler listings organized by interest category; several hundred are published in each bimonthly newsletter. The membership profile questionnaire includes questions about travel habits and preferences ("budget, moderate, deluxe"; "leisurely stay-put trips" to "touring and seeing a lot of places"), as well as reasons for seeking a travel companion ("strictly platonic" to "open to an intimate friendship/companionship"). Membership ranges from six months to two years and includes all services as well as a newsletter subscription. Contact them at: **PO Box 833, Amityville, NY 11701 (516/454-0880).**

•**Partners-in-Travel** produces a bimonthly newsletter filled with travel tips and includes over 200 listings for those seeking travel partners, most over the age of 50. Additional services include the Guest/Home Exchange program for members and Cruise Mates, which matches single people who wish to share shipboard accommodations to avoid paying the singles' supplement. Contact them at: **PO Box 491145, Los Angeles, CA 90049 (213/476-4869).**

•*Great Expeditions*, a "Journal of Adventure and Off the Beaten Path Travel" has a classified ad section—Travel Companions Wanted—with about a dozen adventurous travelers listed in each issue. Write to request a trial issue: in Canada:

PO Box 8000-411, Abbotsford, BC V2S 6H1 (604/852-6170); in the U.S. and elsewhere, PO Box 18036, Raleigh, NC 27609 (800/743-3639).

• *Connecting* is a newsletter for solo travelers that also has ads for companions. Contact: *Connecting*, 1-1866 West Thirteenth Avenue, Vancouver, BC V6J 2H3, Canada (604/737-7791).

Dealing with Money

Because traveling involves continual financial transactions, money can be an easy source of conflict. If you are traveling with a partner whose finances are already mingled with your own, you may not feel the need to keep track of individual expenditures. Otherwise, consider adopting one of these systems to help you avoid struggling over every transaction.

Tally Money at Beginning and End of Trip

On a six-week trip to Greece, my friend and I left home with identical amounts of money. We each changed traveler's checks and spent them during the trip, keeping track *only* of the items that were not common expenditures, such as gifts and personal purchases. On the plane ride home, we counted our money, made adjustments for the purchases, and evened out the imbalance with the remaining cash.

Carry a Common Purse

This system works well for two or more people, and for short-term travel partnerships. Establish a common "purse"—a change purse or zippered pouch. Each traveler antes up an equal amount of money— say twenty or fifty dollars. (It should be enough to cover more than one day's expenses.) Take turns being the banker, carrying the purse and paying for common activities—meals, entrances to museums, bus fares, etc. When the purse gets low, it's time to ante up again. Each traveler uses her own money for personal purchases. This system can also help those traveling on a tight budget: put a day's allowance into the purse and try to make it through on that amount of money.

Both these systems assume a certain degree of reciprocity. That is, the cost of the beer you drank last night is balanced by the dessert I ordered today after lunch. Many travelers assume "it will all even out in the end," in lieu of keeping closer track of individual spending. (Even if the difference is ten dollars over a period of two weeks, you've avoided a lot of mental gymnastics.)

If one traveler consistently consumes much more than the other, adjust her contribution to the common purse.

Record Expenditures

I once shared a room with two Canadian nurses who sat down in the evening and entered all of their daily expenditures into a small notebook. *You had the yogurt, I had tea.* While you may not require so much detail, the key is to find a system that works and is comfortable for you.

Avoid Check-Splitting

Adopting any one of these systems lets you avoid splitting the cost of every restaurant meal. American-style check-splitting is foreign to most other cultures. Waiters around the world are mystified at how "wealthy" Americans spend time squabbling over money in public and find it embarrassing and unpleasant. Adopting a money-handling system makes for a smoother trip and avoids public negotiations.

Go with a person with the same interests; you don't have to know them otherwise. I have a vision problem; I can't read signs on buses and schedules. I traveled with a friend who had a slight hearing problem and that worked fine.

We went to India for two months. I said, Let's not go for the cocoon of the tour group. If forty people are on the tour bus, every time you go to the toilet, so do the rest of them. How many times do you want to wait for forty people to go to the bathroom?

We'd read up before we left, but hadn't made specific plans. So when we arrived we went straight to the Indian travel bureau and asked what we should see if we have two months. The man said, Why don't you start by going to Rajasthan for ten days, and he arranged a private car and driver. It was very reasonable—we spent about half what a tour would have cost. The driver was absolutely wonderful; he took care of us like his own grandmothers.

It was less hassle than taking the train or the bus. Prem took us to hotels all the way across Rajasthan; we stayed in places I'd call Indian businessman hotels. We never had the slightest doubt about the cleanliness or safety. He took us there, and maybe he was getting a cut, but so what? He took us to places where we felt comfortable.

Before we went to the Hill Station at Mussoorie, Prem asked if he could bring his wife and two-year-old daughter along. We stopped off at Hardwar, on the upper reaches of the Ganges River, which is very holy to the Hindu people. The little girl was eighteen months old and had never been to the Ganges. So they took the child and undressed her and immersed her in the river. Then they had her send a paper boat of flowers down the Ganges in memory of her grandmother, who had died a couple of months earlier. It was a very moving experience for us—we felt fortunate to share that moment with them.

Two years ago I started out planning to take a tour of Greece and Turkey. Then I realized that for the same ticket price, I could get a round-the-world ticket. I invited my friend to come along.

In Istanbul, my friend slipped on the marble steps at Aghia Sophia and tore all the ligaments in her leg. I convinced her not to go home, that we could continue the trip—we still had six weeks left. You can cope at the hospital; you can manage. (I'd broken my leg the year before in Austria, so I knew it wasn't the end of the world.) You can get around with a cast on, why not? Just do what you can do.

She was seventy at that time; I was sixty-seven. We had just a bit more than carry-on luggage, and now she was on crutches. We wanted to go to Eastern Turkey, so we booked a tour out of Ankara. (Don't make the mistake of booking tours in advance—it would have cost $1,200 to book it from the U.S., but we paid only $700 because we had booked it in Ankara.) Everyone was wonderful to her because of her crutches. There was a big mountain we wanted to climb. The Kurds wrapped her up in Turkish rugs and put her on a mule and took her to the top to see the sunrise.

You can do things like that if you make up your mind to do it. Having a companion along in a situation like this does help. Younger travelers meet up with younger travelers more easily. But there aren't too many women our age around by themselves. We took a few more taxis than we would have taken otherwise; she stayed and rested a bit more than usual. Instead of going home and sitting around, she finished the trip and had a great time.

Here's my advice to women travelers of any age:

Don't stay home because something might happen. Wear your money belt. Don't take anything valuable with you. Never carry more than walking-around money at any time. Don't do dumb things or make yourself a target with your big handbag. Leave it at home.

Don't worry about seeing every museum. Instead of visiting cathedrals and taking the dull tours, look for posters of concerts in the cathedral. That way you can sit and enjoy it and appreciate the acoustics.

If you've ridden one subway anywhere in the world, every other subway is exactly the same, whether it's Moscow, Madrid, London, or Paris. If you can read a subway map, you can do it. In Russia, I got the Intourist guide to write out the station names in the Cyrillic alphabet, then I just looked at the signs. I had all the time in the world, and I matched them up.

Always carry a small spiral notebook with you. When you go to buy a ticket, have all the information written down—destination, class, type of ticket. You're much more apt to get it right than if you try to pronounce it yourself. Give it to the ticket agent, and they will take care of you very well.

Get them to write down the name or number of the track so you are sure to understand it. If you don't speak the language, the sounds can be difficult to decipher.

On the bus, if you're confused, just hold out your hand with the coins and someone will help you. The bus works the same everywhere.

Most people are nice, and they want to help. If you are nice, they will respond. I've traveled everywhere without reservations—you can always get a bed. Those tourist information places will find you a place for your budget. If they see you are older or you're a woman alone, they will send you someplace where you'll feel comfortable.

I've found that hairdressers are the same the world over. I've had my hair done in Mongolia just as well as at home.

If you are retired, keep your house in order. Keep your bills paid up all the time so you're always ready to go if an interesting opportunity comes your way. If you can afford to go alone, take a friend and pay for her lodgings since double rooms often cost no more than singles, and help her out if she has less money.

Traveling with a Child

Your child can be a delightful travel partner. Sharing experiences across generations offers both of you fresh insights and opportunities for wider contacts. Children are adaptable travelers; the younger they are, the easier they adjust to new environments. Children too young to appreciate museums and cultural events will notice differences in housing, clothes, the quality of light, noises, smells, and street life around them.

Prepare preschoolers and older children by reading books, looking at maps, and discussing the trip in advance. Have them mark the places on a map that interest them, and after you have done the same, use that as a basis to plan your itinerary. Let them organize their own daypack with some select toys and games; help them think about a new interest to pursue on the trip, such as asking local children how to make homemade toys or collecting stamps from each country they visit.

Recommended Reading

A variety of books offer advice and insights on traveling with children. For adventurous travelers planning to bicycle or camp, read *Adventuring with Children: The Complete Manual for Family Adventure Travel* by Nan and Kevin Jeffrey.

For specific ideas on things to do in twelve countries of Western Europe, see *Innocents Abroad: Traveling with Kids in Europe* by Valerie Wolf Deutsch and Laura Sutherland. *Take Your Kids to Europe* by Cynthia W. Harriman explains how to get your children out of school for an extended trip, and provides step-by-step instructions for renting houses in several countries in Europe.

Maureen Wheeler and her husband Tony founded the Lonely Planet series of guidebooks and have traveled extensively in the

"Third World." In *Travel with Children*, Maureen's sensible advice helps demystify the prospect of traveling off the beaten track with young children. She discusses culture shock and poverty and shares tales of their adventures on a half-dozen continents.

Now kids have their own guidebooks, too: the *Kidding Around* series by John Muir Publications offers sixteen titles filled with fun things to see and do for young travelers, providing historical background on places in Europe and the U.S.

Organized Trips for Adults and Children

Adventure travel companies and organizations which offer trips geared to adults with toddlers, preteens and teens include:

Sierra Club offers over a dozen family outings each year (in addition to their outings for adults). Toddler Tromps takes you to the Finger Lakes in New York or Mt. Desert Island in Maine; children six years and older are eligible to hike in the John Muir Wilderness, Big Basin Park and Palisade Glacier in California; service trips provide the opportunity to repair and build hiking trails. Contact: **Sierra Club Outings, 730 Polk Street San Francisco, CA 94109 (415/776-2211).**

American Wilderness Experience offers three-day horseback trail rides into the Colorado Rockies; minimum age for participants is eight. Contact: **PO Box 1486, Boulder, CO 80306 (800/444-0099).**

Appalachian Valley Bicycle Touring sponsors special bicycle outings; young children ride on parents' bikes while older kids pedal themselves. Contact: **PO Box 27079, Baltimore, MD 21230 (410/837-8068).**

O.A.R.S. Rafting Adventures for adults and children offers a variety of trips on U.S. rivers—from float trips in the Southwest suitable for four-year-olds to horseback riding and rafting alongside the Grand Tetons of Wyoming for older children. Contact: **PO Box 67, Angels Camp, CA 95222 (209/736-4677).**

Rascals in Paradise offers group trips, combining three to six groups of adults and children, and individually organized trips to Europe, Asia, and the South Pacific. Special programs offer lessons on snorkeling and diving. Contact them: c/o **Adventure Express, 185**

Berry Street, Suite 5503, San Francisco, CA 94107 (800/443-0799).

Grandtravel is for grandparents who are searching for creative ways to strengthen ties with their grandchildren. Consider a barge trip along the waterways of Holland and Belgium, a tour of English and Scottish castles, or an Alaskan wilderness adventure. Contact them: c/o **The Ticket Counter, 6900 Wisconsin Avenue, No. 706, Chevy Chase, MD 28015 (800/247-7651).**

My partner, Greg, and I traveled for a year in a van. We bought the van in Europe, drove down to North Africa, then went to Malaysia, Thailand, and Indonesia. My stepson, Nick, was with us; he was three when we left and four when we returned. My stepdaughter, Sabrina, who was twelve, joined us for the summer.

We didn't spend much time in Europe; almost all of our experiences were in the "Third World." My one gripe about traveling in Europe with Nick was that he was not very welcome in restaurants. Particularly in Northern Europe—people brought their dogs into restaurants, but they really gave you a dirty look if you walked in with a three-year-old!

Three is a good age to take children traveling; they're not in school yet, they are old enough not to eat off the ground, they're not in diapers anymore, and they have a little more bladder control. But they are young enough that they are still happy to go with the program, whatever it is. They are happy to be with you, as long as you take their toys along. With older kids, you have problems with school absence, and they begin to have their own agendas—they want to be with their friends and do their own things.

Because we are photographers and interested in rural life we tended to go to remote villages where a foreign child was somewhat rare—there were many places where they'd never seen a little kid like Nick. He was a little bit shy; he was protective of his body when people wanted to touch him. But he also made friends easily. Children that age don't need language to play together. Nick would take out his Lego blocks and start playing. Little boys would come and look into the van, then they would sort of work their way to the open door, and pretty soon they'd all be inside, playing together. That happened a lot, in many places.

There were a lot of advantages to traveling by van. We could all sleep in our own beds every night, which is important for a little kid. It provides a sense of security, a feeling of being home. And every three or four months we'd get to a big city and stock up on Nick's favorite foods. Only four times during the year did we rent hotel rooms, and we hardly ever ate in restau-

rants. We didn't have to worry about lice and mosquitos, and we could control our sanitation and health a lot better.

We got a lot of invitations to people's homes. I didn't know this going into it, but Nick was our little ambassador. I don't know if those same people would have struck up a conversation with us if we were just two adults traveling. Also, the presence of a child was a point of commonality. Most people in the "Third World" spend a lot of time raising children— here was a way that we were just like them.

Kids have an incredible facility for picking up language; if you want children to be bilingual, just start speaking a new language to them, and they will learn it. Our kids picked up languages much faster than we did. In one of my favorite pictures, Sabrina has flowers intertwined in her hair, and she's talking and dancing with a Balinese woman. She loved their rituals in the temples and the flowers—she got right into it. And they thought it was wonderful that a little American girl wanted to learn their dances.

One night in Egypt we went out for ice cream and sat down next to a guy named Jean from Rwanda (in Africa) and started to talk. We liked each other immediately. He was a student at the American University in Cairo and spoke good English. He hadn't had a chance to get outside of Cairo, so we invited him to come with us down the Nile valley to Luxor. For a week he traveled with us, and he and Nick became very good friends. We all helped one another—we provided the transportation, he helped us learn more Arabic and learn more about the culture, and he babysat Nick at times. Then, years later, we helped him emigrate to the U.S. Nick is now fifteen, and he and Jean are still very close. And it all started from a chance encounter over ice cream one day.

Another wonderful story from that trip took place in Sicily. We'd just driven up from Palermo into the hills. We picked a town on the map, pulled in and were walking along the street to the bar centrale. In Sicily, a bar is a social center, where they serve food as well as alcohol. We poked our heads in the doorway and a man waved to us, "Come in, come in." He was Pino, one of four brothers who owned the bar. That was the beginning, and we stayed for a week! They took us in and fed us every night. We celebrated New Year's Eve with them. We went to the christening of one of their grandchildren. They would sit Nick up on the counter in front of a big display of these wonderful Sicilian pastries and ask, "What do you want?" They would feed him whatever he asked for. Rice balls, homemade pizza, they made everything. They just loved Nick. Often, the owner's son would take him off for walks around town.

We felt very trusting of people we met—not like in the U.S. where you can't let your kids talk to anyone they don't know. We kept Nick within sight until we'd gotten to know people. But we never worried about him, never like I worry here at home.

Several years after our round-the-world trip, we drove the same van down to Central America. This time we had Nick, our daughter Rebecca who was three, and a twelve-year-old baby-sitter along on the trip. When we were in Mexico, we had major car trouble, and we got stuck for a whole month in Mazatlan. We found a place to fix our van, and they let us live in it right there. So we were living in the diesel yard while they were working on our car. At the time I thought it was a disaster. It was right at the beginning of our trip—we were trying to get to Central America—and we came to a grinding halt in Mexico. Of course now, years later, it's one of our best stories.

We became friends with the mechanics—they would invite us to their homes, we went to the children's birthday parties, we drank beer together at the cantina, it was really fun. Nick was about seven at the time. There was a little boy named Juan who swept out the diesel yard every day and he was also seven. He not only swept out the diesel yard, but he also sold doughnuts from a tray. So here was our seven-year-old and his new friend. But they could only play together when Juan was off work. I think it was great for our kids to see that children in other cultures have many more responsibilities—doing chores, taking care of siblings, even making money to contribute to the family income.

I remember a scene in Nicaragua when we went to visit a neighborhood in Managua that was hit very hard by the earthquake. A lot of the buildings weren't ever really repaired, but poor people were living in them anyway, just squatting there. They were very hospitable to us; right away we were invited to this one house, and they fed us breakfast. And the woman wanted to teach Rebecca how to make tortillas. I have a picture of Rebecca patting out a tortilla when she was three years old, with the woman showing her what to do. The woman was chattering away in Spanish; Rebecca wasn't really answering back, but she understood what to do.

You may not go to a lot of museums if you're traveling with a child—you have to take the child's needs into account. You get on a dawn-to-dusk schedule, which is good for children (as well as good for photography). In many places there's a siesta time, which is good for kids, too. Often we would drive during that time while the kids napped. As most parents know, you just tailor your schedule around your kid's biological rhythms.

Travel really broadens a child's horizons. It is a great way to learn to appreciate all different kinds of people. Our children met ordinary people in ordinary villages in fifteen or twenty different countries. They don't remember everything, but the important parts have stayed with them. And they've picked up a yen for traveling. Some people just never leave home. I don't think our kids will ever be like that.

IV

Creating Your Own Journey

Dig Your Roots

Take a detour off the tourist track down the trail that leads to your own past. Genealogy is no longer just for the Daughters of the American Revolution. Published resources are available to research the history of native peoples and the scores of African, Asian, Jewish, and European ethnic groups that have emigrated to the United States, Canada, Great Britain, New Zealand, and Australia.

Back to the Village

For me, the search was easy. As a second-generation Greek-American, I was trained to politely answer questions in church: "My mother's family comes from Kastoria, my father's family from Keffalonia." I made the pilgrimage to the village of my maternal grandparents as a seventeen-year-old student and to my father's family village years later.

Clinging to the hillside in Macedonia, the wooden balconies of Kastoria's buildings reminded me of Swiss chalets. This was the town John and Anastasia Kideris had left behind. Like many Greeks, Grandpa John opened a small restaurant when he arrived in New York City. For two decades, beginning in 1921, he volunteered as an interpreter at Ellis Island, helping to receive and process the polyglot of new arrivals. He gave the immigration officers free lunches at his cafe, and they returned the favor, letting Papou John smooth the entry of hometown friends. When Papou John pointed out faces from among a sea of hopefuls, they were fished out of the crowd and their papers promptly stamped. Arm in arm, he escorted his townspeople into the new world. And so my grandfather gained the reputation of being fabulously powerful—a man "who could get anyone into America."

Fifty years later, Uncle Chris led me from house to house in the village. The best chair, a traditional spoonful of homemade preserves, and a tall glass of cold water welcomed me to each home. With hair as white as Mount Olympus and eyes as blue as the Aegean, Uncle Chris translated the stories of how my Grandfather John and Grandmother Anastasia had helped each family's sons and brothers, daughters and sisters from the village find a job, a house, even a bride or groom in America.

Those stories brought my grandparents to life in ways that dim memories and flickering black-and-white home movies never could. Papou John was a cigar-smoking back-slapper, always ready with a smile and a joke. Anastasia, his wife, remained a country girl in the big city. She gathered with other village women in New York tenement kitchens, making her famous preserves and working her legendary matchmaking skills across both sides of the Atlantic.

I went to Greece on vacation. I returned with a deeper understanding of who I am. I learned that habits and attitudes I thought peculiar to my family were, instead, typical of my people. I found a place where the model of beauty was, for once, someone who resembled me.

Start Your Research

If you, too, are from a first- or second-generation immigrant family, you probably know at least the town or region that your people came from. But if your family immigrated or was forcibly transported long ago, you'll have to play private investigator and track down some clues. Your best source may be interviews with older relatives. Family Bibles, heirlooms, and written records can provide valuable information. Make notes on everything you find out. Try to go back several generations; seek out the names of your forebears and the towns or counties they came from. If you are searching for an international connection, all you need is one great-uncle from Scandinavia.

You can conduct a scientific investigation, loaded with detailed genealogical charts and corroborating proof. Or scrawl a single name next to a town circled on a map to begin your quest.

Locate Documents

Most of us don't realize how much historical information is readily accessible. In his book *How to Find Your Family Roots*, Timothy Field Beard describes the wealth of resources on hand in public libraries (ask for the genealogy section or room) and archives. Beard lists specific addresses you can write to for birth certificates, death certificates, and marriage records from states and counties in the U.S., Africa, Central and South America, Asia, Australia, the Middle East, New Zealand, the Pacific Islands, the Caribbean, Europe, and the United Kingdom.

Other sources described by Beard include:

- Lists of ships' passengers arriving in the U.S. between 1538-1825;
- Special resources for adoptees;
- The federal census of 1900, which recorded the years of immigrants' arrivals and dates and places of their birth;
- Lists of African-American families in America, 1492-1976;
- Scores of worldwide Jewish genealogies and guides.

With persistence and luck, you can uncover the details of where your relatives were born, their parents' names, places of birth, and occupations.

Borrow Some Roots

If you can't find your own relatives or don't want to, consider borrowing some. A highlight of my second visit to Ireland was visiting the relatives of my friend Maura Bridget Clare Doherty in County Longford. Maura provided me a list of their names and phone numbers; I called several of her Irish cousins to convey greetings from America. One cousin, Imelda, invited me up for a visit. A day's stay on the farm, helping Imelda and her husband, Kevin, feed the cattle, provided a realistic view of life on those picturesque green hills. One delightful evening we met cousins Margaret and Liam at the local pub and traded songs all night. Every man and woman at the pub had a "party piece," a song, poem, joke, or story to contribute to the night's entertainment.

Don't expect much from relatives of friends. Even a cup of tea provides a chance for a unique personal contact. It helps to have some news to share about the foreign cousins. An invitation to stay overnight could be an unexpected bonus.

THEA MARIA

A pounding at the door woke me up that morning. It was cool and dark in my room at Thea Maria's house. The thick white walls kept out the heat and muffled the sounds of Greek village life outside. I pulled back the wrought-iron latch and opened the heavy green door. It was Yannis, the son of the bus driver. Their family ran the village store and were proprietors of the village's only telephone. He had come with a message for Thea Maria.

"Kapios péthane," he told me. Someone has died. He took a moment to explain, with shaking head, that it was a cousin of Thea Maria's, a woman who'd married into another village at the south end of our island of Keffalonia.

I thanked Yannis for coming and watched him skip up the dusty hill past St. Andrew's church to report on his conversation with the American cousin. I dressed slowly and went outside to sit in the shade of the whitewashed stone house, dropping a small cushion to a spot on the low ledge that had become my own. After only weeks in the village, Thea Maria's scolding had molded my habits; I never sat in the sun anymore.

The village had been dead quiet the day I climbed off the bus from Argostoli. I had stood in the center of the deserted road, squinting in the harsh afternoon light, wondering if I would find a place to stay. A woman named Zepatos took me to find my grandmother's first cousin, Maria. She wasn't really my aunt but I called her *thea* out of respect. An old crone dressed in black from head to foot, she scared me with all her scoldings. But she took me in and treated me like the daughter she never had, teaching me much more than the village proprieties. She was tough and often left without me to do the early morning chores in the terraced fields.

I waited for her return from tending the grapevines, or was she picking figs? From my spot on the ledge I stared at the tall cypresses opposite. It was a hillside whose profile I had always known—the rock and leaf realization of a painting that hung over the couch in my grandmother's apartment in the Bronx. From that painting I learned which house was her family's and which was my grandfather's. In a lifetime of Sundays I listened to stories of ancient Venetian invasion, English colonization, and Nazi control. But while centuries of foreign invaders couldn't drive my people off the land, it was the land itself that eventually drove them away.

Since the turn of the century, the village's young and healthy journeyed down the rocky slopes into the bowels of big ships that would deliver them to the good life in Athens, America, or Australia. Those who lingered got a convincing thrust from the giant earthquake of 1953. After that, only the old people stayed behind to clear the rubble and reclaim their homes.

Occasionally a distant relative returns to the home village to see the collection of crumbling stone houses and crinkling old people. Stones fall from rock walls, one by one. And the old Greeks fall, one by one, with a telephone ringing in their wake. Then the toothless old women take off their patched black aprons, skirts, and blouses and put on their Sunday black clothes. Tying their good kerchiefs with a solid knot under the chin, they march off to mourn. I knew what to expect. The death ritual was a weekly event.

Thea Maria ambled down the road balancing the morning's collection of fruit and greens on her head. I rushed to open the gate for her, to tell her the message. By then, of course, she'd already heard. She eased the bundle to the ground and went into the house to wash her face. I filled a bucket at the well and brought the cool water for her to drink. Not knowing what else to do, I returned outside to my place on the ledge.

Thea Maria emerged after a few minutes, dropped her cushion on the ledge and lowered herself down. We sat there, wordless, for a while. She took off her left shoe, inspecting the canvas at the toe where she'd mended it the day before. Then, shoe dangling from hand, she gazed straight through the cypress trees opposite. A ripple of emotion passed across her wrinkled face and settled in her lower lip, which quivered steadily. I wondered if she was grieving for her cousin who had died just this morning, for her sister-in-law Koula who had died two weeks before, or for her husband, Speros, gone since last year.

I studied the gnarled old woman who had taken me in. Silent tears ran down my face as I contemplated sailing on the next day's boat for Kerkyra. When I groped for a handkerchief and blew my nose, Thea Maria emerged from her reverie. "I told you not to sit on the cold stone for too long, now you've caught a cold."

"But I don't have a cold, Thea."

"Then, why is your nose running?"

I thought for a moment. How can I explain to my *thea* all these complicated thoughts and feelings? My Greek is inadequate. Moving my cushion next to hers, I took her hand and said, "You know, I am leaving tomorrow and I am not very happy for that." (I couldn't remember the Greek word for sad.) She turned and looked intently at me. "You mean, you love this place so much that you are crying because it is time to leave?"

"I love not only this village, Thea. I love you."

She gave me a startled look; her lower lip again began to quiver. Tears filled her eyes and coursed down the creased channels of her face. I cried again, not only for leaving but for the lifelong sorrow of a childless woman in a culture where children are the world. I put my arms around her. It was the first time we'd embraced. As we sobbed together she whispered something in my ear, something that at first was hard to hear. *"Mi kles, pedaki mou, mi kles."* Don't cry, my child, don't cry.

The sun pushed the shade across the ledge and dried our tears. Thea Maria returned her gaze to the scrubby mountainside. She reached for her left shoe and slowly put it on. Lifting a corner of the frayed black apron, she delicately blew her nose, got up, and went to the wall where some oregano lay drying. She shook the dried leaves onto a newspaper and positioned them again in the sun. Then she turned to me and said, "Thalia, when you come back to the village, I will be here."

I started crying again. She stood and scolded me in a strong voice, ordering me to get out of the sun and do something useful. So I filled the bucket at the well behind the house while Thea Maria went to put on her Sunday clothes for the wake.

Arrange Your Own Homestay

Imagine staying at a small hotel on the coast of Belize. As you breakfast each morning on the balcony, you watch the local fishermen drag their boats up from the sea, separating their catch into baskets borne away on the heads of women and children. Picture yourself joining them and riding over the waves before dawn, sharing the work and the jokes, your laughter and theirs floating back to shore. If you had a chance to live with a fishing family and work alongside them each day, would you trade your spot on the hotel balcony for a taste of a totally different way of life?

The richest travel experiences cannot be charged on your American Express card. But if you can reach into your back pocket and find a sense of adventure, you can arrange your own homestay anywhere in the world.

Think of it as a foreign exchange program, one that you organize yourself by seeking out a family to live with temporarily. You may be a guest, but more than likely you will make a modest contribution to household work or expenses. Finding a family can be as simple as stepping over that balcony and walking down the beach to say hello.

Many countries have family guest houses where you can organize a long stay. At Japanese *minshukus,* you make your own bed and eat breakfast and supper with a family. On the Greek islands, it is very easy to rent a room with a family. Ask for a special rate if you plan to stay for a week or more. Unlike touring, with its kaleidoscope of many images, a homestay offers the deeper understanding that comes only from staying in one place. There are trade-offs involved—you'll be giving up the luxury and privacy of that local hotel. You may find yourself rolling up your shirt-sleeves to harvest a crop, feed the chickens, or repair a fishing net before it's all over. You may have to adjust your daily habits and behavior to conform to local values; you might be communicating through nothing more than sign language.

Unexpected benefits will materialize—a crash course in international economy unfolds while debating the price of rice at the local market, and different political perspectives are offered with coffee after the evening news broadcast.

Even if you have only a few days or a week to spare, it's worth seeking out a family to live with. The search itself can be fascinating. Many countries have a tradition of offering room and board to out-of-town students, workers, and guests, and inquiries around almost any town will turn up several options.

Without any prearranged contacts, I have organized my own homestays in a bamboo hut in the jungle of Thailand, a mud-walled village on India's western seacoast, and a tin-roofed concrete block house in Mexico's Baja Peninsula. I arrived a stranger with nothing more than a simple request, stayed as short as a few days or as long as four months, and was sent off like a family member carrying away memories and friendships that transcend time and distance.

Locate a Small Town or Village

As a single woman, I find it less threatening and more interesting to arrange homestays in small towns and villages. The lifestyle is slower and people seem to have more time to help out a visitor. Big city life makes both travelers and residents more cautious, so I've never attempted to find a homestay in a large city.

Take day trips or spend a night or two in a hotel to get a feel for the place. Although small rural towns not listed in the guidebooks aren't crackling with excitement, they hum continuously with normal daily life.

Your goal may be a village so remote that you will be unable to locate it alone. In that case you will have to find someone to bring you there, make introductions, and help with the arrangements. People who live in larger towns bordering remote areas often have family or friends "back in the village." Ask for introductions through your innkeeper, restaurant proprietor, or local guides; take someone else along with you.

For example, many guides in the northern Thai city of Chiang Mai offer to lead foreigners on a "tour" of indigenous hill tribes. The guides take a small group of paying tourists to "See Four Hill Tribes in Three Days," traveling by Jeep and staying each night in a different village. One of those same guides may be willing to bring you to a village not visited by any tour groups, advise you on what to take along as gifts, and help make arrangements with a family.

Search for a Family

After a day or two wandering around a coastal town on Baja California's Sea of Cortes, I was sure I wanted to stay. I began my search for a host family by asking at a small corner soda shop. Explaining that I wanted to live in town for awhile but couldn't afford to stay at a hotel, I asked if it would be possible to find a family with an extra room for rent. The shopkeepers seemed optimistic; one directed me to a neighborhood butcher store. The butcher sent me on to a widow who lived on the far edge of town. Hoping to live closer to the central plaza, I continued my search.

For three days I wandered leisurely up and down dirt streets, conversing with women sweeping porches and men repairing cars. A fish taco stand on the main street became my unofficial headquarters. Each day I briefed Don Nacho, the proprietor, on my progress as he fried a piece of yellowtail and folded it into a hot tortilla. On the third day, Don Nacho snapped his fingers with a new idea and disappeared down a side street, leaving me in charge of the taco stand. Returning a few moments later, he closed shop in order to introduce me to Doña Tito and her large family. I moved into their house the next day and left four months later.

Choose Single or Double

Because most people live in homes without much extra room, it is much easier to find lodging for one than for two. If you are traveling with a companion, decide if it is absolutely mandatory for you to stay in the same house. If you can locate hospitality in two homes in the same town, all the better. You will have two families to meet and twice as many contacts to enjoy during your temporary residency.

Determine Your Bottom Line

Is it important for you to have a private room? Think about it before you are invited to share space with a little "sister" or "brother." In some countries, people may offer to put you in the same bed with the little tyke. Are you willing to walk through the yard with a flashlight at night to find the toilet, or do you draw the line at inside plumbing? There's no right or wrong answer here, but it helps to be clear about your needs before starting your search.

Remember that hospitality is highly honored in most parts of the world; people will try to accommodate you if they sense you need a roof over your head.

Organize Your Meals

I try to arrange for both room and board. Sometimes my hosts insist that I should cook my own food because they fear I will not like the local cuisine or they cannot imagine what I might want to eat. Cooking your food over a wood fire out back behind the house can be a real learning experience. After your hosts watch you stumble around for awhile, they may invite you in to dinner.

Help shop for the groceries or increase your financial contribution if you are eating with the family. Try to figure out what their most expensive purchases are—coffee? sugar?—and supply the household with those items.

Consider Your Length of Stay

No matter how flexible you try to be, unexpected circumstances can make your homestay less than ideal. You may be such a curiosity that you will literally have no time or space to yourself. (In one rural Indian village I was constantly followed by curious children—even to the outdoor privy.)

In order to hedge against possible problems, make an initial arrangement for a short period of time—a few days to a week, with an understanding that both parties can renegotiate later. Again, the ethic of hospitality may virtually prohibit your hosts from indicating anything other than willingness to have you stick around. But if you see that your presence is making the workings of the household difficult or is using up precious resources, you will want to end your visit.

Pay Your Way

This can be the most difficult issue to resolve and requires sensitivity. Families accustomed to taking boarders will be direct in discussing an actual price for your contribution to the household. But many will agree to take you in with the idea of "working it out" later on. That leaves you with the task of calculating your contribution.

Take time to do your research. Ask local people for help; find other local boarders and tactfully solicit their advice. Your eventual contribution should be far less than you would pay at a local hotel, and could come in the form of cash or a gift.

Before going to an Akha village in Thailand, I was advised to bring scissors, needles, thread, and some coffee as gifts. In Mexico, my host family refused to accept any money from me during a lengthy stay—I bought them a small appliance instead.

In calculating a fair cost, I try to think in terms of the local economy and then add a "gringo supplement" that accounts for my different standard of living. Avoid giving lavish sums of money—it makes people feel uncomfortable and sets up unrealistic expectations for the next traveler.

Aside from gifts and financial contributions, you can pitch in and participate in the work of the household. Find a daily task to make your own, whether it be grinding corn or washing the dishes. Offer to tutor members of the family in English if they show an interest; if you will be staying for a while, set up some informal sessions and include the neighbors.

The ideal homestay is a genuinely reciprocal arrangement. Don't abuse someone's hospitality if all you want is a low-cost hotel. Seek families out when you genuinely want to share part of your life and make a positive contribution to theirs.

Organizations That Arrange Homestays

Servas is an international organization designed to foster world peace through personal interaction. You can join as a host or traveler; both are screened through recommendations and personal interviews. Travelers must call or write ahead to arrange a free two-day stay with hosts in any one of ninety-seven countries. You are expected to spend some time with the hosts, often international travelers themselves, who range from farmers to scientists to teachers to political activists.

Stay with a fashion designer in Italy, on a sheep ranch in Australia, or with a feminist in Brazil. Listings provide information on the host's age, sex, and occupation, the languages they speak, and where they've traveled. Applying as a traveler and receiving the lists of hosts for countries you plan to visit requires a month or longer. Joining is well worth the effort, as is the forty-five dollar membership fee. Hosts in highly-visited tourist areas are deluged with requests, but many others wait all year for a single traveler. I recommend Servas highly, especially as a safe alternative for independent women travelers. I've never been disappointed.

In the U.S., contact: **U.S. Servas Committee, 11 John Street, New York, NY 10038 (212/267-0252).** In Canada, contact: **M. Johnson, 229 Hillcrest Avenue, Willowdale, Ontario M2N 3P3 (416/221-6434).** In England, Scotland, or Wales, contact: **Ann Greenough, 55 Jackson Avenue, Leeds, Yorkshire LS8 1NS (0532/665-219).** In Ireland, contact: **Luke Plunkett, 5 Priory Drive, Stillorgan, County Dublin (01/288-0567).** In Australia, contact: **Desmond Harkin, 16 Cavill Court, Vermont South, Victoria 3133 (03/803-5004).** In New Zealand, contact: **Ray Scott, 15 Harley Road, Takapuna (09/489-4442).**

The Friendship Force is another nonprofit group that organizes two-week homestays for Americans in forty-five countries to help promote world peace. You pay transportation and fees, but the housing is free. Contact: **Friendship Force, Suite 575, South Tower, One CNN Center, Atlanta, GA 30303 (404/522-9490).**

The Experiment in International Living has a long history of arranging foreign exchange programs for students in nineteen countries and is committed to integrating disabled people into its programs. For a fee of $100-$400, the nonprofit organization will organize a one- to four-week homestay for one or two independent travelers. You pay fees and transportation costs, lodging is free.

For those over sixty years of age, it offers **Elderhostel Homestay**, a one-week homestay combined with two scheduled weeks of classes and field trips. Background information provided by you assists in proper homestay placement. Current homestay sites are Bali, Indonesia, Ecuador, England, Germany, India, France, Ireland, Mexico and Switzerland. Contact: **The Experiment in International Living, Federation Office, PO Box 595, Putney, VT 05346 (802/257-7751).**

International Homestays Foreign Language/Study Abroad Programs promise "100 percent total immersion." Live for one to twenty weeks with a language teacher and her or his family, learn local customs, make social contacts, and pursue common activities in any one of seventeen countries as you study Spanish, French, Portuguese, Italian, German, Swedish, Dutch, Russian, Chinese, or Japanese. Contact: **PO Box 903, South Miami, FL 33143 (305/662-1090).**

A new series of travel guides unlocks the doors to thousands of homes in the Baltic States, Czechoslovakia, Hungary, Bulgaria, Poland, and Romania. The **People to People Guides** by Jim Haynes read like personal ads. Each guide is organized by city and lists hundreds of people from diverse backgrounds who want to entertain solo travelers. They may not all be able to offer homestays, so don't make assumptions without corresponding first. Each host describes her or his age, profession, family, language skills, and interests, in listings like this one from Romania: "I come from a family with a long-standing tradition in law practice. Have studied foreign languages. Expelled for my family's bourgeois origins and their staunch democratic ideals, but still finished studies. I translate and work with the movie industry."

LEX Homestay can make arrangements in Japan for singles, couples, retired people, and adults traveling with children. Contact: **LEX America, 68 Leonard Street, Belmont, MA 02178 (617/489-5800).**

DOÑA TITO

I came to Mexico and fell in love.

I didn't fall in love with the museum curator who pursues me like a treasured artifact. Nor with the handsome policeman with bristling black mustache who wants to drive me to the beach on his official motorcycle.

No, the one who has captured my heart is Tito Baeza de Romero, the forty-nine-year-old mother of a large family who took me into her home two months ago as a paying guest. She is a beautiful *prieta*—dark skinned with thick black hair and silver streaks twinkling at her temples. She has laughing eyes and a smile made crooked by the loss of a few teeth on one side.

Doña Tito announces to her friends and relatives that she wants to adopt me, which pleases me greatly. She fixes coffee for both of us in the mornings, when the family has gone off to work and school. We talk about life and the day ahead. She includes in every declaration of future plans the conditional phrase, "if God is willing." "If God is willing, I'll make fish stew for lunch." Or, "We'll go to the beach at Puerto Escondido on Sunday, if God wants it."

Each time I leave the house, she solemnly blesses me, saying *"que le vaya bien."* When I return home, she quizzes me immediately, "Where have you been?"

"Out for a walk, to visit Yuyi."

"What did you eat?"

"Only a cup of coffee."

"Ah, good, I'm saving something special for you."

She coquettishly lifts the lid on the pot and offers a peek at the food she's guarding on the back of the stove. She clears a spot on the end of her crowded kitchen table, orders me into my chair with a nod of her chin, and serves me a fragrant bowl of chicken and rice.

Doña Tito is the center of a universe populated by legions of relatives, and friends made into relatives through the intricate network of godparenting. She rarely leaves home except to attend mass at the mission church or to buy some cloth to sew clothes or curtains. She sends her youngest son, Manuelito, to the market several times daily for everything else. But even without leaving the house, she knows all that's happening in town within minutes of the event.

All the world comes to her. Her mother and brothers walk across the side yard to the kitchen window, rattling the glass and leaning over the sill, bringing their problems along with the vegetables to be minced and chopped at the kitchen table.

Her neighbors come, day and night, to use the telephone in the living room. The little notebook where they log the calls is a record of neighborhood news and emergencies, a testament to long-distance love affairs.

Her sisters-in-law and *comadres* stop by during their morning shopping to compare arthritic aches and pains. They discuss their favorite cures and trade recipes for the midday meal.

Doña Tito likes showing me off to the women who visit. She comes to my room or outside to the table where I am writing and timidly asks if I have time to drink coffee with her and her guest. Of course, I will do anything to please her. As I take a seat in the kitchen she announces, "This is Thalia, she's traveled all over the world and speaks six languages!"

"Well, not exactly, Doña Tito."

"Don't be modest," she scolds me. "Tell my *comadre* how the people in India eat rice with their hands. Tell her about that place you lived in the jungle." She loves my stories, and tells some of them better than I can. "Show her the photos of your brothers, you should see how handsome they are!"

After lunch we sit on the shady porch, slapping mosquitos from our arms and legs with a small towel as we wait out the heat of the day. We drink a cup of coffee, light and sweet, and tell stories. She delights in repeating certain tales. "Remember when my brother came to visit from La Paz?"

"Yes, Doña Tito, I remember."

"What did he say to you, when he learned you are not married?"

"He said it was too late, the bus has already left the station."

"And what did you tell him?" She starts laughing even before I respond.

"I said, Uncle, don't worry, another bus arrives every hour."

She tips her head back and cackles, throwing the towel over her face to conceal her open mouth. Her shoulders rock up and down, her chest is quaking. She lifts her right foot several times and stomps it on the concrete floor.

"Ah, Thalia!"

I love it when she laughs like that.

Organize a Trip Around Something Special

Grab a hook and haul yourself onto the side streets. You need a key, a password, an excuse to knock on someone's door. Whether it's weaving, dance, jewelry-making, natural healing, or cooking, choose a subject and really explore it. Find the experts and attend their meetings and schools.

Livia Szekely is a landscape gardener. She organized a trip to the British Isles to explore her passion for gardens and to research the possibility of attending graduate school there. "I signed up for a week-long garden tour that was advertised in one of the horticulture magazines. It allowed me to get into private gardens that I couldn't have seen on my own. Then I bought a book called *Gardens of England and Wales Open to the Public* (available at most British bookstores) and let my search for a graduate program dictate my route. I saw gardens designed by Vita Sackville-West, Rosemary Verey and Gertrude Jekyll. On sunny days, one of my favorite things to do was to sit in a quiet corner and paint. I got inspiration from those gardens."

Arthur Frommer—*yes, Arthur Frommer*—says, "Most American vacations are trivial and bland, devoid of important contact, cheaply commercial, and unworthy of our better instincts and ideals." He's right, and his book *The New World of Travel* is a fantastic resource packed with ideas for off-the-beaten-track adventures and experiences for all ages. I recommend it highly.

The following are some of my ideas as well as ideas I've collected from talking with women travelers. They're offered not as patterns for you to follow but rather as fuel to spark your own imagination.

Immerse Yourself in a Time and Place

Take yourself to a place that has captured your fancy—whether it is Berlin, the Yukon, or Kyoto—and track down the sites that intrigue you. Get lost in Paris in the 1920s, when Gertrude Stein and Alice B. Toklas held Saturday evening salons. Read the work of your favorite writers of the period, and keep notes on cafes and street addresses to search for. Or buy guidebooks such as *Expatriate Paris* by Arlen J. Hansen, which organizes the major sites and landmarks of Paris in the '20s into neighborhood walking tours.

Track down the homes of the Bloomsbury Group—many are open to the public—or buy a guidebook that will locate them for you. An excellent one is *Virginia Woolf—Life and London, A Biography of Place* by Jean Moorcraft Wilson, which takes you past Woolf's houses and haunts on seven walks with descriptive text culled from her writings.

Make a visit to the Yorkshire home of the Brontë sisters. Ramble for miles over the bleak and beautiful Pennine moorland that they loved. Prowl the cobbled streets of Haworth village, visit the Georgian parsonage where Charlotte, Emily, and Anne Brontë lived, and the village church where they are buried.

I've known travelers who like to tune into earlier eras of the places they visit. Martha Banyas scours used-book stores for vintage travel guides and literature, dating from 1900 to the 1940s. "I make notes on the places they mention to visit, which are usually not the same destinations the books mention nowadays. It's like traveling back through time to a different historical, cultural, and religious context."

Take a Women's Art Tour

Peek into the home and life of an artist you admire. If you were fascinated by *Frida*, Hayden Herrera's biography of Frida Kahlo, visit her cobalt blue house in Coyoacán and see her paintings in the museums of Mexico City. Track down the paintings and murals of Vanessa Bell while traveling through England, or visit the former home and sculpture garden of Barbara Hepworth in Cornwall. Wander the spacious landscape of northern New Mexico near Abiquiu, and scan the changing colors of the Sangre de Cristo mountains that inspired Georgia O'Keeffe for more than forty years. If you were enchanted by *Klee Wyck*, Emily Carr's book about her travels among the Northwest tribes of British Columbia, then go there yourself to experience the power of the giant totem poles that dominate her paintings.

Enjoy women's art on a multinational journey. Seek out the works of Angelica Kauffman in Switzerland, Gabriele Münter and Käthe Kollwitz in Germany, Judith Leyster in Holland, Anna Ancher in Denmark, or Harriet Backer in Norway. Visit the National Museum of Women in the Arts in Washington, D.C.

Plan a Spiritual Pilgrimage

If you are interested in Celtic native religion or early Celtic Christianity when women's power was honored, then tour the sacred sites that for many still possess spiritual energy. Several guides to them exist, including *Goddess Sites in Europe* by Anneli S. Rufus and Kristan Lawson and *A Traveler's Key to Sacred England* by John Michell. The latter is part of an excellent series of guides to sacred places which includes *A Traveler's Key to Ancient Egypt* and *A Traveler's Key to Medieval France*.

Or visit historic synagogues, Jewish neighborhoods, and landmarks throughout Europe. Read *A Travel Guide to Jewish Europe* by Ben Frank for insight into a people's shared identity across more than a dozen countries of Europe.

Attend a meditation workshop at an ashram in India, a monastery in Thailand, or a retreat center in Switzerland, Italy, Britain, or New Zealand. For information on meditation centers that offer ten-day silent retreats with healthful vegetarian food for a minimal fee, read the *Yoga Journal* or *The Meditation Temples of Thailand: A Guide* by Joe Cummings or *Buddhist America: Centers, Retreats, Practices,* edited by Don Morreale.

Venus Adventures sponsors goddess-oriented tours for women to sacred sites around the world. Contact them at: **PO Box 39, Peaks Island, ME 04108 (207/766-5655). Hawk, I'm Your Sister** is a women's travel company that combines wilderness canoe and raft trips with spiritual retreats. Paddle through Big Bend National Park, follow Sacajawea's route along the Upper Missouri, or study medicinal plants as you travel by dugout canoe through the Amazon jungle. Contact: **PO Box 9109, Santa Fe, NM 87504 (505/984-2268)**.

Seek Out Women-Only Places

Spend time in the company of women. Feminist organizations, bookstores, restaurants, and women's clubs exist around the world and are listed in special guides such as *Women Travel* edited by Natania Jansz and Miranda Davies. It combines over one hundred first-hand accounts of contemporary women travelers (including a Chinese woman's experiences in Sicily, a New Zealand woman who cycled across the Nubian desert in the Sudan, and an Englishwoman who worked in a fish factory on the northwest coast of Iceland). The comprehensive listings of contacts and organizations such as Casa de la Mujer, a women's center, and Cine Mujer, a women's film collective, in Bogotá, Columbia; the Bangladesh Mohila Samity, which promotes equal status, education, and employment opportunities for women; the Women's Association of Yemen; and WIN (Women in Nigeria) provide valuable leads for women travelers.

Other useful books are *Women Going Places* (formerly *Gaia's Guide International)* and feminist guides to specific countries that you can more easily pick up locally, such as: *Frauenkalender*, a feminist calendar and guide to Germany, which can be obtained through **Emma Magazine, Kolpingplatz, No. 1A, 5000 Köln (21-02-82)**, and a feminist guide to Spain which can be obtained through *La Sal de las Doñas*, **calle Valencia, No. 226, 08007, Barcelona**.

Women's Baths

Tucked in a secluded part of Hampstead Heath, a beautiful park in London, is the **Women's Pond**, where topless (but not bottomless) swimming is the rule. Across Europe, public bathhouses for women (or with women-only days)—sometimes called Turkish baths—still exist in many towns, complete with sauna, steam room, and showers. They range from the humble (but usually delightful) to the opulent, such as London's women-only **Sanctuary** and Berlin's **Hamam** in the

Schokofabrik (Women's Building). Budapest has scores of bath-houses, fed by thermal and mineral springs. In Morocco and across North Africa, the steam baths are called *hamam* and remain one of the few places for unencumbered interaction among women.

Women's Centers and Cafes

Women's centers and cafes, located primarily in Western countries, are great places to get recharged, meet local women, and get advice, assistance, and good tips on what not to miss. Some are modest vol-unteer-supported projects. Many are solidly established, such as Kyoto's **Bioti**, a vegetarian restaurant and women's information cen-ter. A few are large-scale operations such as Berlin's **Cafe im Frauen-stadtteilzentrum**, a former chocolate factory that now houses a women's theater, sports center, cafe, steam room, sauna, and a women's arts and crafts center, and Geneva's **Centre Femmes**, which has a restaurant and bar, terraced garden, library, video archives, ex-hibitions, and workshop space.

Listen to the Music

Music lovers can save lots of research time by consulting the *Music Lover's Guide to Europe—A Compendium of Festivals, Concerts and Opera* by Roberta Gottesman. A calendar of events and map keys help you organize your own concert tour from among 600 events at 300 locations in eighteen countries.

Go to School

Do you harbor a secret desire to be an outstanding chef? A first-rate photographer? Use your vacation as an opportunity to sign up for classes in cooking, skiing, language, wine appreciation, or art history.

La Verenne, the famous Parisian cooking school, holds bilingual, hands-on summer classes at the Château du Feÿ in Burgundy. Shaw's *Guide to Cooking Schools* provides listings of many schools that are popular with travelers.

If you're focused on photography, attend the Chenik Brown Bear Photography Camp, where the world's largest concentration of brown bears fish for salmon each summer, or join Ecosummer Expeditions' tours, which balance outdoor adventure and photography. Shaw's *Guide to Photography Workshops and Schools* lists more than 200 workshops in over two dozen countries.

Four hundred overseas language and other centers are described in *Vacation Study Abroad*. Study Spanish for twenty to thirty hours per week in Antigua, Guatemala, while you live with a family; take the fifteen-week course at the Instituto de Lengua Española in Costa Rica; or choose from a variety of courses at one of nine locations in Spain (including Seville, Granada, Salamanca, and the Costa del Sol) offered by Lingua Service Worldwide of New York.

Shaw's *Guide to Writers Conferences* describes over 850 writing workshops. Of particular interest is the **The Flight of the Mind Writing Workshops for Women** which offers an outstanding summer program for women writers on the scenic McKenzie River in the foothills of the Oregon Cascade Mountains. For information send a first-class stamp to: **The Flight of the Mind, 622 S.E. Twenty-ninth Avenue, Portland, OR 97214 (503/236-9862).**

Study Tours

Study tours provide a nice challenge. They offer lectures from experts in the field and often require participants to do background reading in advance. They may be sponsored by an organization you already belong to—your library, zoo, university extension program, sister city program, environmental organization, or world affairs council. **Academic Travel Abroad** organizes over a hundred programs a year for many of these institutions. Contact: **Academic Travel Abroad, 3210 Grace Street, N.W., Washington, DC 20007 (202/333-3355).**

Elderhostel offers short-term academic programs for people sixty years of age and older. Costs are kept low through campus living. Most programs last one week and offer one to three courses of study during that time. Programs are offered in every American state and

Canadian province and in forty-five other countries. Special arrangements are made for physically disabled participants. The catalog of offerings is over a hundred pages long, and a short video is available upon request. Contact: **Elderhostel, 75 Federal Street, Boston, MA 02110 (617/426-8056).**

Folkways Institute offers field-study tours in cultural and natural history led by naturalists and academic guest lecturers. Some trips are limited to participants over fifty-five; others welcome all ages. Offerings include a culinary and cultural tour of Italy, studies of the history and culture of Nepal, and cruises down the Nile and through France's Burgundy country. Contact: **Folkways Institute, 14600 S.E. Aldridge Road, Portland, OR 97236 (800/225-4666).**

Sierra Club organizes over 300 outings in over twenty-six countries, divided into five categories (light to strenuous activity). As many as 75 percent of participants are solo travelers. Contact: **Sierra Club, 730 Polk, San Francisco, CA 94109 (415/923-5630).**

Study Cruises

Skip the shuffleboard and the slot machines. Instead, spend your shipboard time studying ancient cultures and archaeology, astronomy, or marine biology with naturalists and cultural historians in the Mediterranean. Contact: **Swan Hellenic Cruises, 581 Boylston Street, Boston, MA 02116 (800/426-5492).**

Small expedition ships travel to the Seychelle Islands along the Great Barrier Reef in Australia and to the Antarctic. Shore visits on Zodiac landing craft allow exploration of remote rivers, inlets, and beaches for observation of marine life, birds and wildlife. Contact **Sea Quest Cruises, 600 Corporate Drive, No. 410, Ft. Lauderdale, FL 33334 (800/223-5688).**

Residential Campus Programs

Residential study courses abound throughout the world. You can study Shakespeare at Oxford or art history at Cambridge, attend a Danish folk school or study traditional Appalachian crafts such as stonemasonry, quilt-making, and log home construction in West Virginia. Contact the **National Registration Center for Study Abroad,** a consortium of overseas schools in sixteen countries **(414/278-0631).** Some of these are for women only, such as **Kvinnohogskolan** (Women's School), **Storsund 90, S-781 94 Borlange, Sweden (0243-237-07).**

Focus on Film

International women's film festivals are held each year in Amsterdam and London. **La Festival des Films des Femmes** is held annually in a Paris suburb. For information contact: c/o **Maison des Arts, Place Salvador Allende, 94000 Créteil, France (49-80-38-98).**

Search Out Women's History

Do battlegrounds, castles, and cathedrals bore you? There's much more to history than the remnants of men's wars and conquests. Study women's history, and use your travel time to search for important sites in women's lives.

On your next visit to London, buy *In Our Grandmothers' Footsteps: A Virago Guide to London* by Jennifer Clarke or *Our Sisters' London: Feminist Walking Tours* by Katherine Sturtevant, and plan a week's worth of walking tours: past Caxton Hall, where the suffragettes held the First Women's Parliament; to the home and clinic of early birth control activist Marie Stopes; and into the militant women's stories set at Westminster Abbey and the Tower of London. Jennifer Clarke's *Exploring the West Country: A Woman's Guide* is highly recommended for travel in a beautiful part of England that includes Cornwall, Devon, and Somerset. Expand your explorations throughout the British Isles with *Local Heroines: A Women's History Gazetteer to England, Scotland and Wales*. Author Jane Legget guides you to the birthplaces, former homes, schools, places of work, sources of inspiration, graves, and memorials of over 500 prominent and obscure artists and actors, suffragettes and politicians, trade union activists and welfare workers. The **Fawcett Library** in London is an impressive women's archive with an extensive collection of suffragette memorabilia and documents. It's at the City of London Polytechnic, **Calcutta House, Old Castle Street, E1 7NT**. Call for hours **(071/283-1030, ext. 570)**.

Create your own tour of the remaining *beguinages* (independent women's communities) in Belgium, which date back as far as the twelfth century. Independent of both husbands and the church, thousands of women lived cooperatively and supported themselves by running schools, spinning, weaving, and lacemaking in Bruges, Leuven, Diest, Ghent, Antwerp, Arschot, and Kortrijk. Many of the *beguinages* are gone, but about twenty of them still exist. They are described in *Are You Two...Together?: A Gay and Lesbian Travel Guide to Europe* by Lindsy Van Gelder and Pamela Robin Brandt.

Focus a trip to Crete on learning about the Minoan civilization, the last culture with a nondominator form of social organization. Visit the ruins of Knossos, where ancient art and architecture come alive in partially reconstructed buildings that foster easy imaginings of the way things were.

Look for a feminist tour company, if you don't want to organize your own trip. **Frauen Unterwegs** (Women on the Move) in Berlin takes small groups of women (ten to twenty) on European tours of various kinds, as well as a shorter "Feminist Berlin" tour. You can contact them at: **Potsdamer Strasse 139, 1000 Berlin 30, Germany (030/215-1022)**.

Pursue Professional Interests

Ask your professional association, club, or union for international contacts and help in arranging meetings. China is one of many countries that regularly arranges introductions between foreign visitors and their Chinese colleagues. Take advantage of "sister city" relationships to meet people who share your professional interests. **Sister Cities International** provides a directory of sister cities worldwide. Contact: **120 South Payne, Alexandria VA 22314 (703/836-3535)**.

Attend an international conference or event that interests you. The International Feminist Bookfair is held every other year in a different country. Contact the **Permanent Secretariat, c/o Carol Seajay, Feminist Bookstore News, PO Box 882554, San Francisco, CA 94188 (415/ 626-1556)** for information.

Follow the Footsteps of Intrepid Travelers

Travelogues chronicle the journeys of daring Victorian women who set out alone to travel across Africa, the Middle East, and Asia. Virago Press in the U.K. and Beacon Press in the U.S. have reprinted many of these marvelous books, including Mary Kingsley's *Travels in West Africa*, Alexandra David-Neel's *My Journey to Lhasa*, and five volumes by Isabella Bird.

Mary Kingsley left England for West Africa in 1893. She collected beetles and fish, explored a section of the Congo, and negotiated the deadly rapids of the Ogowe River in a canoe. A century later, Caroline Alexander followed Mary Kingsley's route, recording her observations in *One Dry Season: In the Footsteps of Mary Kingsley*.

Modern-day women adventurers abound. Draw inspiration from books written by Dervla Murphy, Helen Winternitz, Mary Morris, or Jan Morris.

The first time I went to Africa was in 1971. I participated in a program called Operation Crossroads Africa. I was a freshman in college, and I received a scholarship and some assistance from a professional business-women's association. Operation Crossroads Africa was founded by a minister to provide interracial opportunities for folks from the United States to go to the Continent and have an educational work experience. The summer I went over, there were 150 of us, black and white, high school and college students, from all over the country.

For me, it was a very emotional return to Africa. From the moment I got on the plane in New York, headed for Africa, it was like a dream. Most of us were very moved when we landed in Senegal, especially the black students. People were kissing the earth, looking for stones or pieces of earth to pick up and touch. I brought some rocks back with me. It was an incredible feeling.

The ten people in my group were assigned to a small village in Nigeria named Osi-Okero. We helped the villagers build their maternity hospital from the ground up. We cleared the earth, made the bricks, and laid the bricks, shoulder to shoulder with people of the village. The chief allowed our group to live in his compound to show his consent to our contribution to the community. That's where we lived for the summer, sharing meals and participating in the life of the village. The people were very warm and gracious and were glad to see African Americans participating.

Together with students from the University of Ife and students from the University of Ibadan we put on a cultural performance, featuring poetry from Africa and America. At night in the village when we finished our work on the hospital, we gathered around candles, studying our lines and working on the dialogue.

I don't think any of us really knew or understood the magnitude of what we were about to do until we actually got out on the stage. We were greeted by a standing-room-only crowd; people were lined up in the street trying to get into the building to see the African-American students and our peers from the Continent perform the poetry of Langston Hughes and other

African Americans. It was absolutely incredible. I still have a big poster at home that publicized that event—even now when I look at it I get real strong feelings.

When we left, the hospital was three-quarters finished. We had put in the window frames, but not the windows. In fact, when I look back, I'm still amazed at how much we were able to accomplish. What we did was a result of a collective effort; everyone worked on this common vision of what was to be. I've often wondered what it looks like now. Maybe some day, if I'm fortunate, I'll be able to go back and take a look.

That summer was the first time that I had traveled outside the country and the second time that I traveled anywhere alone; it was an opportunity to get to know myself. There I was, having to count on my own inner resources and find out what my strengths were and deal with my weaknesses and fears and all of that.

That trip influenced the direction of my life. I have no doubt about it. It had a lot to do with the way I see the world and people in it. I learned that we are all tied together; what affects one of us affects all of us. There are so many artificial barriers that get set up between people, and we allow those barriers to keep us from knowing one another. It was an opening-up experience for me, opening me up to the world and my place in it.

The other part of it is that when you go some place like that, you have to be prepared to see real poverty, suffering, and degradation. The idea of the "ugly American" is real, and hard to overcome if you don't feel it is you. It was a time for me to become more aware of the ironies and injustices that we allow to exist in the world.

Quite a few years later, I returned to Africa as a political activist in a very different mode. My second trip was a study tour put together by the American Friends Service Committee. We went to observe the impact of South African policies on the surrounding states—Zimbabwe, Mozambique, Botswana, Lesotho.

It was another incredible journey. In South Africa we were traveling from Lesotho down to the Transkei, where we had planned to meet with some church representatives, when we became aware that we were being followed. We were pulled over by members of the South African defense force—the police. The armed black officers searched our car and let us know that they would be monitoring our movements. We went on and were stopped again, late at night on a lonely road with no lights or people. Several cars came literally from nowhere and surrounded us. Again, police got out, some in uniform, some not, with automatic weapons and shotguns held on us. They searched our car, searched our luggage, and went through the pages of our books. This was a very tense time, in 1985, just prior to the state of emergency being declared.

We were probably a real suspicious group of people—four blacks in a car with a foreign license plate. The car was packed with luggage, yet clearly we weren't tourists. Once it was established that we were Americans, affiliated with AFSC, they became even more interested in who we were and why we were there. When it became clear that our movements were going to be monitored, we changed our itinerary. We shredded anti-apartheid literature that we were carrying. We did not go to see the people we were planning to see, not wanting to bring harm to anyone.

The third time we were stopped, we literally quaked with fear. By this time no one really knew our movements because we had changed our plans. They took us to this little house, which turned out to be an out-of-the-way police station, took us into separate rooms, and interrogated us.

We had no idea it would be that dangerous when we accepted an invitation from Bishop Tutu to attend one of the church-sponsored meetings there. But we wound up on a road, four of us facing a dozen men with guns pointed at us. Again, it was one of those opening-up experiences, where you end up coming to terms with fear. You get a sense of what you're made of. And we all four came away feeling like we were brothers and sisters.

We also had very warm experiences with people there. Several people would look at me with my hair worn short then as I do now, and say, "You're one of us, who are your people?" As soon as I opened my mouth, they'd say, "Oh, you're American!" There was that warmth. We got constant invitations to visit people in their homes. It's good to bring things over to give away—books, educational materials, and clothing. But they must be given with love and respect.

The most important thing I learned from my travels to Africa is to be totally open to the experience. No matter where you are, don't make assumptions about people or their politics. Once I got into a conversation with the chambermaid in our hotel, and she turned out to be the leader of a large women's organization with over 300 members.

For the African-American cultural community, returning to Africa is very high on the agenda; the Caribbean is also attractive. Or, we go to Europe to see the lost and stolen artifacts from our ancient cultures.

Get Involved

Seize opportunities to get involved with people around you. Anything of mutual interest can inspire conversation—even a crochet hook. Sandy Polishuk recounts this story:

> I always travel with a crochet hook. One spring, I
> bought a ball of crochet cotton and made a string bag on
> the train from Holland to Paris. When the weather got
> warmer, I stuffed my sweater and down jacket in the
> string bag; it was lightweight and easy to carry over my
> shoulder. My new bag was so pretty my hosts in Corsica
> each wanted their own. We found more string in the
> market and I happily obliged them. When I got to Spain,
> a friend asked to trade some of her homemade goat cheese
> for a bag. I worked out a goat head design for hers.
>
> On a train in northern Spain I was using two colors to
> make a geometric design on a change purse when I
> discovered the woman sitting next to me was also
> crocheting. We showed each other our work and used
> sign language to explain just what we were doing. My
> Spanish was very limited, but I said lots of "muy
> bonitas." Another connection made beyond language via
> the crochet hook.

Teach English

Drop in on classes where students are studying English, or any subject you can help teach. Guests are almost always welcome. I met teachers and visited English classes in Nepal, Mexico, Indonesia, and Greece. In China, where it's rare to encounter English speakers on the street, English classes provide a welcome venue for personal conversation. Visiting our friends who taught English at two schools was a highlight of Mary's and my interaction with the Chinese:

> *At the Science Institute, we agreed to attend Linda's class several times during one week, for two hours each visit. The first visit was mostly small talk, but I suggested a ground rule: they could ask me anything about myself or the United States if I could ask them anything about China. By the second day, the more interesting topics were approached. I asked about their personal experiences during the Cultural Revolution, and they asked me questions like: What do Americans do on dates? How does divorce work in America? Is it true that after divorce, the father usually raises the children? Are all soldiers homosexuals? Most of these questions arose from generalizations created from a single news story or American film.*

In Malang, Java, a unique dormitory-style hostel served two functions. The Bamboo Den/Webb Institute, offered low-cost accommodations (one dollar per night) if travelers agreed to attend at least one conversation class while there. Local students had a constant parade of British, Canadian, American, and Australian accents to decipher.

Teaching English as a second language is a favorite way of earning money for long-term travelers. Read about the requirements, training, and opportunities in *Teaching English Abroad* by Susan Griffith.

Haul That Boat

Pitch in and help people who need a hand. While walking along the beach in Goa with my Austrian travel partner, Eva, we spotted a man and a boy struggling to beach their boat. Goa is the "little Portugal" on the central west coast of India.

> *We helped a man and boy push an outrigger fishing boat from the surf. Other family members arrived, and*

*we joined in untangling the fish from the golden nets,
sorting them into baskets for the market in Margao.
Sebastian Fernandes and his wife invited us up to their
house. A long pantomimed exchange brought out an
invitation for Eva and me to go out fishing on the boat
the following night. We met Sebastian and his nephew on
the beach at 3 A.M. and pushed off into a star-encrusted
night. A single candle lantern hung from a tree-limb
mast. After lowering the nets, Eva and I napped in the
bow of the boat, moonlight washing over our faces as the
waves gently rocked us to sleep. We returned at 8 A.M.,
and Sebastian insisted on giving us a share of the catch;
we feasted on a huge platter of lobster, crabs, prawns, and
fish for breakfast.*

Eva and I spent most of a week visiting daily with the Fernandes family. The older children, who studied English in school, got plenty of extra practice as they struggled to translate our wide-ranging conversations.

Explore New Interests

Let your enthusiasm lead you down twisted roads and back alleys. Pursue subjects you happen upon while traveling; find out all you can by meeting local experts, artists, and craftspeople.

How I Became an Art Collector

*We're in Ubud, a Balinese arts and cultural center.
Hundreds of weavers, wood-carvers, and painters reside
in the villages nearby. Mary and I are especially enchanted with the paintings, which range from traditional
Balinese-Hindu legends to contemporary scenes of rice
paddies with exquisite detail. There is great variety, and
some are not very expensive; we're going to buy some
art.*

*We've visited a large gallery and the museum and
written down names of our favorite artists. Then we try*

*to track them down. It's like going to the National
Museum of Art and finding out that all the painters live
in the neighborhood! Each morning we set off on foot or
riding rented "pushbikes" up narrow lanes. We stop
repeatedly to ask for directions—"turn past the monkey
forest"; "go straight beyond the second temple"; "keep
going through the rice paddies"—until we find our
destination. Sometimes a child is sent to guide us to the
proper house. If the artist is at home, we politely ask to
see their work. We may be invited for coffee; we sit and
talk, all the while gazing out over the terraced rice
paddies. There is no pressure to buy, we can think it over
and return another day. We ask for advice about where to
stop for lunch. Every meal in Bali is a great experience:
giant prawns with ginger and chilies, barbecued chicken
with papaya in coconut milk, gado gado, fresh fruit
shakes, black rice pudding for dessert.*

Cross that invisible line between observing a country and its people
and interacting with them. Be adventurous and curious.

The Spices of Life

*Eva and I wandered along the main street of Cochin. It
is a major southern port and the historical locus of
India's spice merchants. We decided to learn all we could
about spices. We walked up and down the pungent
streets, pausing at the doorways of buildings to peer into
courtyards covered with mountains of black pepper,
ginger, nutmeg, turmeric, and cardamom being sorted,
shoveled, or bagged. One spice merchant, the son from
Vasanji and Son, invited us to his office for a cup of chai
(Indian boiled spiced tea). He sent his assistant outside
repeatedly to fetch samples until he had before us the
twelve spices that go into a cup of chai. He told us about
the spice market of New York, where these bales were
destined; ginger is down, pepper up these days. As a
special treat, he made us a pan and waited expectantly
for us to pop it into our mouths. (Pan is the Indian*

version of chewing tobacco, a collection of spices, betel
nut, lime paste, all wrapped in an edible leaf that you
hold in your cheek and chew.) Unsure of our abilities to
use the spittoon, we bade our farewells and ran out to the
street to dispose of our tasty treat.

Embark on a search for the perfect crème caramel, steamed dumpling, or gazpacho. It may transport you to the kitchens of hidden restaurants and even into the home of the chef's mother.

Volunteer

Find local contacts who share your concerns about political, social, and economic issues. Offer to attend meetings and exchange information. Not an expert in either field, I talked with women lawyers in India about feminist legal issues and with members of the Ghandi Institute on nuclear power and the environment. The updates I provided, based on information gleaned from reading newspapers back home, sparked lively interchanges.

If you are a member of an international organization such as the Women's International League for Peace and Freedom or the World Wildlife Federation, inquire with your national headquarters for contacts with local chapters before you travel.

Help Other People

While studying Spanish in Guatemala, legal aid lawyer Lee Ann Ward was shocked at the exploitation of local women weavers by foreign buyers. After learning they earned only ten cents for several days' labor, she stayed to help organize a weavers' cooperative and develop direct markets for their distinctive goods. When she left the village two years later, a new school and thriving weavers' cooperative were firmly in place.

In India, I volunteered at a rural development organization called Bhagavatula Charitable Trust. I arranged my stay in advance and made a donation to cover the cost of my food and lodging.

Volunteer Vacations: A Directory of Short-Term Adventures That Will Benefit You...and Others by Bill McMillon lists almost two hundred organizations that sponsor over two thousand projects annually in the areas of public health, medical and dental assistance, environmental work, marine research, executive and technical assistance, archaeology, and community development worldwide. In some cases, fees paid to the organization are tax deductible. Some of the best known nonprofit organizations that rely on volunteer labor for achieving their goals include:

• **Habitat for Humanity**—Imagine returning from vacation with sore muscles, callused hands, and a picture of the house you helped build for a family who needed it. Habitat for Humanity offers volunteers opportunities to do just that—for one to three weeks in the United States and Canada, or longer periods of time in over thirty countries, located in Africa, South America, Asia, and the Pacific Islands. Contact: **Habitat for Humanity, Habitat and Church Streets, Americus, GA 31709 (912/924-6935).**

• **Operation Crossroads Africa**—This group sends college and high school students (including those with visual, hearing, mobility, and other medical disabilities) to rural Africa and the Caribbean to build medical clinics, day camps for children, and to assist with archaeological and agricultural projects. Contact: **Operation Crossroads Africa, 150 Fifth Avenue, New York, NY 10011 (212/242-8550).**

Save the Planet

Among the excellent organizations that offer trips with a focus on environmental concerns are:

• **Earthwatch Institute**—Paying volunteers assist scientists and share the costs of environmental and archaeological expeditions around the world. The current catalogue lists 141 projects needing volunteer assistance; no previous experience is necessary. Observe koala bears in Queensland, Australia; study dolphins in Hawaii; measure leatherneck turtles in St.

Croix, the U.S. Virgin Islands; track endangered species in the rain forests of Brazil. Earthwatch staff work with potential volunteers with disabilities to find creative ways to maximize their participation on the projects they hope to join. Contact: **Earthwatch, 680 Mount Auburn Street, Box 403, Watertown MA 02272 (617/926-8200).**

•**Smithsonian Research Expeditions**—Join curators at museums or in the field. Recent expeditions include monitoring an active volcano in Costa Rica, researching giant tortoises of the Mojave Desert, and excavating Paleo-Indian remains in rural Virginia. Contact: **Smithsonian Research Expedition Program, Smithsonian Institution, 490 L'Enfant Plaza S.W., Rm. 4210, Washington, DC 20560 (202/287-3210).**

•**TERN, the Traveler's Earth Repair Network**—TERN links overseas travelers and hosts concerned with reforestation, forest preservation, and sustainable agriculture. Sponsored by Friends of the Trees, TERN will supply lists of names and organizations for travelers interested in making overseas contacts. For information on fees and services, contact: **Friends of the Trees Society, PO Box 1064, Tonasket, WA 98855.**

•**Youth Service International**—Young women and men aged seventeen to twenty-five are selected to participate in international expeditions that promote human service and environmental conservation. YSI participants have helped replant trees in a Czech forest destroyed by acid rain, conducted wildlife surveys in northern Slovakia, and worked to protect golden eagle nesting areas in the High Tatras Mountains. Contact: **Youth Service International, 301 North Blount Street, Raleigh, NC 27601 (800/833-5796).**

Take a Political Tour

If you want firsthand exposure to social problems and economic issues and their solutions in Africa, Asia, India, and South America, go and meet with local activists, political officials, and social workers.

You can organize your own political tour as Mimi Maduro and her husband did.

> *We spent our honeymoon traveling to Vietnam. We were both drawn there—Michael as a Vietnam veteran who works with vets, and me as a child of the sixties who had horrific images indelibly imprinted on her mind. We took our nephew Chris with us—he is twenty-three, the same age Michael was when he went to Vietnam.*
>
> *We didn't want to take a tour, so we called the William Joiner Foundation, which studies war and its social consequences. They gave us ideas on how to go about making contacts as independent travelers. At their suggestion, we wrote to the Vietnamese government, describing ourselves and who we wanted to meet. Through a series of faxes and phone calls to the Vietnamese Mission to the United Nations, our visit was set up. Mr. Cuong met us at the airport, helped us bypass a lot of bureaucracy, arranged our journeys, and set up homestays for us all over Vietnam. We were astounded and very grateful for all the assistance we were given as two American citizens interested in healing the wounds of the past.*
>
> *We visited several Vietnamese veterans and their families and learned a lot about how vets are treated there, which is very different from how vets are treated in the U.S. The heart-to-heart contact was really special.*
>
> *I had two major pursuits. In Hanoi, I met with members of the Vietnamese Women's Union. We discussed family planning, poverty, and health-care issues. Despite the differences, we found many points of commonality—it meant a great deal to all of us.*
>
> *In Saigon we met with the head of the Vietnamese Writers' Union. The Joiner Foundation had sponsored a short-story writing contest in Vietnam, and 4,000 manuscripts had been submitted. The manuscripts were carried out in these teetering piles; people had written*

*their lives on scraps of paper, by hand and with broken
old typewriters. Only a hundred of the entries were from
women, yet women won two of the four prizes!*

*We were able to make a $50 donation to the writers'
union to be given as first prize in the contest. This was a
way in which a small sum of money, given appropriately,
had a large effect. Because of the exchange rate, the prize
money equaled an annual salary for an average worker—
it allowed a writer a whole year in which to write.*

*It turned out during the conversation that the head of
the writers' union and Michael were both stationed at
Tay-Ninh during the war. Their faces lit up as they
realized that over two decades ago they were fighting
each other; now we were sitting down and having tea.*

Several organizations offer a range of political tours. Generally, housing is modest, and participants are expected to read and study in preparation for the trip. Contact: **Plowshares Institute, P.O. Box 243, Simsbury, CT 06070**. Send a self-addressed, stamped envelope for information, or call **213/651-4303**.

The Center for Global Education organizes travel seminars to the Middle East, Central America, and other locations. Ten- to fourteen-day trips expose participants to a variety of points of view on local problems. Contact: **The Center for Global Education, Augsburg College, 731 Twenty-first Avenue South, Minneapolis, MN 55454 (612/330-1159)**.

Global Exchange Reality Tours take you to meet farmers, religious leaders, women's groups, and government and opposition leaders on tours such as: "Culture, Politics, and Religion in Haiti"; "Grass-roots Organizing in the Philippines," and "Environment and Alternative Medicine in Cuba." The nonprofit organization also provides resources, organizing ideas, and contacts to facilitate lifelong partnerships between tour participants and the groups they've met. Contact: **Global Exchange Reality Tours, 2141 Mission Street, No. 202, San Francisco, CA 94110 (415/255-7296)**.

AT BHAGAVATULA CHARITABLE TRUST

I got off the train at Yellamanchili, an hour outside Visakhapatnam, India. A short rickshaw ride down a dirt road from the station took me to the office of the BCT, where I climbed into a van that hustled me down back roads, past paddy fields and bullock carts to Haripuram Farm. The farm was the hub of the organization's work—to help the rural poor in twenty-seven villages of the Indian state of Andhra Pradesh climb out of poverty.

Parameswara Rao, the organization's founder, greeted me at the farm and introduced me to Sujata, a top organizer who offered me a short tour. Young and elegant in her sari, she showed me the quarters where the staff lived and the guest room that would be mine for the next two weeks.

I had been a community organizer for years, working with citizen groups and women's organizations around the United States. While issues changed, the task was always the same—building citizen leadership to tackle the problems of unresponsive corporations and government. My tools were simple—I called people on the telephone from the organization's office and met them in coffee shops and meeting halls to discuss strategy, make plans, and build organization. Invited to observe community organizing at BCT, I wondered how the principles of organizing I knew would apply in this place, where the issues and conditions seemed vastly different. I followed Sujata for several days as she walked from village to village, meeting with local leaders.

In Kummarapalli I absorbed the rhythms of women grinding spices on large flat stones, of men harnessing water buffalo to work the rice paddies, the sound of laundry being slapped against rocks, the chattering of children doing their chores. Our arrival in Mamidevada provided an excuse to take a short break. The villagers offered me special treats—warm buffalo milk and short pieces of sugar cane. I swallowed the thick warm milk as best I could, then stripped the bark off the cane with my teeth and chewed the pulp as a crowd solemnly gathered to witness my delight.

But Sujata was working. She squatted beside a woman in front of her mud-walled home. They conferred in low voices and drew figures in the dirt. Messages would be passed from person to person; there were no telephones. In the time I might have made forty or fifty phone calls at home, we walked to two villages and met with three or four women. I was awed by the slow pace and wondered how long it would take to get things done. What could they accomplish on foot with no telephones?

Quite a bit.

Thrift societies, organized by village women, have broken the stranglehold of the money lenders and enabled families to buy their land and invest in farm animals and basic equipment. Child care centers and nutrition programs crack the cycle of illiteracy. Wasteland development projects reclaim eroded land and return it to productive use. Appropriate technology projects, such as windmills and biogas, make use of precious natural resources.

The village women were the most valuable natural resource to be "discovered" by BCT. They were the keys to success for most of the projects. At one village's annual meeting, wives and mothers reviewed the past year's progress and made plans for the future. A BCT staffer translated the proceedings into my ear, but the prioritizing of plans, discussion, and voting were all as familiar as my meetings back home.

Top priority was placed on reorganization and expansion of BCT's training programs. I had just completed a year training American women to run organizations and political campaigns and offered to lend a hand in designing the new programs. I was to assist Raghavarao, the head trainer, in his task.

We reviewed the training needs of widows and "untouchable" women who aspired to be health care workers and para-veterinarians. Women who saved a few rupees each week in the thrift society now wanted to read and write in order to keep track of their savings, give loans, and develop lending policies. Our next work session revealed many common principles of organizing and training. Raghavarao and I were sparked by the interchange of ideas and experiences. We worked long hours each day, drafting and redrafting training programs and curricula. In a week, we had designed the Basic Training Program, a Dairy Training Program, Para-Vet Program, and Thrift Management Program.

Whenever I think now about my time there, I remember the end of one day. I felt overwhelmed by the task and doubted that my work could actually be of assistance. Then my eyes drifted to a sign on the wall—a hand-lettered plaque read, "Your feet should be in one village, your eyes and mind to the whole world."

Step Off the Beaten Track

After months of travel in Southeast Asia, I felt like just another ant, following an established, well-marked track. The geography of Indonesia, Malaysia, and Thailand determined the curve of the track. All the other traveler-ants got their marching orders from the same, well-known budget guidebook. Some journeyed from north to south; the rest passed in the opposite direction, reading the book from back to front. We met along the road, eating and sleeping in all the recommended places, sharing tips and updating information.

At first it was comforting to follow the track. The book explained Balinese culture and Javanese history. Although I was far from home, I was surrounded by a comforting cocoon of Westerners. The book predicted prices, told us where to go, what to eat, and where to stay. It was a good guidebook, packed with helpful information; yet I found it limiting me to the places mentioned in the text. After a while, I wondered if I would ever meet a local person or family outside a restaurant or lodge—someone who hadn't had the same conversation with me as they'd had with the many travelers who'd passed through before?

Most people in Indonesia, Malaysia and Thailand live in small villages never mentioned in the book. I wanted to meet those people and stay in their villages, even if there was "nothing special" to see or do. It was ordinary daily life that interested me. I shut the guidebook and buried it in my pack.

I spent the next fifteen months traveling mostly off the well worn path. I dug out the book every few weeks when I needed a rest or when, exhausted by my attempts to communicate in yet another language, I longed to converse in English. Then I would head for one of those travelers' way stations that are tucked in beautiful corners all over the world. I would sleep late, eat an American breakfast, and spend a day on the beach with vagabonds from Canada and France, trading paperback books and travel tales.

Soon I would unfold the map and begin plotting the next part of my journey. With a little practice, I learned how to leave most other travelers behind.

Get Away from Beaches and Paved Roads

Just a short distance from most famous beach resorts lies another, uncrowded world. Follow the crooked line on your map. Look for dirt roads and dead-end lanes that tour buses can't negotiate. Only a few kilometers inland from the sea of sunbathers on the Spanish coast are tranquil towns without resorts and tourists. Mountain villages of Jamaica, like those of many other islands, are rarely visited even when the beaches are crowded. Seek the road less traveled to a destination in the interior.

Drive your own vehicle for free access to out-of-the-way places. Traveling by car or van can be economical, especially for a family or small group. Barbara Gundle explains how her family did it:

> We bought an empty Mercedes freight van and put everything in it—bunks, a stove, a little oven, windows and skylights for ventilation, a sink with a foot pump for water, and a solar sailboat-type shower that sat on the roof. If you don't want to do all the work yourself, there's a market in Amsterdam for used vans; you can fly to Amsterdam, buy a used Volkswagen camper, drive it around Europe, and then sell it at the end of your trip.
>
> It was a very cheap way to travel; our biggest expense was gasoline. Of course, we had to buy the van, but overall it was much cheaper to sleep in it every night than to pay for lodging each night for a year. We shipped the van three times: from Egypt to Singapore, from Singapore to Sumatra, and from Java home. That was a major expense, but still, it was a very cheap year.
>
> I was concerned that traveling in our own car might be a bit isolating, but it really wasn't. We often picked up hitchhikers, which was a good way for us to meet people.

One time, we stopped for a guy hitchhiking at a 1,000-foot high pass in Guatemala. As soon as we stopped, he motioned to the side of the road, and ten other people jumped out. They were all carrying metates, those big bowls used for grinding spices, made out of volcanic stone. They were on their way to the market, so we loaded all their metates in the van. By then the van was so heavy, we were worried about making it safely down from the mountain.

Instead of going to a hotel, where mostly Americans and Europeans were guests, we slept almost every night in a village, where we'd be the only strangers. So every night we'd have conversations with local people. We bought our food in the markets, just like they did; we bathed in the rivers with them, we did our laundry in the rivers. We were basically living in the streets, which is how a lot of people live; so we had plenty of contact.

Thailand was great because fairly early on we figured out about the Buddhist wats, or temples, in every community. It's part of their tradition to welcome travelers off the road. Every little village has one, and they are sort of removed, generally with a stone wall and some grounds, and are very quiet places—refuges. We realized that we could always find the local wat and have a place to camp for the night. We were always welcomed with open arms. In the little villages, it was so quiet we could hear the monks chanting their prayers. And then they would come out and bring us little hospitality gifts, like soap. We'd usually pull in at dusk and leave in the morning. Thailand was one of our favorite countries for that reason.

Nothing bad ever happened to us. The worst thing was in Sumatra, in a village called Barstogi, the home of a former head-hunting tribe. Of course, they're not head-hunters any more, but the people seemed to have a mischievous sense of humor. We asked the headman if we could spend the night in the village, as we had learned

was proper, so we could hike up this volcano early the
next day. He said yes, and showed us where to park the
van. Then some kids asked if we wanted to hire them to
watch the car. And we said, no thanks, we don't need any
help. We went to sleep and about five in the morning we
heard voices and looked out the window and saw kids
standing around. They started rocking the van, and then
they let the air out of our tires. And we realized, "Oh,
wrong decision, we should have paid them to watch our
van." We had a tire pump, and we pumped up the tires.
And that was the most trouble that we had in a year.

You don't have to travel far afield to get off the beaten track. Even in countries like the United States, you can go beyond the obvious tourist destinations to discover fascinating places. In *Going off the Beaten Path: An Untraditional Travel Guide to the U.S.*, author Mary Dymond Davis describes places few guidebooks ever mention: sites associated with noted environmentalists (how *do* you get to Walden Pond?), resource-conserving buildings and structures (from ancient cliff dwellings to modern solar structures), and peace sites, as well as natural areas and their wildlife.

Choose the More Difficult Transportation Options

Most tourists, due to time limitations or lethargy, won't expend much energy to get around. Greece is a classic example. Some say the Greek islands are overrun with tourists. But the vast majority herd onto a few well-known islands, those with daily ferry service from Piraeus. Use a ferry or bus schedule to research the less crowded spots—the ports where ferries stop only once a week, the towns with bus service just once a day. Visit an island you've never heard of, one that is reachable only by boat via another island. If you have to walk a half-hour or more to reach your destination, few others will be there.

Eschew the cruise ships and join local passengers on ferries that travel:

• Across the Caribbean—Wend your way from Grenada to Mustique to St. Vincent on mail boats and schooners. Snorkel the coral reefs, catch the Saturday market in Dominica, or wander seventeen miles of pink beach on Barbuda.

•To the Arctic Circle—Coastal express steamers depart nightly from Bergen, Norway. Jump off at any of thirty-five ports and book a room with a family; get back on when you're ready to complete the four-day journey to the Arctic Circle. Travel in the early summer and see the Midnight Sun.

•Across the Saimaa lake region of Finland—Sail on the traditional double-decker lakeland steamer to visit the castle town of Savolinna and attend the International Summer Opera Festival held within the walls of the medieval castle each July.

Just Get off the Bus or Train at a Local Stop

If the view out the window is captivating, get off the train and look around some more. Wherever there are people, there is bound to be food and a place to stay. If you end up sleeping in a temple or church, the bus station or police station, it might just be the biggest adventure of your trip.

Seek Offbeat Accommodations

Convents throughout Italy, France, and Spain offer spotless rooms at very reasonable prices. Independent traveler Elizabeth Kaufman describes her experience in Italy:

> I stayed in a convent in an old basilica in Florence. I got the name from an article in the New York Times travel section. It was a gorgeous place with huge hallways, marble floors and staircase, although a bit starkly furnished. It was uncrowded, in the middle of the summer. I had a spacious private room with a full bathroom, breakfast and dinner, all for $30 a day, which was a bargain in Florence.
>
> There was a nice garden-filled courtyard where the nuns raised their vegetables and fruit trees. It was

peaceful inside, compared to the noisy streets. The meals were at set times and you had to be in by 10 P.M., so that was a bit restrictive. The nuns spoke Spanish, French, Italian, or German, but not English.

Although just a fifteen-minute walk from the train station, the convent was in a nice neighborhood away from the tourist scene downtown. As guests of the convent, we felt welcome in the neighborhood square; it was fun to watch the local kids play around the square and see the neighbors shopping on Saturday.

Some families stayed at the convent, but most of the guests were single women travelers. I met a lot of really nice women. Two middle-aged French sisters were travelling together through northern Italy for the summer. One was a teacher, like me, and we compared notes on class size and course requirements.

Another was a high school teacher in her early fifties from northeastern Spain. We took several day trips together to small towns in the Tuscan valley. She spoke Spanish, French, and German; I only spoke French and English. So we communicated for four days in French. She had a guidebook written in German, and she'd translate the sightseeing information into French for me. We still keep in touch.

Universities and private homes all provide opportunities to meet people more easily than standard hotels.

Join your national chapter of the **International Youth Hostels Association,** and gain access to over 5,300 hostels in fifty-nine countries. You'll pay from thirty-five cents to twenty dollars a night for a dormitory-style room with access to a self-service kitchen and dining area. Some private family rooms are available. There is no age limit on membership; in Europe especially, travelers of all ages stay at Youth Hostels. It's a great place to meet temporary traveling companions and trade information. Membership is twenty-five dollars (ten dollars for those under eighteen and fifteen dollars for those over fifty-four). In the U.S. write to **American Youth Hostels National**

Office, PO Box 37613, Washington, DC 20013 (202/783-6161); in Great Britain: **Youth Hostels Association of England and Wales; Trevelyan House, 8 St. Stephen's Hill St., Albans, Herts, AL1 2DY England (071/ 836-1036)**; in Ireland: **Irish Youth Hostel Association, An Oige, 39 Mountjoy Square, Dublin 1, Ireland**; in Australia: **Australian Youth Hostels Association, Level 3, Mallett Street, Camperdown, New South Wales 2050, Australia (61/565-1699)**; and in Canada: **Canadian Hostelling Association, 1600 James Naismith Drive, Suite 608, Gloucester, Ontario K1B 5N4, Canada (613/748-5638)**. An excellent directory with detailed information on each listing is *The International Youth Hostel Handbook*.

Home Exchange Programs

Avoid tourist zones by temporarily trading your home for another. Subscribers to home exchange services list detailed information about their homes or apartments in membership directories in order to exchange living space with others worldwide when time, space needs and preferences coincide. Weekend swaps to one-year exchanges are possible; sometimes a car is included.

Ruth Gundle and Judith Barrington traded their home in Portland, Oregon, for a house in London for a three-month trip.

> *We didn't go through an organization. Our exchange happened quite serendipitously. When friends of Judith's from London who were visiting the States heard that we were planning to take an extended trip to England the following year, they told us of friends of theirs who wanted to come to the Northwest. So we wrote them and asked if they were interested in trading houses and cars. They wrote back saying that they had never considered going to the Northwest but, since we mentioned it, it sounded like a great idea! We made detailed arrangements through the mail, each of us taking special care to make sure car insurance coverage was adequate.*
>
> *They left London the day after we arrived, so we had a day to meet each other and go over details. It worked out*

*splendidly. We each had house-sitters, lodgings, and a
vehicle for the entire trip, all at no cost. They had a great
time exploring the wilderness areas we recommended and
loved poking around in the shops and cafes in our
neighborhood. We had alerted friends to look in on them,
many of whom invited them to dinner or to interesting
events. On our end, we had a lovely four-storey terraced
house in one of London's most interesting sections, with
a gorgeous walled-in back garden where we ate our
breakfast under a flowering honeysuckle. An unexpected
bonus was a living room full of first editions of
Bloomsbury writers, one of whom had been a close friend
of the mother of our absent host.*

Some organizations that arrange home exchanges are:

•**Vacation Exchange Club, PO Box 820, Haleiwa, HI 96712
(800/638-3841).**

•**The Invented City, 41 Sutter Street, Suite 1090, San Francisco, CA 94104 (800/788-CITY)** in U.S.A., **(415/673-0347)**
worldwide.

•**Worldhomes Holiday Exchange, 1707 Platt Crescent
North, Vancouver, BC V7J 1X9, Canada (604/987-3262).**

•**The ACCESS Foundation for the Disabled** provides travel
information and services to people with disabilities, including
an international residential exchange program for people with
mobility impairments. Contact: **(516/ 887-5798).**

Utilize an Unusual Mode of Travel

If a particular mode of transportation entices you, then make your
way by bicycle, train, freighter, ferries, on foot, canoe, or kayak. An
unusual travel style will distinguish you from the masses of tourists
and draw local people to meet you.

Walking Magazine lists over fifty companies that offer walking
tours of the United States and forty-two other countries. An eight-day
walking tour of Burgundy allows multiple wine tasting stops while a

van transports your luggage. Or, buy *On Foot*, Adam Nicolson's book of guided walks in England, France, and the U.S., and wander on your own.

Britain has over 12,000 miles of public footpaths. Feudal rights of access still exist, and marked footpaths are indicated in Ordnance Survey Maps, which can be purchased in local bookshops. You can wander on your own, or follow one of the Countryside Commission's twelve "long distance paths" that are popular with walkers in England and take you through particularly beautiful areas. Books can readily be found giving the routes and recommended places to stay along the way. Walking from village to village through fields, over moorland or downs, or beside streams or the sea, is the ideal way to see England.

Marcia and Philip Lieberman's book, *Walking Switzerland: The Swiss Way*, explains how you can hike across Alpine areas and stay in mountain huts, Alpine centers, and local inns.

Join the legions of women who have bicycled across China, the United States, and in virtually every country of the world. Virginia Urrutia, at age seventy, hired a taxi to carry her baggage and cycled over the Andes in Ecuador. Read her story in *Two Wheels and a Taxi*. Combine cycling with train travel in Europe; you can rent bicycles easily in France, Holland, and Belgium. Or join **Backroads Bicycle Touring**, which organizes bicycle trips in several countries for solo travelers at every level of ability. Contact: **Backroads Bicycle Touring, 1516 Fifth Street, Berkeley, CA 94710 (800/245-3874)**.

Robyn Davidson purchased and trained camels for her eight-month trek across 1,700 miles of Australian outback. She wrote *Tracks* about her experiences.

Christine Dodwell bought a horse and rode through remote sections of Turkey and Iran. She wrote *A Traveller on Horseback* about her adventures. If you're not prepared to organize your own trip, contact **Fits Equestrian** at 800/666-3487 in the U.S. for guided equestrian vacations in Africa, Australia, the British Isles, the Caribbean, Europe, Mexico, New Zealand, Russia, South America, and the U.S.

Book a seat on the Trans-Siberian Railroad or the Orient Express for a ride through the classic age of train travel. Sit back for an opulent tour of India on a resurrected royal train, or hold on to your seat over thirty-six bridges and through eighty-six tunnels as Mexico's fabled Copper Canyon train hurtles from the Sierra Madres to the sea.

Cross the ocean on a working freighter—as one of perhaps a dozen passengers you'll likely enjoy the comfort of a spacious cabin, share your meals with the ship's officers, and get a close-up view of the workings of a cargo ship. *Ford's Freighter Travel Guide*, updated semiannually, is the classic source of freighter-passenger service, including fares and schedules.

Ursula Walker is a seasoned freighter traveler:

> *I've traveled alone back and forth to Asia from various ports in the United States, on all nationalities of freighters. I love it—I always have to be dragged off the boat kicking and screaming.*
>
> *The principal advantage of freighter over cruise ship or even ocean liner travel is that the staterooms have size: a comfortable bed, a small bathroom, a window to look out of, a sofa, chest of drawers, a desk.*
>
> *Go alone and everybody will be interested in you and concerned about you. Get a stateroom to yourself if you can: it is worth the extra cost if you need to be alone at least some of the time, and if you have writing or studying to do. (And I think you must have work to do to keep from going nuts on a freighter.)*
>
> *One really memorable trip was from the Bay Area to Singapore on a Norwegian freighter. Every night I sat next to the captain at dinner, and the food was divine. Imagine all the lox you can eat....*

Naturalist and guide Esther Lev traveled by kayak among the Fiji Islands:

> *Traveling by kayak was a wonderful way to visit Fiji because we approached villages the way the Fijians did— by boat—and we were able to visit places that tourists*

didn't see. We planned to camp on deserted beaches, but every time we thought we'd found one, people came out to greet us. Somehow they always knew that we were coming before we got there; we dubbed it the coconut telegraph.

As part of local custom, the first people we met on each beach escorted us to their village, so we could perform the kava ceremony with their chief and request formal permission to camp on the beach. Kava is a root that is mashed into a powder and then made into a drink. For the ceremony, you sit in a circle around a big kava bowl. The chief sits at one end of the circle, and the kava pourer says, "Bula?" and you clap your hands. After participating in the ceremony a few times, I was sick of kava—it tasted like mud with pepper in it. Still, we drank it.

One day it was raining very hard. We had paddled far that day and were crossing a large bay to a place where three villages were clustered together at the other end. Toward the middle of the bay, we could see what must have been half the villagers—men, women, and children—standing on the beach in the pouring rain, waiting to welcome us. My kayak was the first in, and a little girl couldn't wait for me to pull up on the beach— she ran out into the water in her short cotton dress. She asked me where I was from, and I answered, "America." She jumped right onto my boat and hugged me, welcoming me, which made me cry. She and I became friends— she went with me everywhere and taught me the names of animals in Fijian.

My first big trip was hitchhiking around New Zealand with a friend for six weeks. We were both in wheelchairs. No one believed we were hitchhiking; they'd drive by and just wave. We carried bungee cords so our chairs could pack easily into cars or trucks.

We spent six weeks traveling the North and South Islands. Our longest wait for a ride was three hours. Every night (except two or three) we were invited to stay in people's homes who we met hitching. People fed us and gave us grand tours of their communities. Just yesterday I got a letter from one of the families that I met twelve years ago—we still stay in touch.

I don't think either of us had ever heard of someone in a chair hitchhiking. It was great fun, two of us in chairs traveling together. It evens out because you help each other in different ways. People with disabilities don't always have to find a nondisabled partner.

Of course, traveling with a nondisabled friend is another way of experiencing a place. They can help us get to inaccessible places. One time when I went to China, my friend Evelyn was with me, and she was a bicycle enthusiast. We wanted to get to the outskirts of Beijing and explore the narrow winding streets. Evelyn rented a bicycle; I sat behind in my wheelchair and hooked onto the back of the bike with my two canes and we went around Beijing like that—she towed me.

We rode down quiet alleys, where we saw people mending shoes, selling fruit, talking to their neighbors. We stopped to admire an old man's cane— it was beautifully carved. I showed him mine. We smiled and our eyes met—one of the rare moments in travel where differences melt in an instant.

Another time I traveled solo for four weeks, visiting France, Spain, and Italy. The great part of traveling alone is that it's really liberating to have a rail pass and go anywhere you want. I was always getting off at tiny towns that I'd never heard of. I felt comfortable scoping out the station to find the people I wanted to ask to help me get on the train.

In northern Spain, at San Sebastian, I met a Spanish woman in a wheelchair. We spent half our time talking about Basque independence, the other half about independence for disabled people. Neat things happen when disabled travelers meet other disabled people overseas. There is instant recognition, real camaraderie, and a strong bond between disabled people all over the world, and between women.

Finding places to stay was hard sometimes, but I tried to keep from freaking out. I figured if I had to, I could always go to the police station and sleep in the jail.

One time I had to leave my hotel in the middle of night to catch my plane. No one was around to help me; I ended up crawling down two flights of steps and pulling my backpack and chair down behind me.

So few places are accessible, but I want to go exploring anyway. I have a weak bladder, but I don't let it keep me home. Now I sit back and remember all the crazy places I peed: under the Eiffel Tower, behind the Great Wall of China. I remember those places more vividly than I remember the museums.

You have to ignore the nay-sayers and have a sense of adventure. A friend and I wanted to go to the top of the Acropolis. On the way there, we met two Canadians who hauled us up on the back wheels of our chairs, popping wheelies all the way. Someone took a photo and the next day it was in the newspaper.

Traveling in a chair, I feel more vulnerable. I can't run away if someone wants to get me. But people look after me because I stick out in a crowd. I'm careful when I'm out alone at night. I like to go on streets where there are other people, and streets that are well lit. I glance behind me.

Eating alone can be hard, too. People look at you like you're a reject.

I get stared at a lot; in Spain I got tired of it. Finally I confronted some men, and asked "Why are you looking at me?" They said they were trying to figure out if I was traveling alone, it was so unheard of in their country. What looked like harsh stares were not; it was the beginning of a good conversation.

I heard of a quad guy who hitched around Brazil. And a woman with a ventilator who has traveled to Paris and back. Everyone's disabilities are different—it's important to figure out what your needs are and what works for you.

Remember, there are disabled people everywhere, of every age. It's as though you have disabled friends all over the world, if you want to take advantage of the opportunities. Contact people and organizations, and go and see them!

Sign Up for Adventure

Gain confidence as you acquire new outdoor skills in the company of other women. Women of all ages and skill levels meet challenges and make new friends in groups offering women's outdoor adventures and international travel. More than fifty women's outdoor adventure companies offer a diverse array of trips. They include:

•**Adventure Associates**—All-women outdoor adventure trips include a ropes course leadership training as well as wilderness training weekends in the Pacific Northwest. Coed overseas adventures include culturally responsive travel to Morocco, Kenya, Costa Rica, and Tanzania. **PO Box 16304, Seattle, WA 98116 (206/932-8352).**

•**Alaska Women of the Wilderness**—This group offers courses and seminars as well as trips, all of which are designed to promote self-reliance in the outdoors. **PO Box 775226, Eagle River, AK 99577 (907/688-2226).**

•**Her Wild Song**—Travel across snowy mountains and winter lakes by dogsled and cross-country skis. Or, study writing along the banks of the Penobscot River in Maine during a week-long canoe trip. **PO Box 6793, Portland, ME 04101.**

•**Lost Coast Llama Caravans**—Hike into wilderness areas without a load on your back—a llama will carry your gear. **77321 Usal Road, Whitethorn, CA 95489.**

•**Mountain Mama Pack and Riding Company**—Take a horse trail ride or a longer pack trip into the mountains of northern New Mexico. **Route 3, Box 95G, Santa Fe, NM 87505 (505/986-1924).**

•**Off the Beaten Path**—"Transformational wilderness journeys for women" include sailing the San Juan Islands and hiking through old-growth forests in Oregon's Cascade Mountains. **PO Box 83, Vida, OR 97488 (503/896-0222).**

• **Outdoor Vacations for Women over Forty**—Women of all skill levels are invited to join over two dozen nature and outdoor adventures, including sailing from Key West, Florida; rafting the Snake River in Idaho; and cross-country skiing through Glacier National Park in Montana. International trips feature walking the Lake District in England and hiking in Austria. A multigenerational windjammer cruise invites participation by mothers and daughters, grandmothers, granddaughters, aunts, and nieces. **PO Box 200, Groton, MA 01450 (508/448-3331).**

• **Paddling South**—Learn to kayak as you travel the secluded Sea of Cortes coast along Mexico's Baja Peninsula. Visit fishing villages, see frigate birds, and try to spot migrating whales. Other adventures include horse-pack trips through Baja's cactus garden valleys and kayak trips among the islands of Fiji. Both coed and women-only trips are available. **4510 Silverado Trail, Calistoga, CA 94515 (707/942-4796)** or **(707/942-4550).**

• **Sea Kindly Sailing Charters**—Take a sailing trip in the Florida Keys or farther, in a variety of sailing ships. **999 First Coast Highway, Box 10, Fernandina Beach, FL 32034 (904/227-3826).**

• **Womanship**—Learn to sail or improve your skills on daylong, weekend, or week-long cruises on the waters of Chesapeake Bay, Nova Scotia, Florida, the Pacific Northwest, or the Virgin Islands. **137 Conduit Street, Annapolis, MD 21401 (301/269-0784).**

• **Womantrek**—Trek through Scotland, Bolivia, or Tibet. Tour China, France, or Nova Scotia by bicycle. Raft the Colorado River—no experience necessary! **1411 East Olive Way, PO Box 20643, Seattle, WA 98102 (800/477-TREK).**

• **Women in the Wilderness**—Learn outdoor skills while living close to nature. Women in the Wilderness is "dedicated to having fun" and to "encouraging women's spirit of joy and adventure." **566 Ottawa Avenue, St. Paul, MN 55107 (612/227-2284).**

•**Woodswomen**—Offering over seventy different trips internationally and in the United States, Woodswomen seeks to encourage the spirit of adventure in women. Basic trips offer opportunities to learn new skills such as bicycle touring (along the Mississippi River) white-water rafting (in Wisconsin), dogsledding (northern Minnesota) and rock-climbing (Joshua Tree National Monument). International journeys include a wildlife watching trip in the Galapagos Islands and a chance to study Celtic mythology in Ireland. **25 West Diamond Lake Road, Minneapolis, MN 55419 (612/822-3809).**

Coed adventure tours that will be of interest to women with special needs and their friends include:

•**Environmental Traveling Companions**—Outdoor adventures organized for people with special needs include kayaking, white-water rafting, and Nordic ski trips. Contact: **Fort Mason Center Bldg, San Francisco, CA 94123 (415/474-7662).**

•**Wilderness Inquiry**—Canoe, kayak, raft, and dogsled trips are offered for people of all ages with mobility impairments. Some financial aid is available. Contact: **1313 Fifth Street S.E., Suite 327, Minneapolis, MN 55414 (612/379-3858).**

A thorough guide for people with disabilities is *A World of Options for the '90s: A Guide to International Exchange, Community Service, and Travel for Persons with Disabilities* by Mobility International U.S.A.

I've always liked adventure. One of my first adventures was when a friend and I drove in a Jeep from St. Louis, Missouri, to Anchorage, Alaska, in 1967. We left St. Louis with $300 and a credit card, and it was wonderful. I loved learning something new, seeing something new, meeting people who were different from me, observing the difference in the land.

Adventure means learning, it means encountering things you could not foresee and figuring out how to address them—finding some way to get through it, if it's scary, or just being novel in your approach if it's a more mundane obstacle. Adventure is a creative process. When you put yourself in a place that's totally different, you reveal yourself to yourself.

In a single year, I've had two big adventures. Both were personally illuminating. The first was a wilderness experience which involved rock-climbing. I don't like heights, yet I found myself climbing up the side of a cliff. Looking down, I thought, I can't do this, it's too hard. It was scary and also really rewarding. When I made it to the top, I cried.

The second was a sailing trip from Hong Kong to the Philippines. There were thirty-two of us from the U.S., Hong Kong, Britain, and Singapore. There were some young people in their twenties, and the oldest person was around seventy, with a bunch of us in our fifties. The ship—a 135-foot brigantine—had three big square sails like the old-fashioned sailing ships had. Someone had to climb up in the rigging to let them down or put them up.

The biggest sail is called the drifter. When you put it out there you look at it and say, "It's so beautiful." There's nothing else to say. The ocean was so blue, I didn't believe anything in the world could be that blue. It was bluer than the bluest sky I'd ever seen, bluer than anyone's eyes, blue like something dyed, except this was something living, vibrant. How can you tell anybody about this? They have to see it, they have to feel it. Because it's not just the sight of it, it's the feel of it.

Everyone had to take their turn on the "watch"—four hours, either on bow watch, working in the galley, navigating, or on stern watch. If you're up on the stern watch, and you see a tiny light off in the distance, once you really believe it's a light, you go back and tell the helmsperson, "There's a light off the port bow," or, "There's a light off the starboard." Then you have to keep looking out for it. For a while all we did was put up sails and take them down, to learn how to do it. "This is a halyard, this is a down-pull, this is the foresail." In the chart house, everybody on the ship learned how to navigate, and everyone learned how to manage the wheel. We all learned some sail theory and how to tie knots.

Achin and Ming, two Chinese men who had been hired to work on the ship, were sitting on the sorry seat the second night out, and I was sitting there too, wondering if I'd get seasick if I went below. These guys started singing in really lovely voices and I recognized the song, "How Great Thou Art," one of my dad's favorites. They were singing in Chinese (they didn't speak any English), and I started singing in English because I didn't speak Chinese. When I joined the singing, they just lit up and their voices took off. Then we did "Amazing Grace"—it was like touching some other part of the world to sing with those guys.

I saw whales, dolphins, flying fish, cuttlefish, sea snakes, jellyfish, all kinds of things. One of the high points of the trip for me was steering the ship—I steered it right into the little harbor town of Bolinao, on the island of Luzon. We came into Bolinao on the 4-to-8-A.M. shift, so I got up at 4 o'clock in the morning and stumbled around in the dark, but as soon as I got outside the weather felt wonderful on my skin. The captain—who never did get my name right—was saying, "320, Kathryn."

"Aye, Captain, 320." And I moved the wheel back and forth, and every time he told me to change course, I repeated his instructions back to him.

"Bring her to 300."

"Aye, captain, 300."

He got us to just the right spot, and then said, "Drop anchor." I dropped the anchor, and then he said, "Midships. Good job." I felt great—I had done it—I had just brought a large ship into harbor.

We stayed for three days before we sailed back. My brother, who had been in the Philippines when he was in the service, had told me, "It's like being at home." And that's what it was for me, as a person of color. People acknowledged me as another human being; they looked at me clearly, without trying to be coy about it.

Riding the bus was great. We were sitting in the back, and I thought it was full. And then the driver stops and waves two more people in. And I think, okay, great, and we move down the bench a bit. He stops again and waves two more people in, and here comes somebody with a basket of mangoes, and here comes somebody with a couple of kids, and everybody just moves down to make room. And then we stop again and one of the guys in the front swings up onto the hood of the bus so an older man can get into the front seat. And then somebody gets on the other side of the hood. And then we were full. My definition of full was way off—it was American full. When there's caring and connectedness, people can practically sit in each other's laps. And when there's not, everyone needs a lot of space.

On the return trip, we encountered a big storm. We were running into the wind; it was a gray day, and it felt like we were flying. That night, I was on the watch from 8 P.M. until midnight. The ship was moving fast, we had lots of sail on, and it scared me to watch the bow of the ship tip down, and wonder each time if it was going to come up or if we were going to head for the bottom. I stood there with one foot in the galley and one foot on the deck and clipped my harness into a handrail. You clip in when you're on watch, especially at night or if there's bad weather, so that if you fall off your feet, or fall overboard, you'll still be connected to the ship. I could see the whiteness of the whitecaps on the waves, and then the waves would hit the ship and wash up on the deck, and I watched the phosphorescence wash on and off the deck. It was marvelous, it was like riding a living thing, like a horse, except a horse doesn't rock you from side to side at the same time you are rocking forward and backward. I held on to the wall with one hand and let the ship take me for a ride. I stayed on bow watch an extra shift, I enjoyed the storm so much.

You never know what you can do until you try to do it. The one thing I knew I probably wouldn't do was climb the rigging, and I even questioned that once I was on the ship. I did other things, even when I was afraid. Like climbing on top of the carriage house, where the mainsail is. There were a couple of times when I literally crawled across the roof on my knees because I was afraid of being tossed off by the rocking of the ship. Then I'd clip on to the wire and stand up. I don't have any knees left at fifty-one years old, so there's no point trying to do what I could have done at twenty. But it doesn't mean I can't do it at all, I just have to figure a different way to do it. The thing I kept repeating to myself was, trust yourself, trust yourself to find a way. Trust yourself to be able to handle almost anything, and allow someone to help you when you can't handle it alone.

V

Lessons of a Traveler

Socially Responsible Travel

International tourism has become the biggest industry in the world. The Center for Responsible Tourism educates travelers on the impact of mass tourism, especially when "First World" travelers visit "Third World" countries.[2] They urge travelers to consider the effects of our travel choices on local cultures, people, and the environment and to be aware of the ethical issues involved in cross-cultural travel. For more information on how your travels can promote multicultural understanding and world peace, purchase the *Alternative Tourism Resource Guide*, which is available from **The Center for Responsible Tourism, 2 Kensington Road, San Anselmo, CA 94960 (415/258-6594).**

Environmental Concerns

The huge number of environmentally conscious tourists seeking encounters with wildlife in natural habitat can inadvertently lead to the destruction of fragile natural areas. Attend to the damage your footsteps cause by making a donation to a local environmental organization. Ask travel agents and tour organizations if they follow guidelines for environmentally responsible travel—tour operators should be able to discuss a region's specific environmental concerns, such as endangered species, habitats, and ecosystems. They should have a strategy to limit the negative impact of their tour groups on the surrounding environment and contribute part of the fees they collect to environmental organizations. And they should provide background information on natural history to group participants.

Ecotourism is a strategy designed to protect the earth's flora and fauna through carefully planned, ecologically appropriate tourism. Dwight Holing, author of *EarthTrips: A Guide to Nature Travel on a Fragile Planet*, explains it this way: "The idea behind ecotourism is simple. Protected natural areas attract tourists. That brings money to the region, which translates into jobs for local people. This gives government and local residents the economic incentive to stop uncontrolled logging, poaching, and slash-and-burn farming." Kenya and Costa Rica are two countries that have pegged economic growth on setting aside large park reserves to attract thousands of tourists annually. Holing's *EarthTrips* contains a continent-by-continent sampling of opportunities to join nonprofit and commercial tour operators in nature tours. Special "conservation alerts" highlight ways you can direct your travel dollars toward making the crucial difference in saving endangered ecosystems.

Cultural Concerns

Travelers' desire to have authentic encounters with "real natives" can indelibly change the culture and values of indigenous peoples. Don't buy sacred items or ask to buy items that are being used in someone's home. Be aware of the feelings of local people; prevent what may be offensive behavior (especially when taking photographs). Make no promises to new friends that you cannot follow through on. Educate yourself about the working and living conditions of the people, the political system, and the role of women in society to gain a true understanding of what you are seeing. In *Handle with Care: A Guide to Responsible Travel in Developing Countries*, Scott Graham thoughtfully discusses some of the more difficult issues facing socially conscious travelers.

Economic Concerns

Studies show that less than half of every tourist dollar actually stays in the country where it is spent. International hotels import their own managers, construction materials, liquor, and food supplies from Western countries. Local employment is restricted to the lowest tasks; maids and busboys are seasonal workers who receive no benefits.

You can direct your spending into the local economy by patronizing locally owned hotels and restaurants. This may mean fewer advance reservations, but it doesn't mean lower quality. Whenever possible, order locally produced food and drinks rather than imported ones. Buy indigenous handicrafts rather than those manufactured elsewhere. Use local transportation (buses and taxis) rather than special tour buses. Participate in exchange or homestay programs. Talk to your travel agent or tour operator about your concerns for socially responsible travel.

Working Assets Travel Service is a full-service travel agency that donates 2 percent of its profits to organizations working for human rights, peace, economic justice, and the environment. Contact them at: **230 California Street, San Francisco, CA 94111 (800/332-3637).**

Co-op America's Travel Links is a tour agency that specializes in responsible travel and can help you book lodgings at locally owned hotels. Contact them at: **14 Arrow Street, Cambridge, MA. 02138 (800/648-2667).**

Confronting Poverty

If you'll be visiting a country with extreme poverty, think ahead about how you will react to your personal encounters with the poor. Some travelers tithe 10 percent of their daily expenditures to give to beggars, placing that amount in a pocket and distributing it throughout the day. Others prefer to share bread or fruit. You may feel that the most responsible course of action is to make a donation to an organization or agency working directly on the issue.

Spending or inappropriately giving away lavish sums of money or gifts can disrupt the local economy. Rather than tossing pens or candy to children, why not provide an assortment of school supplies to a local school?

Getting Acquainted with New Cultures

When you enter a country you agree to live temporarily by its customs and rules. Some of those may seem strange or even objectionable, but as travelers our aim is to experience the culture, not to change it. The task is to maintain your own integrity while not insulting your hosts.

When two cultures meet, both sides may bring along stereotypes and preconceived notions about the other. Like it or not, Western culture is our major export worldwide. Our television programs, films, music, and dance trends precede us to places we would like to imagine as "remote."

> *While hitchhiking up the east coast of Peninsular Malaysia, Mary and I stopped overnight in the small fishing village of Marang. As I sauntered down the moonlit main street for a walk on the beach, the villagers hurried past me in the opposite direction, crowding into two thatched palm restaurants. I circled back around to see what had drawn so many eager participants. Inside the restaurants, all chairs faced east, with one or two sarong-clad villagers perched on each one. The crowd was hushed, all eyes riveted to the action on Marang's two television sets. A toothy woman motioned me inside to get a peek—*Dynasty *was on TV!*

Just as you may feel that *Dynasty* does not represent you and your life, be aware that images you have of other cultures may not truly represent theirs. Counteract misleading TV and movie images of the West by providing real information about your own life. Break down stereotypes you have of others by constantly reviewing your assumptions as well as your actions.

Prepare

Read up on customs and manners before you leave home. Dozens of helpful and entertaining books demystify everything from greetings to gift-giving worldwide. Elizabeth Devine and Nancy Braganti have written several excellent books including: *Traveler's Guide to Middle Eastern and North African Customs and Manners*, *Traveler's Guide to Latin American Customs and Manners* and *Traveler's Guide to European Customs and Manners*.

Seek out someone who is from or is familiar with your destination, and solicit their advice. After you arrive, use appropriate opportunities to ask people for guidance.

Observe, then Act

Practice being super-observant during social interactions. Model your behavior on the actions of those around you. Listen before speaking; check your assumptions before concluding. Your presence as a foreigner should not radically change what is going on around you. All activity should not be centered on you. Avoid interrogating others.

Greetings

How do people greet one another? By shaking hands, kissing each other on the cheek, or bowing their heads? Does the greeting differ between sexes, in family and business situations? When in doubt, adopt the most polite form. Cris Miller, codirector of Adventure Associates, describes this encounter in Africa:

> *The first year I spent any time with a small clan of Masai, we happened to be there while young men were being initiated into warriorhood. I was then very unfamiliar with the social customs. When we walked into the village, the elder men came up to greet us—they held our palms and spit into them. It was shocking and*

surprising and because of the language barrier I couldn't
quite clarify what this meant. Later an interpreter
explained that in a very dry or arid region, the sharing of
water is an honor, quite a nice way to be greeted. I had no
idea that was going to happen; it was the sort of thing
you could easily misinterpret, given our customs about
spitting.

Gestures

Efforts to communicate across language barriers often involve the use of gestures. Yet your own gestures and body language can have different meanings far from home. Roger Axtell's informative book, *Gestures*, points out that:

•The American goodbye wave may be interpreted as the signal for "no" in many parts of Europe and Latin America.

•The gesture used for hitchhiking in America—clenched fist with upraised thumb—is obscene in Australia and Nigeria.

•The American "OK" sign can mean "zero" in France, "money" in Japan, and refers to part of the anatomy in Brazil and Germany.

•People in the Middle East and Latin America tend to move in more closely during conversation due to a different sense of personal space.

Axtell points out that only one of the thousands of physical signs produced by humans is universally understood—the smile.

Eating

Food etiquette varies greatly. During my travels I was instructed in one country to "eat every bit off your plate to show you liked the food"; in another I was admonished to "leave some food behind to show that the host provided enough for everyone." Observant travelers can figure out what's right in each situation.

Coping with different eating styles can present unusual challenges.

Helen Winternitz, in her book *A Season of Stones,* describes one such experience in a Palestinian village:

> *Each of us tore pieces from wheels of peasant bread,*
> *using these to scoop up the food. The Palestinians*
> *managed gracefully. I spilled rice on myself more than*
> *once and finally had to wrestle the chicken meat free with*
> *both hands in an unavoidable breach of etiquette. In the*
> *darkness I tried to wipe the grease from my hands onto*
> *my legs without, I hoped, anyone noticing.*[3]

She also points out differences in mealtime conversational patterns:

> *We drank our coffee in silence. Not talking, leaving*
> *gaps of time in a conversation, was permissible according*
> *to the Palestinian etiquette. I was not accustomed to it*
> *and tried to come up with something to say.*[4]

Nepalese custom does not include mealtime conversation. Marijo, an American nurse, and I learned this the hard way—we invited two Nepalese students out for lunch to thank them for showing us around Kathmandu. Each time we initiated a topic of conversation, they stopped eating, put down their utensils and politely responded. Finally we realized our mistake, quit the conversation, and let everyone finish their meal.

Time

The Western sense of time and our cult of efficiency lead tourists to advise clerks worldwide on "improved" ways of handling ticket lines at the train station, application procedures for visas at consulates, and almost anything else. Be aware that behaviors that bring results in Western cultures may breed resentment overseas. High technology is not necessarily an indicator of a higher form of civilization. Recognize that others operate with a concept of time that may be different from your own; slow down and enjoy experiencing the slower pace.

Cleanliness

Judgments about cleanliness invite others to judge us as well. Some Western habits are considered filthy elsewhere in the world. The fact that we may enjoy washing ourselves while sitting in a tub of dirty bathwater mystifies many. The practice of blowing one's nose on a piece of paper or cloth that is carried around in one's pocket is considered less than civilized by some cultures.

Family and Gender Roles

In traditionally patriarchal and paternalistic societies, women travelers unaccompanied by men confound social mores. We may be treated as "honorary" men—invited to sit and eat with men while women and children prepare food, wait, or eat elsewhere. You may not want to insult the hospitality of the hosts, yet feel awkward about accepting special privileges not granted to other women. I always try to join the women in their tasks, although I have sometimes been prohibited from doing so. This can be difficult to resolve during a short visit; I have found it easier to work my way into participating in women's roles over time.

In sharing details of my life with women from other cultures, I have encountered incomprehension and pity for the choices I have made to be economically independent, single, and childless. In cultures where women are defined as wives and mothers, those of us who are not must make special efforts to find common ground.

Before you fall back on old assumptions about the behaviors and capabilities of children, notice how they are treated and how they assume responsibilities. Mildred Widmer Marshall made these observations during a 1937 trip, recounted in *Two Oregon Schoolma'ms Around the World*:

> *Getting the mail required rowing across the fijord, a*
> *distance of about half a mile. Lisabet was very adept at*
> *handling it by herself. Her father had taught her to row*
> *when she was five, and she had been going alone when*

the water was not too rough ever since she was six, to get the mail and bread from the store. She also worked in the fields to help with the haying. She milked the cow and bicycled two and a half miles to Hauge to bring home fish and other items. Her mother also taught her to knit. She was a very accomplished and independent little eight year old.[5]

Follow Cues

Some cues are obvious and easy to follow: when you see shoes piled at the door of a home or temple in Asia, remove your shoes and add them to the collection before entering; bow in response when others bow in greeting you. Cover your head or shoulders when entering a strict Catholic church; keep your head uncovered in a Buddhist temple or Shinto shrine.

At other times, you really may not know when you're right or wrong. As Dervla Murphy points out in *Muddling Through in Madagascar*, it's best to follow the lead of local people.

> *One's behaviour in a village should, as far as possible, be guided by the people. Especially in remote areas, it is easy unwittingly to insult, frighten, desecrate or appear to threaten. Thus when the chief led us through his hamlet, it was advisable to follow exactly the path he took. Had we deviated to examine something of interest we might have infringed on an area forbidden or "vazaha"—a sacrificial site or Vazimba grave (not easily detected by the unknowing eye), or a sacred cairn, spring or tree. If we did give offence this would be no trivial matter. The whole terrified community would feel obliged to organise expensive and inconvenient rituals in an attempt to undo the damage.[6]*

When observing festivals or rituals, refrain from joining in without a specific invitation from the participants, especially if the rites are religious in nature.

Ask for Advice

When sitting at a meal or visiting someone's home, ask one person in the group, a woman if possible, to be your mentor. Request direction instead of assuming you know the proper etiquette. Before you do something, ask (or look questioningly at) her to determine if it is a wise move.

Be Open to Curiosity about Yourself

Edith Durham, who traveled extensively through the Balkans at the turn of the century, recorded this exchange in her book, *High Albania*:

> *For months I had been incessantly questioning about manners and customs, now I was myself the victim. I was asked all about all that I did, and then "why?" The thing that bothered everyone was my straw hat; they had never seen one before. "Why do you wear wheat on your head?" Everyone broke a little bit off the brim to make sure it really was "wheat."*
>
> *"Do you wear it in the house?" "Do you sleep in it?" "Do you wear it to show you are married?" "Did you make it?" "Are all the women in your vilayet (province) obliged to wear wheat on their heads?" "Is there a law about it"...*
>
> *"I wear it because of the sun," I said desperately.*
>
> *It occurred to me that if there was a Devich Anthropological Society it might report that it had found traces of sun worship in the English, and mysterious rites connected with it that no questioning could elicit.*[7]

Let Go of Expectations and Judgments

In Mexico, I bought a birthday gift for Yuyi, a young woman who I tutored in English. I presented the package and waited expectantly to see if she liked the hair ornament I had chosen. She placed the gift out of sight and thanked me warmly. I felt disappointed and a bit hurt. Later, she explained that it was considered bad manners to tear a gift open in front of the person who had given it.

Expectations arise automatically. They can be hard to let go of, or even anticipate. When you find yourself expecting a particular attitude or action, test it out in the form of a question—will you open the gift now or later on?

While you're at it, let go of judgmental statements and thoughts. As experienced travelers say, "It's not good or bad, just *different*." No one drives on the *wrong* side of the road; in some countries drivers use the left side, in others the right.

We all want to be treated as human beings, not as one-dimensional stereotypes. If you don't want to be considered a "rich tourist snob," neither does anyone you encounter wish to be thought of as a "poor ignorant native." Linda Besant, reflecting on her travels in West Africa, put it this way:

> The entire trip outside of Western culture will be difficult unless you are willing to set aside your assumptions about how life is. Things that you stand on as being ultimate truths may not be ultimate truths in a place you visit, according to the lives of people there. And, for me, that's one of the most valuable things about traveling. When my assumptions are undermined, it helps me know myself and learn what I unconsciously think about life.

Be Humble

Travel is humbling. It leads many of us away from the land where we are part of a privileged majority and allows us to experience what it is like to be in the minority. Some will journey in the opposite direction, finding themselves, for the first time, in a place where they fit in. Both experiences can be profound.

When I wandered the streets of Xi'an, in central China, my flowered cotton skirt caused a tropical sensation in a blue-gray sea of women and men dressed alike in Mao suits. I returned to my hotel, trading my skirt for gray slacks. On my next walkabout, I met a young mother on the street. She turned her baby's head toward me so I could meet the toddler. The child's face filled with horror; she wailed loudly at her first encounter with a round-eyed monster. Later that day, I knelt beside two young schoolchildren to say hello. They examined me shyly, their voices low and cautious as they fingered the wavy brown hair on my head. When they discovered that I also had hair on my forearms, their shrieking attracted the rest of the class. I was a freak.

My year in Asia taught me humility. I came from one of the richest, some might say advanced, societies of the world. Yet my survival skills were limited to a handful of office-bound activities I called my "work," which I exchanged for money to provide for all my physical needs. Those skills were useless in rural villages, where women my age could grow cotton, spin, weave, dye, and decorate their families' clothing; where children used machetes with confidence, harvesting jungle plants for dinner; where teenagers hunted small game with slingshots.

It made me humble to accept hospitality from people so poor that they couldn't buy two chicks, to take food from people I could never repay. I was humbled to learn that ancient cultures view the United States as a child-country, spoiled by excessive wealth, growing up like an ill-mannered bully.

The humble traveler leaves behind her possessions, her pride, her assumptions. Carrying no more than a simple humanity, she is a student going out to learn the lessons of the world.

I've lived in Kenya for years, working as the head of a medical clinic near the shores of Lake Victoria, and I have traveled quite a bit around East Africa. Tanzania, Kenya, and Uganda are among the safest places for a woman to travel alone that I've encountered. I've found it easy to get to know the women riding on the matatu or on the bus or walking down the same road I'm walking. Talking through sign language, through smiles, through laughter, through playing with a baby strapped to someone's back, helping to carry bundles, you can establish rapport. I've always felt, in any situation, that I had women I could turn to. And traveling alone, it's nice to have company and to have someone to get off the bus and pee with.

There is a slower time frame here; the rhythm of the day is much more relaxed, and once you're into it, it makes a lot more sense. Not many people have little desk calendars around here. So it's a process of stepping down your expectations of how many things you can see or get done in a day. Knowing that I will make social faux pas and big errors, I've learned to laugh at myself at least five or six times a day. Here in Kenya, people are generally very willing to laugh with you.

As a stranger, I often get looked at, stared at, and questioned. I've come to expect that, and to feel it's okay, even if it's a bit uncomfortable at times. Like when I sit out on the shores of Lake Victoria and read, children will circle around, staring at me. I think they will soon go away, because how interesting can it be to watch me read? Well, very interesting, I guess, because they'll stand there for hours watching me turn the pages, touching my hair, looking at my skin. The other side of that is that people will go out of their way to help you and give you answers and introduce you and take you places that you can't find—whether it's an office building or a dala out in the middle of nowhere.

There's a hospitality and warmth here that's lovely to be around. The people have a grace of living that we in the States have lost or maybe never had. There's a quickness to forgive. One time I inadvertently offended some members of our mobile clinic committee, and a clan elder of the area leaned over and told me, "Dat's all right, Carrie, mistakes are for humans."

I came to Africa to meet the people, not to see the wild game, but I did take a camping trip to a big game park where I met a Masai gentleman who was a game scout. He ended up coming with me in my Land Rover for three days during which he told me fascinating tidbits of information and folklore. I got to see things with him that I never would have seen because I wouldn't have known how to read the grassy spot in the distance that meant a lioness was there with a pride of cubs. Camping is a great low cost way to see the game parks, and you should definitely hire a guide.

An attitude that's really important for women traveling anywhere is to know that you belong there—you belong doing what you're doing. I can't tell you how important it's been for me in situations when I've been questioned by customs authorities or officials or even the clan elders. In my bones I feel it's right for me to be here—and to be here by myself. I try to convey a quiet confidence that I know what I'm doing and I can take care of myself. I represent a different culture, and in my culture women travel alone more often—I've learned to share that freely and willingly. I respect other people's cultures and I expect the same respect for mine.

I believe that if a woman's got an itch in her feet and a yearning in her soul to travel, she should come to Africa. Once you're here among the people, you won't find it intimidating. I've seen women who have come to visit me just blossom; they encounter challenges and they rise to meet them. All of a sudden they'll say, "Oh, I didn't know I could do that, but I do now."

Accepting Hospitality

The Greek word *xenos* means both stranger and guest. As a traveler and stranger, you may find yourself invited by people worldwide to share the hospitality of their homes. "In the Sudan there's the desert tradition," says Rosemary Furfey. "If someone has come across the desert, you welcome them. I've ridden on buses in the Sudan, and when we stop for the lunch break, people offer to buy me lunch, even if they don't have much money. It's a genuine friendliness and openness—they want to share their country with you."

The strong ethic of hospitality in many cultures demands that an invitation be extended, even from those who can ill afford to feed or take care of you. A popular guidebook explains that Fijian culture dictates people always invite a stranger into their home, whether or not they can afford to do so. The book recounts the story of a family whose child missed a term at school because they had spent her tuition money taking care of an uninvited guest who had stayed for a month.

As a traveler, you should be acutely aware and highly responsible about the impact of your visit on a family or village. Customary lengths of visits vary from culture to culture. An American saying admonishes that "house guests, like mackerel, stink after three days," while an appropriate visit may be a month in southern Europe, two months or more in Asia.

When accepting a spontaneous invitation from a new acquaintance, plan to stay for just two or three days. Hosts will invariably protest when you declare your intention to leave; in fact, they may never admit that it is time for you to go. A tactful way to depart is to explain that your schedule demands that you meet a friend, catch a train, or see the flowers while still in bloom. If your hosts agree that, yes, you shouldn't miss the flowers in the north this time of year, take it as an immediate signal and pack your bag.

Being a Guest

What do hosts get in return for your visit? The pleasure of sharing their home and town, their food and way of life. The entertainment of watching you and learning about your culture. Perhaps the fun of showing off their own private foreigner to the neighbors. Try to co-operate in all activities, and accept invitations to visit their friends, attend church or temple, or drink tea when someone drops by.

Don't, however, feel compelled to do everything—whether it's shooting at animals, jumping off a high bridge into the river below, or smoking opium. State your limits firmly and in a friendly manner.

Be especially alert when traveling in poor regions. When staying with rural farmers, food supplies may seem plentiful. Just remember, those bags of rice or that stack of corn may have to last the family until the next harvest.

Contribute something to the household during your stay. Hosts may be insulted by an offer of money; rarely will they be offended by willingness to work or a thoughtful gift. Subsistence farmers living in an almost cashless economy may need certain implements—tools or plastic buckets, for example.

Ask to accompany family members to the marketplace. They may forbid you to make purchases while you are with them (as well as try to buy anything that you ask about or admire). But if you observe what they buy, from whom, and at what prices, you can return on your own and purchase food to contribute to the household. Stock up on the more expensive, nonperishable items, like coffee, sugar, and canned milk.

Everyone cannot or will not invite you to their home. Many Europeans live in crowded quarters and entertain by inviting others out for meals. Even after being treated to meals by others, a woman traveler may find it difficult to assert that it's her turn to pay. But don't take an initial refusal at face value. In most cultures you are expected to over-come even emphatic refusals and reciprocate.

In most parts of the world, if you invite someone to join you for a meal, they will expect you to pay for it. The American custom of split-ting meal costs (inexplicably known as "Dutch treat") is not viewed positively in most countries. (In Holland I was invited to an "American party"—a potluck dinner.)

"Come and Visit, Any Time"

Some Western travelers sponge their way across the world, secure in the belief that most of the people they've stayed with will never be able to take them up on the return invitation.

Be aware of what it really means when you invite someone to visit you. Western countries can be incredibly expensive places to visit; few people in the world have the resources to support their travels and lodging. Don't give your name and address freely to casual contacts unless you are truly willing to house and feed them when they show up at your door. A letter or telegram from a completely unfamiliar name, announcing their date of arrival, can be a sobering bit of news.

Of course, do invite new friends and those who have extended hospitality to you. Give them your bed, cook their meals, take time away from your normal schedule to show them the sights. But be aware that for those desperate to establish a foothold in a Western country, friendship with a traveler can raise high expectations.

Sandy Polishuk explains her experience with a friend from Russia:

> When I went to Moscow I met a woman who invited me to visit her home. She took me to an art show with crafts from all the different republics and invited a close friend over to meet me.
>
> After I returned home, she sent me nice long letters with photographs, and then a package with a half-dozen gifts for my birthday. I wrote and asked what they needed, and made up a big package which their government returned six months later. She sent frequent letters and gifts; in one letter she asked if it was all right for her to refer to me as a friend. I wrote back and said, sure, we are friends. I couldn't keep up with all the letters she sent me; then she started sending telegrams and calling on the phone.

*Suddenly I realized she wanted me to sponsor her
whole family so they could emigrate. A woman who
knows the culture well explained to me that the word
"friend" is taken very seriously there, and I had meant it
more casually.*

We travel all over the world inviting people to visit us. But what happens when they want to come? What are their expectations?

Sponsoring a visitor from the "Third World" is a big commitment. Signing immigration papers or writing a letter of invitation for the purpose of acquiring a visa indicates a promise of financial responsibility. That means that you have agreed to guarantee payment for health care, housing, and other necessary expenses should they be unable to pay for them. Aside from financial demands, significant social and emotional needs may be placed upon you.

NASDROVIA!
OR, THIRTY HOURS IN BUCHAREST

It seemed like a good idea at the time.

Romanian Air Transport's bargain-basement fare to the Middle East from Bangkok required a thirty-hour layover in Bucharest. Included in the ticket price were free meals and lodging at a deluxe downtown hotel and the prospect of my first hot bath in months.

My flight arrived at Otopeni International Airport too early to be called morning. In the deserted terminal, wide women with babushka-wrapped heads methodically mopped the floors and traded words in low tones. I spent the first three of my thirty hours studying their technique, forced to wait for additional passengers before claiming the promised ride into town.

Airline officials eventually collected forty transit passengers and dispatched us on a noisy bus through the vacant countryside and into the drab city. We were deposited before a grand old hotel half a century after its prime. When my turn came at the massive front desk, the thin clerk asked politely if I would share a room with another female.

"Yes, of course."

He pointed indifferently toward a tall slender woman in her mid-thirties, with dark wavy hair, who stood alertly at one side of the desk. Dressed in a fur jacket and leather boots, wool skirt and sweater, she looked like an image from a newspaper photo from Eastern Europe.

He reached up and gave her the key and then waved vaguely in my direction. She fixed her coal black eyes on me as I walked toward her; then the corners of her mouth tweaked in a half-smile.

We politely shook hands, exchanged names, and then carried our luggage toward the once-gilded elevator. Maria was the only female member of a Polish trade delegation bound for a trade fair in China. A mother of two, she hoped to do well at the trade fair and improve her position in the delegation. We entered the room and settled our bags. I immediately ran the hot water to fill the huge tub. My enchantment with the bath amused Maria. Conversation and steam wafted through the partly open bathroom door as I soaked and scrubbed.

She knew little about China, and we discussed what she might encounter there. She was amazed that I was wandering around the globe alone, without a set itinerary, limited only by money in how far I could go. I asked about her life in Poland; she indicated that things were very difficult there. But, she added darkly, here in Romania, they were even worse.

I dressed to leave for a day's walk in the city. It was 9:00 A.M., and I had less than twenty-four hours left. Since we had been issued only one key to the room, we arranged to meet that evening for dinner. Map in hand, I stepped out on the city's wide boulevards.

I hadn't planned to visit Romania, hadn't read or studied or asked any questions. I struggled to remember what history I could, and searched the streets for clues to the story as I wandered.

Marble fountains were planted in the center of wide squares; wind whistled where water had once run. Cream-colored buildings surrounded the square, dark streaks from rusting wrought-iron balconies striped their facades. Conversation slowed and then halted as I approached a huddle of shoppers on a street corner. Large signs over old-fashioned stores proclaimed goods for sale; hand-lettered updates in vacant front windows seemed to notify otherwise.

The bustling activity of the outdoor market drew me away from the subdued streets. One section was crowded with vegetable farmers, their boots redolent with the pungent perfume of the countryside. The flower market was an island of brightly clothed Gypsies with flowered picnic umbrellas hovering over each stall. An olive-skinned woman reached authoritatively into plastic buckets, selecting flowers and tying bouquets with muscle-flexing alacrity.

A 4:00 P.M. homing instinct delivered Romanians to local beer halls, where they leaned elbows on chest-high counters as they stood drinking from frosty liter-sized mugs. The people, like the buildings, were constructed on a monumental scale.

My dearth of Romanian *leis* prevented me from joining the beer-hall crowd and drove me back to the hotel for dinner. A note outside our room promised the key if I knocked next door. Maria answered, opened the door wide, and introduced me to her co-workers, Alexei and Stefan. All in their thirties, they were the junior members of the delegation.

Stefan was tall and fair haired, with fine features. He bowed formally, from the waist, and issued an invitation, "Please be so kind as to join us for a drink. We would like to talk about China."

I glanced at Maria's hopeful smile.

"Just one," I agreed, stepping into the room.

An open bottle of Polish vodka presided over several glasses on the desk. Alexei, shorter than Stefan and a bit more rumpled, retrieved an additional water tumbler from the bathroom, and poured the clear liquid into the four thick glasses. In unison, they hoisted their drinks, exclaimed, *"Nasdrovia!"*, tilted their heads back, emptied their glasses in a sweeping motion, and banged them down on the desk.

I took a large sip of mine.

"No, no," Alexei said. "You must...finish." He poured another round and demonstrated proper technique: say *nasdrovia* (loudly, as if you weren't worried about disturbing anyone else in the hotel), tilt your head back until the glass is empty, then emphatically put it down.

Stefan remarked in Polish, something about *Amerikanskis*, and I thought, "All right, they think I can't do this."

I stood up, looked from one to the other, pronounced a strong *nasdrovia*, tipped the glass back, and dumped two inches of liquid fire into my throat. Whew! No wonder they slammed the glass down.

"Ver-ry, ver-ry good," beamed Alexei, pouring another drink. "Now, you must eating." He went to the bed and unlatched his suitcase, a Polish Samsonite that opened flat, each half packed solidly under ribbed straps that held the contents in place. One side was filled with his neatly arranged clothes. The other was stocked with several more bottles of vodka, nestled in among long salamis, cheeses, loaves of dark bread, and bottles of pickled food.

"Romanian food very bad, must bring good food from Poland. And, Chinese food...," he moved his head slowly from side to side as he sliced salami and bread and opened a jar of pickled onions.

"Always between drinking is eating, it helps cure the big head."

We ate, we drank, and we talked. My glass was filled the moment I emptied it. Clearly I was out of my league. I never drank straight liquor, what was I doing? I could see them watching as I was offered each round. Twin impulses seemed to keep me going—my stubborn pride, and my hesitance to refuse the hospitality of these new friends. We shouted *nasdrovia* in unison, then raced to be the first to empty the glass. The thick tumblers machine-gunned onto the table.

At 11 P.M. I wavered on unsteady feet and told Maria I had to leave. At the same time, Stefan jumped up to answer a quiet tapping at the door. He turned toward us and shrugged his shoulders apologetically. "It's the assistant director."

"Our superior," Maria whispered urgently. He'd heard they were entertaining an American and wanted to join us for one round.

I demurred. But Maria leaned over and spoke into my ear, "Please be so kind as to stay for just one more drink; this will help our position with the assistant director."

"Okay." I tried to sit erect as the bureaucrat stiffly entered. His English was surprisingly poor, compared to my friends'. An emissary of another generation, he spoke Russian instead. I held my glass up for the toast.

"Nasdrovia!"

We talked politely for a few minutes about farm machinery and crop dusting, his words efficiently translated by the junior members in the room. At 11:30, another soft knock rapped at the door, an aristocratic face peered in.

Maria turned to me again. "Oh, here is the director. Please be so kind...."

I was bleary-eyed and dizzy. "Sure, why not?"

At midnight, I tried to remember if I'd ever actually passed out from drinking. Unsure, I joined in another round and toasted the arrival of the assistant minister.

We sang Polish songs. I made up the words as I went along and wondered where all these people were coming from? No one ever left the room; how did the rest find out what was going on? And, just how large was the delegation?

Finally, the "minister himself," as my friends referred to him, strode in. The Poles stood and quickly bowed. His manner was courtly, his English as impeccable as his finely tailored suit. He sat beside me in a chair hastily vacated by the assistant director, and put his hand out for the glass that was instantly placed in his grasp. We traded observations on cities around the world.

By 1:00 A.M., the assistant director was weeping, begging me in roughly translated Polish to go home and convince my government not to destroy the world. "No matter who starts the next world war," he insisted, "Poland will be the first country blown off the map."

By 2:00 A.M. we were into the last bottle of vodka. The "minister himself" was falling in love. He invited me to Warsaw, offering to send a limousine to meet me at the airport. He would put me up at the finest hotel, take me to the opera, and to all the exclusive restaurants. When I protested that I didn't travel with a suitable wardrobe, he offered to have the clothes tailor-made in advance.

I could hardly stand, barely walk, and could no longer speak my native language fluently. I summoned Maria into the bathroom for a consultation. "Maria, I really like you. For you, I drank with the assistant directors and the directors, I toasted the health of the assistant minister and the 'minister himself.' But even if it would somehow help you get a promotion, I will not go to bed with the minister!"

Her eyes widened with shock, and she shook her head repeatedly. "Oh no, please. You must not, do not....Here, let me help you back to our room."

I said goodnight and shook hands all around. The Poles took turns slapping me on the back. Was this their way of saying farewell, or were they administering another anti-hangover remedy?

Maria shook me awake the next morning. I had fallen asleep with the telephone receiver in hand, trying to book a wake-up call before passing out. With a suppressed smile, she pushed me into the shower and helped pack my bag.

My head was huge and outweighed my backpack. I could barely open my eyes. The prescribed vodka-to-salami ratio had clearly been out of balance. I put on my sunglasses and consoled myself with the thought that perhaps I had snatched America's vodka drinking reputation from utter disgrace.

Maria walked me to the elevator and hugged me like a dear friend. "Thank you for being so kind last night."

"It was fun. I just hope I didn't embarrass you."

"Oh no, Thalia. Everyone was very impressed."

"Impressed? With what?"

"That's what they were saying in Polish when they were patting your back. They'd never before seen an American girl drink so much vodka."

Hospitality, national pride, my desire to please. Everything had to have its limit. I just wondered if hangovers did.

Bargaining

It's comedy. It's drama. It's commerce. It's a way of life. Rather than calmly considering a sterile series of price tags under fluorescent light to a gentle background of canned music, you are thrust into a noisy marketplace and forced to confront a stranger selling the very item you desire.

What's the struggle all about? Bridging the gulf between buyer and seller by finding the one price to satisfy both. Bargaining is not a scam developed to bedevil tourists; it's a centuries-old tradition that is the normal mode for transacting business in many parts of the world. Besides, it is a social activity—it will give you an excuse to make contact with new people and have fun.

Unaccustomed to bargaining, we Westerners flinch at the prospect and pray not to disgrace ourselves. We suspect that we will pay more than others for the same item. To some degree, that is true. A stranger will always pay more for a chicken than the farmer's cousin will. But bargaining with skill and a sense of humor will bring you closer to the local price faster than you may think.

Read your guidebook or ask other travelers whether bargaining is common at your destination. If it's North Africa, the Middle East, Asia, Southern Europe, South America, Central America, or Mexico, you will likely be bargaining quite a bit. In countries where bargaining is the rule, there are a few exceptions—government craft emporiums, drug stores, Western-style supermarkets, and hotel gift shops.

What's at Stake Here?

Pride

Neither you nor the merchant wants to be shamelessly taken advantage of or insulted. You both want to emerge from the interaction feeling good. In *Changes in Latitude: An Uncommon Anthology*, Joana McIntyre Varawa points out how she and her Fijian husband, Malé, approached bargaining from different cultural perspectives:

> *Shopping in Labasa, Malé bargains over a 50¢*
> *difference in a pair of shorts or a T-shirt. The prices of*
> *everything slide around like a greased pig. Once I bought*
> *a $30 dress for $8; another time the same storekeeper*
> *wouldn't budge past 25¢. Malé drags me from store to*
> *store in search of the best price. It doesn't matter whether*
> *I want to pay the difference and get going, preferring*
> *efficiency in the heat to the 50¢, it is a matter of prin-*
> *cipled pride with him.*[8]

Each traveler must decide for herself just how long she is willing to negotiate; everyone has a limit. Whatever you decide is what's right for you.

Money

Just how much? Are you haggling over the equivalent of a cup of coffee or a day's wages? (Or does a cup of coffee back home equal a day's wages round here?)

Responsibility to Other Travelers

Basic economics teaches that the price charged is a function of what the market will bear. If other travelers have willingly overpaid, your price will be higher. If you overpay, others will be expected to also.

Somewhere between pride and value, history and circumstance, a smile and a scowl, lies a fair price for most items. If you work to make every transaction mutually beneficial, both parties can walk away satisfied.

How to Bargain

Look first. Is there something that interests you?

If you don't like what you see, why bother to ask? Some Westerners, accustomed to knowing the price of everything, ask incessantly
for prices of things they will never buy. This wastes time and irritates
merchants.

When you see something you like, ask for a price.

The price quoted by a merchant is a starting point, an invitation to
bargain. If you want to look further, do not respond or counteroffer
at this point. Simply walk away. Shake your head or say no. The vendor may yell a second price as you leave, interpreting your departure
as shrewd bargaining strategy. (Some shoppers make a ridiculously
low offer as an attempt to end the discussion. I don't do that because
it engages the bargaining process and makes it more difficult to back
out. And what do you do if your offer is accepted?)

*When you are ready to buy, respond to the opening price by making a
counteroffer.*

Your offer indicates that you will buy if a mutually acceptable price
is found. If your offer is too low, the seller may appear disgusted and
dismiss you as not serious about buying. Usually, each offer is met by
a counteroffer. Relatively large adjustments in price may be followed
by smaller and smaller adjustments.

Once either side accepts the other's price, the deal is closed. If you
never close the gap between your price and theirs, you're off the hook.

Here's a typical example:

Buyer:	How much?
Seller:	This is a very fine mask. 100 baht.
Buyer:	Oh, too much. Very expensive.
Seller:	Okay. How much?
Buyer:	I don't know…25 baht.
Seller:	No, no. 80 baht. Good quality. See, how nice? 80.
Buyer:	Other masks cost 40. I'll give you 40.

| Seller: | This mask is special, very old. Special price, just for you, 75. |
| Buyer: | Very old, and in bad condition. 50. |

And so on. The two will likely agree on a price somewhere between 55 and 70 baht, depending on who's more stubborn.

It's difficult to predict how high above your first offer the final selling price will be. This varies by place and also by individual. Many shoppers assume they will wind up paying about 50 percent of the first price quoted. That is often true, but at times the price paid can be as little as 20 percent of the first price quoted.

Time is a factor. When in a hurry, you'll find you can bargain quite efficiently, but you may not find it worthwhile to linger over the last few cents. On the other hand, a deal can be drawn out for weeks, if you can return periodically and don't mind risking the loss of your precious item to another buyer. Persistence is usually rewarded.

If you find yourself getting angry, go away and come back an hour or a day later.

Buying Food and Other Necessities

When buying produce at a local market, you have the advantage of witnessing local people shop. Stand by and observe a few transactions, or ask a shopper how much they paid as they leave the stand. This obligates the merchant to charge you the same price.

Observe the behavior of other shoppers. Do they select their own vegetables, or does the vendor choose for them? Touch food only if it seems an accepted practice and if you plan to buy it. Ask about unfamiliar foods, but be prepared to buy if something is cut open for you to taste.

Produce merchants may bargain by offering greater quantity for the same price. This can be a problem if you're traveling light. Either stick to the quantity you want, or plan to give extra food away.

Buying Handicrafts and Gifts

Don't make significant purchases without some study. Prices and quality of most handicrafts vary widely. "Fixed price" gift stores and government emporiums are a good source of comparison to the local market, where prices should be lower. As you shop around, keep mental or written notes on prices. Even if you wander into a shop and see price tags attached to every item, inquire if those are "fixed prices." The shopkeeper may indicate a willingness to bargain.

Use your shopping time to get educated on the finer points of the craft. Ask the merchants questions, "How can you tell high quality lacquerware?" "What makes a good rug?"

If you enjoy buying jewelry or semiprecious stones, get educated at home, not abroad. Do not rely on the merchant's authenticating tests such as stones scratching glass, a drop of acid, or stamped gold or silver marks. Verify your purchase with a government agency or gem-testing laboratory. If possible, pay by credit card and get an itemized receipt describing the gems in great detail; these will help you recover your money if the gems are fake. Be aware that it may cost you $200 to set that amethyst you bought for $15. The bottom line is, would you still want it if it turned out to be fake?

Handicrafts vary greatly by region; don't assume you will find "another one" later in your trip unless you are destined for the area where the craft originates. If you really like something, and the price is right, buy it. If you encounter a better deal later on, buy that one as a gift for someone else. If it was worth $6, it's a real bargain at $3.

Many markets are open only one or two days a week. Don't assume you can come back without knowing the schedule.

Beware of vendors who approach you at historic sites. They may be selling fake antiquities at exorbitant prices, or real antiquities, which could land you in jail.

Itinerant vendors may hand you an item and then refuse to take it back, as a way of forcing the purchase. If you don't want that ceramic peacock, simply put it on the ground and walk away.

Don't buy handicrafts made from ivory, tortoiseshell, leopard fur or spotted cats, reptile skins, birds and bird feathers, animal teeth or coral. Merchants may assure you of the legality of the sale, unaware that international treaties regarding protection of endangered species may subject the items to seizure and you to a substantial fine.

Pottery glazes can contain lead; be cautious about buying dishware. After returning home, call your local health department and obtain a test kit before using dishware for serving food or beverages.

Bargaining for Services and Accommodations

Always ask a local person what the fare or rate should be before contracting for services. Ticket clerks at train or bus stations can usually provide an estimate. If fares are not fixed, be prepared to bargain fiercely with taxi and transport drivers. Late at night, when options are limited, your safety and security may be worth the higher fare.

Many varieties of local transport, ranging from vans to pickup trucks to river taxis, charge a point-to-point fare system for everyone except foreigners, who can get taken for an extra ride. Rather than bargaining, your task is to find out what the real fare is; then insist on paying no more than that.

In small hotels and guest houses, always try for a better price or a better room for the same price. In areas with lots of local competition, check two or three places before settling in. If you decide to stay for several days, negotiate a preferred rate. (In some countries, prices for accommodation are fixed by the government and posted, but that doesn't always preclude on-the-spot adjustments.)

The Finer Points—Tips and Techniques

➤The best hagglers are accomplished actors. They scoff, laugh, appear outraged or angry. Don't be intimidated by them. Study and learn from their methods. Keep your sense of humor and join in the spirit of it.

➤Merchants want to close the deal. Any delaying tactic, such as acting unsure, saying you want to shop around or come back another day, may elicit a lower price.

➤Don't show how interested you really are in the item. Point out its flaws.

➤In some parts of Asia, the first sale of the morning is auspicious, a good or bad omen for the day. Once they've commenced bargaining, a merchant may go far to complete the sale. Take advantage of that "morning price" by planning your big purchases for early in the day.

➤Have small bills on hand when going to market. The ten minutes you spent working to get the merchant's "best price" could be undercut the moment you pull an eye-popping bank note from your pocket.

➤When planning a specific purchase, put exactly what you intend to spend in one pocket. When you're ready to make your final offer, turn your pocket inside out to show "this is all I have to spend."

➤If you have the cash, make a low offer in U. S. dollars or other non-local currency. Stable foreign currencies may bring you a better deal. Just double-check your math; local merchants are probably more adept at hopscotching between exchange rates than you are.

➤Sometimes the need to save face can predicate a stalemate. Both parties have stated their final price, and neither will budge. Divert from arguing price and ask for a small bonus item to be "thrown in" to clinch the deal.

➤When faced with many good choices, make an offer for two or three at a real bargain price. Vendors often give quantity discounts.

➤Ask others not to contradict or undercut your statements. Keep discussion of potential purchases, likes and dislikes, private. (I've derided the quality and beauty of a potential purchase, only to have a friend enthusiastically assure me it was more than worth the asking price.) Assume that vendors understand your private conversation.

➤Don't let lack of language skills hold you back. Offers can be communicated via pencil and paper, a pocket calculator, or by holding up fingers. Merchants know the vocabulary of commerce. Just make sure the terms of the sale are understood. Are you buying two for $20, or two for $20 *each*?

➤You may get better bargains without a big audience of foreigners or locals. Too many witnesses may keep the merchant from making a good deal.

➤You may be served refreshments as part of your shopping visit. Accepting hospitality does not obligate you to buy, although you probably shouldn't stay for dinner without having a purchase in mind.

Seek out opportunities to practice bargaining before you leave home. Yard or garage sales, bazaars, used-car lots and swap meets are all places to negotiate prices. After you return from your trip, you may find yourself negotiating more than ever before. After all, every price tag is just the asking price!

Without Language

The language frontier is exciting to cross. Familiarity with language can enhance your experience, but don't let the lack of language skills keep you at home. Don't feel compelled to know the language before you go someplace; do feel compelled to try to learn some words and phrases.

Some travelers seem to have a natural facility with language. But everyone can learn at least some words of greeting. Even a laughable attempt does generate at least a laugh—and that's a start.

Language Study

You need not devote years of study to language classes, although any time invested will surely pay off. Consider these easy alternatives:

- •Buy audio tapes, or borrow them from the library. Listen to them at home while dressing in the morning, or while commuting to work. Just getting accustomed to the sound and rhythm of the language will give you a real boost toward understanding.

- •Inquire with travel agents or a community college about language classes for travelers, which focus on key phrases for verbal communication rather than grammar and written ability. (Those over 65 years of age may be able to audit community college classes at no cost.)

- •Bring a phrase book and a pocket dictionary along, or purchase them at the airport. Start studying on the plane.

- •Devote some of your travel time to language classes. Investigate residential language programs that place students with local families. Hire a private tutor, or offer to trade language tutoring hour for hour with someone who wants to study English.

•Take advantage of natural study opportunities—long train and bus rides are my favorites. Get out your notebook, ask fellow passengers to teach you words or numbers, write them down and repeat them over and over. These sessions can be really fun and make the time pass more quickly.

For a high-tech, high-priced alternative, AT&T's **Language Line** provides language interpretation over the phone in 140 languages, twenty-four hours a day. In the U.S. and Canada, call **800/752-6096**.

Sign Language

Where written and spoken language end, another form of communication begins. It's possible to ask for directions, buy food, find a place to sleep, make new friends and converse with non-English speakers, all without even a rudimentary knowledge of the language. Shared experiences create shared language—with words replaced by eye contact, smiles, shrugs, hands pointed north, figures etched in dirt. In her delightful first book, *Full Tilt: Ireland to India with a Bicycle,* Dervla Murphy recounts an important lesson of a first-time traveler:

> *When you ask for fried eggs by making noises like a hen after laying, followed by noises like something sizzling in fat, the whole household is convulsed with laughter, and not only are fried eggs served, but you are unanimously elected as one of the family.*[9]

I've been astounded by the complicated explanations, discussions, and arrangements that can be conducted through signs, even without a single mutually comprehensible word.

Some ways to ease nonverbal communication:

•When arriving in a remote place without language skills, remember you may seem strange or dangerous. Repeat at least one or two words of greeting, or smile constantly. Keep hands out of pockets; extend an open hand to show you carry no weapons. Move slowly and reassuringly.

•When asking directions, repeat the name of the place you are seeking over and over. (Don't point in a likely direction; you may get confirmation of wrong information.) Don't ask for a faraway destination, as the person may never have been there. Ask for the next likely place on the way.

•If pronunciation is tricky, have your destination written on paper or in a small notebook to show.

•Use sounds and gestures to imitate what you want. Request for toilet facilities are rarely misunderstood; gestures that show you are hungry, thirsty, or sleepy are among the most universal. But be aware that some gestures that are innocuous to you may be insulting in another culture.

•Draw pictures on sand or paper. Be aware that maps are abstract representations that not all cultures share.

•Resist the temptation to shout; increased volume does not increase comprehension.

Making Friends without Language

➤*Show and Tell*—Share a pocket-sized photo album with pictures and postcards from home. This is a great communicator and conversation starter and allows others to understand a bit about your life.

➤*Simple Games*—On a train, or when visiting a home, offer to play a simple game, especially with children. Carry balloons to inflate for instant volley games. Look for games that can be demonstrated easily, like the ball and cup toss, jacks, soap bubbles or Frisbee.

➤Ask for help, or offer some.

IN THE AKHA VILLAGE

We rode the bus from Chiang Mai through the lush green hills of northern Thailand into the heart of the Golden Triangle. A couple of hours after leaving town, the Dutch traveler sitting beside me waved the driver to stop at a wide place in the road. We got out beside a small thatched shelter.

"Now what?"

"We wait."

"For what?"

"A truck that may be going a few miles up toward the village. The road is muddy during monsoon season, so the truck will take us as far as it can go. We'll walk the rest of the way up."

Short, dark people emerged from the shadows and joined us in the little shelter. Some of the men were dressed in Western trousers and T-shirts. Others wore homespun jackets and pants the blue-black color of indigo, trimmed with red and white appliqued designs. Then a woman walked straight out of the pages of *National Geographic*. I tried not to stare at her magnificent headdress. Rising from her head like a conical tower, it was crafted from row upon row of silver coins and beads, red and white buttons. Tassels fashioned from dyed fur and feathers hung from its sides.

Geert saw me watching the woman. "Wow," I said in a low voice.

"Just wait," he responded.

I'd met Geert on the tropical beach of Koh Samui, an island off the southern coast of Thailand. I'd told him that my traveling partner, Mary, would soon be leaving for other adventures and described my dream of traveling alone and visiting remote villages. He offered to take me to the hillside village of the Akha tribe where he'd spent the previous three months.

Geert would help organize my stay in the village and remain available for advice and support the entire time I was there. He was enthusiastic about my goal—to make friends and live as independently as possible.

Two men arrived in a small green pickup truck. They pointed

uphill and motioned to the group that had gathered at the thatched bus stop. The Akhas piled into the back. I followed their lead, taking a seat on the open side, placing my pack between my feet on the truckbed. The pickup revved its motor and sprang up a dirt track into the hills.

The truck careened from one edge of the muddy track to the other, swerving wildly as the tires bounced out of deep ruts and spewed mud into the air. Akhas and foreigners crisscrossed arms, holding on to each other to keep from getting bounced out. The rear wheel below me skidded off the road and hung for a breathless eternity in thin air; my gaze was sucked down the steep jungle ravine to the twisted wreckage of a Land Rover a hundred feet below. Two silver teeth punctuated an Akha man's smile once we regained solid ground. A red pom-pom atop his wool beret marked time as he sang a low tune.

Truck wheels chewed deeply into mud until they could go no farther. I welcomed the chance to get my feet on the earth. The diminutive Akhas walked gingerly atop the crusted mud; my foot broke through on my first step and I sank to my ankle in the slippery goop. Everyone laughed.

After an hour's climb, we reached the village, perched below the crest of a hill. We stopped at a sort of central square, a flattened piece of earth with benches on three sides. I circumspectly looked around. Three main streets radiated from the square, following the contours of the land. Bamboo houses stood neatly along wide avenues, each house built on a platform jutting out from the hillside with one end propped up on stilts. Children carried wood in baskets and water in large gourds; no one was idle. An Akha man who had come up with us spoke some English and would negotiate my stay with a village family. Geert would remain as interpreter; he knew but a dozen words of Akha. We walked together down one avenue and entered a fenced compound through a bamboo gate.

I was introduced to Azo and Apu. Azo was the headman's brother, and a respected elder of the tribe. About forty years old, he was lean and strong with a distinguished face. Looking into his calm eyes was like gazing down a well a century deep. Apu, his wife, sized me up with awe. She pantomimed an observation that she was half my height, then motioned me into the house with a high-pitched laugh, displaying her red, betel-nut-stained teeth and lips to full advantage.

I felt blind when I entered the dark house. The bamboo floor swayed lightly under my feet. I was relieved when Apu motioned for me to sit down. She was preparing rice and vegetables, and when my eyes became accustomed to the slanted rays of light that filtered through slats in the walls, I offered to help. She put a knife and some greens on a chopping block before me. I methodically began to perform my task. Moments later, Apu swept aside my dainty movements and finished it with three well-placed chops of her machete. A fierce squawking outside was silenced by a loud "thwap." Chicken for dinner. Azo brought the gutted carcass inside.

We ate from a low bamboo table on the men's side of the house. Serving bowls in the table's center held cooked greens, bamboo shoots, the chicken dish, and hot chili sauces. We used chopsticks and Chinese flat-bottomed spoons, taking turns to scoop food from the common bowls. Reaching into baskets set on the floor, we grabbed handfuls of steamed rice and molded them into little cakes before taking a bite.

After the meal, the small table was moved aside. Rice and food that had fallen on the floor were swept through a wide crack to the ground below, where pigs and chickens gobbled up the remains. A perfect eco-system: no garbage.

Some neighbors came to meet the *farang* (foreigner). We sat, staring and smiling at each other until I retrieved a child's toy from my pack. A ball on a string hung below a plastic cup; the proper toss would place the ball in the cup. The toy was passed round and fierce competition ensued. Later, I joined the women on their side of the house while the men lit a small kerosene lamp, lay back against their bedrolls and smoked.

The Swing Festival started the next morning; it was a harvest celebration that marked the beginning of the Akha New Year. Men of the village gathered at a high promontory in early morning fog to build a tall swing from four saplings stripped of bark and branches. After planting the four poles in a square, they shimmied up and lashed the tops together into an arch. They hung a swing from the center of the arch, choosing the heaviest from among them to test it.

We went to the headman's house and drank a bowl of fragrant

rice whiskey with breakfast as young people gathered outside. The teenagers rhythmically pounded large sections of bamboo against a flattened tree trunk, making a steady beat to accompany their songs. For three days, the Akha wore their finest traditional clothing and stayed home from the fields. One by one, each villager took their place on the swing, singing a new year's song as they teetered over the cliff. Teenage girls swung tandem and flirted with young men. On the third day, Apu brought me to the swing. She helped me balance on the narrow seat and pushed me off into the sky. I leaned my head back and sang the swing song, imitating the words I had heard a hundred times in the hours I'd stood watching. When I came back to earth, a toothless old woman wearing heavy silver neck rings nodded and drew me to her side. I'd made a new friend.

Then the festival was over and it was time for work. Apu left her finery hanging on pegs inside the bamboo house, slipped on her oldest homespun jacket and pulled a pair of torn men's trousers underneath her skirt. She placed a fitted hood on her headdress and chose work clothes from my pack for me. Geert rigged large baskets on either side of a child-sized packhorse. Apu gave me a bamboo-and-rattan basket to carry, showing me how to support it with the woven tumpline across my forehead. It was an odd sensation, hanging the basket from my forehead instead of my shoulders.

We followed winding paths away from the village, up a hill and along the top of a tree-covered ridge. Apu stopped along the trail to harvest fresh greens and bamboo shoots for dinner. She darted from side to side, checking traps she had set days before. On one steep hillside, she sang out a triumphant cry. A trap had been triggered, and she ran for the prey. She lifted the log that had smashed the animal, and held it up for us to see. The scaly carcass was about a foot long, covered with crawling white maggots.

It had been dead too long; Geert and I covered our noses against the sickening stench. Apu smiled and patted her stomach, reassuring us that it would be tasty to eat. "No, no!" we responded. We held our noses, pantomimed bad stomachs from eating something so foul. She laughed merrily, lopped off a giant banana leaf with her machete, wrapped the animal in the leaf, and tossed it into the basket behind her back.

She reset the trap, showing us how the log would crash down on the next animal to pick at the bait tied to the Y-shaped trigger. We adopted the sound she used to imitate the falling log as the name of the stinking carcass that had been its victim. We called it the Blap.

We tried to reason with Apu. She should throw the Blap away. It was no good. She laughed and walked on ahead, singing an Akha song in her bell-like voice. Geert and I hung back, muttering.

"She can't cook that thing, it'll kill anyone who takes a bite!" I said.

He smiled, "Shouldn't we try to be good guests and eat it? Apu must know what she's doing."

"Listen," I retorted, "when Ano shot that iridescent jungle beetle out of the tree with his slingshot and roasted it on the fire, I ate it. I ate the chicken feet and the pig and the dog meat during the festival. And I never once complained. But I'm not going to eat that...Blap."

We arrived at a terraced hillside and set to work, hacking corn off stalks with machetes and tossing the ears over our shoulders into the carry-baskets. I got accustomed to swinging the heavy blade and quickened my pace. But the increasing weight of the corn in the basket pulled my head back until I could only stare straight up at the sky. I stumbled along, straining my eyes to spy the next ear from the corner of my vision. Apu spotted my predicament and scurried over, relieving me of my burden with a suppressed grin. It was time for lunch.

Apu unfolded our midday meal from banana leaf wrappings and opened a round basket packed with the nutty-flavored mountain rice. She lit a fire, let it burn down, and tossed the Blap onto the smoldering embers. Several minutes later she pushed the blackened thing away from the coals with a stick. Once it cooled, she peeled the scales from the carcass, smiling and nodding, telling us again how delicious it would be. She wrapped it again and returned it to her carry-basket.

I was relieved to avoid eating the Blap. But I feared it was only a matter of time before the beast appeared on our dinner table. As we shucked corn during the afternoon, I repeated to myself, "I am not going to eat that thing no matter what."

When we returned from the day's work, Apu sent me down to the village shower. Bamboo pipes sluiced water from a spring into a narrow gorge. Certain times were reserved for women to wash, others for men. The Akha girls laughed shyly when I arrived; I followed their custom and wore my sarong while showering. Afterwards, we fought mock battles with the children who'd come to fill their containers with drinking water.

I was suspicious about the dinner that simmered on the fire when I returned. Geert leaned across the divider from the men's side of the house and said, "Don't worry, she got rid of that Blap thing. It's fish for dinner tonight." I vowed to ask about the Blap before every meal.

By the light of the kerosene lantern, Apu slapped one rigid arm on top of the other and told the story of the Blap. Then she mimicked my head tipping back under the strain of the carry-basket to another round of laughter.

"How many days' walk to my home village?" I was asked in sign language.

"Not possible to walk," I pantomimed. "You must fly over the ocean." I took out my notebook and drew a picture of an airplane. Everyone seemed perplexed; they had seen planes up in the sky, but they were so small. How had I gotten inside?

Life slipped into a familiar routine. I spent most days working with Apu, harvesting and shucking corn. She sang Akha songs as we walked toward the fields and taught me the names of plants and flowers. One afternoon on the path back to the village we heard a terrible roar. Apu vaulted into the brush and dragged me behind her. The entire jungle seemed to shake as an elephant came charging past, hauling a felled tree that was chained behind it. A "flatlander" man ran behind the elephant with a whip. We huddled among the leaves, waiting for the spectacle to pass. Apu took me off the path and showed me a logging camp. It was the only time I saw the smile disappear from her face.

For several days, I stayed home from the fields, bouncing our neighbor Abu's baby as she wove cotton cloth. She outfitted me in her extra clothes; the open black jacket, trimmed in white seeds and red beads, was a bit short but fit fine over my T-shirt. The gathered skirt barely covered my thighs. The towering headdress weighed several pounds and swayed each time I moved, its silver coins, buttons, and beads tinkling beside my ears. I joined a group of chattering women trimming headdresses, tying on dyed monkey fur and chicken feathers and making brightly colored pom-poms from store-bought yarn.

I lost track of time. Life flowed in an unceasing pattern of work, each day rung in by the sound of the foot-treadle mortar, husking mountain rice for breakfast.

Finally, I had to leave. Everything seemed poignant that last day, even the gray monsoon clouds that rolled in across the valley. We returned from the fields a bit early for my special farewell feast. Once again I marveled at the mysterious array of delicately sea-soned forest plants, meats, and fish that had been stir-fried, pickled, or smoked over the men's hearth. I swept the floor after dinner one last time. Later, we played the ball and cup game that had become our favorite.

The next morning I packed to leave. Azo sharpened my knife on his special whetstone, indicating that no journey should be initiated with a dull knife. The two women, Apu and Abu, strung white seed necklaces with tiny dried gourds trimmed in colored yarn. Tears clouded my eyes when they placed the farewell amulets around my neck.

We took some last photos; Apu imitated a *farang* by posing Western-style and mugging for the camera. In gestures and a few Akha words, I thanked her for her hospitality, her friendship, the lessons she had taught me, the delicious meals she'd cooked.

Her face cracked an impish grin. She pantomimed a question about the farewell dinner. "Did you like it?"

"Yes, very much." I patted my stomach. "Delicious."

She tipped her head back and chuckled, lips exposing her red teeth. She patted her stomach, showing the sign for "delicious" again and again. Then, she gave me a devilish smirk. She slapped one arm down on top of the other—Blap!

Romance and Sex

A romantic encounter with a foreign stranger may be an expressed or secret goal of your trip. Even when it's the furthest thing from your mind, a fascinating character speaking softly into your ear with a musical accent might turn your head. After months of traveling completely alone, just the prospect of a warm touch can be too inviting to pass by.

Romance

A cross-cultural flirtation or romance can offer an inside glimpse into the habits of another people. But heterosexual women beware: you may find yourself participating in a mating ritual without knowing the meaning of all the messages you convey. The uncomplicated flirtation you were hoping for can escalate quickly into a situation that you didn't intend. Try to be clear about your thoughts and feelings at all times.

If you are a lesbian traveling outside lesbian circles you may find it difficult to identify who is gay. Don't make assumptions based on your own cultural cues. And make sure you understand the culture's attitude toward lesbians before you begin a flirtation.

Sex

Cultures collide in bed. You and your sex partner each heed unwritten rules on bedroom behavior and have culturally influenced needs and expectations. Communicating those across a potential language barrier can be delightful or frustrating.

Be aware of what you're getting into; many cultures do not embrace the concept of casual sex. Making love may be considered an engagement to marry.

If you choose to have sex during your trip, you should be prepared to supply condoms or dental dams and make their use a condition of sexual intimacy. Male attitudes toward condoms remain negative in many parts of the world. Your partner may be unaccustomed to discussing contraception in an open manner. (See "Staying Healthy" in Chapter VI for a discussion of AIDS prevention.)

Heartbreak

Love weaves a magic spell on a tropical night under a full moon; palm trees sway rhythmically to a warm breeze and anything seems possible. Keep your expectations in check, and don't get too invested in your holiday romance.

Even if you decide to travel with your new-found love for a while, a long-term relationship will rarely ensue. You've each got your own plans, lives, values, and cultures. One day, after a shorter or longer period of time, it is likely that you'll each go your own way.

BABI

I was seventeen the first time I went to Greece. I'd come from Spain, where I'd been living in a village on the Costa Brava as an exchange student. I met my godmother, Connie, and we traveled north to the Macedonian town of my maternal grandparents.

Kastoria clung to a craggy hillside that descended into a blue-green lake. The main street was lined with furrier shops; mink coats, rabbit gloves, and hats sat poised behind dust-streaked windows.

My Uncle Chris took me around to meet family members and old friends of my grandparents. I had been thinking and dreaming in Spanish, and the abrupt switch to speaking Greek knotted my brain and twisted my tongue to muteness. Someone introduced me to a guy named Babi, who attended university in Italy, and we found it easy to bridge the gap between Italian and Spanish in conversation.

Babi invited me for a walk around the lake at Kastoria. The lake was shaped like a figure eight, and we had plenty of time to compare our very different experiences of growing up as we made the circuit. We made the walk again a few days later, talking about American pop music and life in the United States. I told him that I was enamored of village life in Spain and Greece; he pointed out how old-fashioned and limiting it could be. I can't remember now if we ever held hands.

Thursday was market day, and my godmother's cousin Foni said we'd be going after breakfast. She instructed me to wear a nice dress. We went to the lake's edge where farmers from the area sold their produce. Foni waved her hands as she haggled for a large fish. She winked triumphantly at the good price as she handed me the fish to carry.

A hefty woman threaded her way past the stalls, greeted Foni, and then assaulted me with a crushing hug and a sloppy kiss on the cheek. I stood beside Foni as she and the woman carried on animatedly, half-listening while observing the market around me.

From time to time the women paused, patting my arm or cheek. I nodded and smiled back at them. Occasionally, I plucked a few words from the rapid stream of dialogue that flowed right past me. I recognized one word after it was repeated several times—*nifi*. It meant bride. But I hadn't caught the name of who in the village was getting married.

Finally I asked in Greek, *"Pya eene ee nifi?"* Who is the bride? They exploded with laughter, *"Pya eene ee nifi?"*

"Pya eene ee nifi?"

The unknown woman grabbed me by both shoulders, slowing the pace of the Greek words as she increased their volume. "You! You are the bride, and my son Babi is the groom." I stared blankly. She tried again, "My son is going to be your husband!" It seems that after two unescorted walks around the lake, we were betrothed.

The conversation picked up speed without me, as they discussed engagement parties and made wedding arrangements. I stood silently beside Foni, holding the newspaper-wrapped fish.

Thoughts stomped my head like the rear hooves of an angry mule. I felt sorry for Babi, who would doubtless be quite embarrassed by the whole situation. But then—he'd told me he wanted to come to America—could he be a willing participant in the plan? A more horrifying thought insinuated itself in my brain. What if I had been pushed and pulled through all the preparatory motions for a wedding, ignorantly nodding and smiling and being polite and never quite understanding what exactly was happening? When would I have finally realized that they were marrying me off?

Standing there in my grandparents' village, I felt a long way from home. I'd just spent my first summer on my own; it couldn't be the last. I didn't want to dedicate the rest of my life to washing Babi's socks.

Fear choked me and wouldn't let go. For two days, the word *nifi* was muttered over my head and behind my skirts whenever I walked through town. I couldn't tell if they were joking or serious. On the third day, I realized there was only one solution. I packed my bags and left for Thessaloniki on the afternoon bus.

VI

Safe Passage

Handling Sexual Harassment

Women traveling alone (or in pairs without the "protection" of a male) generate special kinds of interest, and more than the usual offers of hospitality. You probably look forward to encountering a variety of people during your trip. Chance meetings can seed new understandings, sprout into a change of plans, and blossom into true friendships. Yet it's difficult to remain open and accessible when persistent men with inappropriate attitudes create uneasy, annoying, or even fearful situations.

Whether from fantasy, personal experience, or as a result of stories they've heard, some men view single female tourists as willing and adventurous sex partners. Their implicit assumption is that women travel alone to look for sex. Other men seem compelled to go through the tiresome motions of feigning interest in or threatening a woman to prove to themselves and any onlookers that they are truly "masculine." I call this the "rooster strut."

Before You Go

Research Your Destination

Women can, and do, travel in every country of the world, but some countries require more adaptation than others. The first rule for women travelers is: *do your homework*. Make sure you know exactly what to expect. Your experience in a Muslim country will vary drastically from your experience in Scandinavia. Your plans and expectations as a visitor to these destinations should be adjusted accordingly—while you may feel comfortable traveling solo in one country, you may prefer to travel with a companion in another.

Utilize all available resources. ***Women Travel: Adventure, Advice and Experience***, edited by Natania Janz and Miranda Davies contains first-person accounts of women's short- and long-term stays in over seventy countries, as well as a summary of laws, the status of women, and a listing of women's organizations in each country. It's a terrific resource—read the selections pertaining to your destination, or use it to help determine your travel choices.

Browse through the guidebooks in the travel section in your bookstore or public library and look for those that discuss sexual harassment and the special needs of women travelers. (See "Selecting Guidebooks" in Chapter VII.) Books such as Kevin Chambers' *Traveler's Guide to Asian Customs and Manners* help you prepare for cultural attitudes and religious and social customs. Talk to other travelers, especially women, who have visited your destination. Post a note on a college or community bulletin board, or write a letter to the travel section of your local newspaper to locate travelers with helpful tips. Returned travelers will often share practical advice in exchange for a chance to relive a journey with an appreciative audience.

Don't assume that the countries most "familiar" to you will be the places of least harassment. Many women think of Europe as an appealing, nonthreatening travel destination. But southern European men can be annoyingly tenacious in their pursuit of women tourists, much more so than men from places that may seem initially more intimidating to visit.

Pack Appropriate Clothing

Clothes that are acceptable at home may make you a magnet for problems in another culture. Clothes carry culturally specific messages—think of the many assumptions you make daily about people you encounter based on their clothing. Plan a basic, conservative travel wardrobe that will serve in a variety of situations, and augment it with special items as you go along. For warm climates, I recommend a combination of pants and loose cotton skirts that reach well below the knee, topped with baggy, short-sleeved-shirts. (The skirts are especially useful in "Third World" countries with variable toilet conditions.) In colder climates, clothes that layer over thermal underwear provide the maximum warmth while minimizing weight and bulk.

Analyze the way women dress in each country you visit. You don't have to adopt native dress, but you may want to follow the principles behind it. If a few minutes' study reveals that women's shoulders and legs are always covered, then cover those same parts of your body as well. With a bit of research you'll realize that wearing trousers can help you blend in in rural China, but not in Malawi. Some clothes advertise your status as a foreign tourist—expensive running shoes, for example.

Travel Light

The most experienced travelers carry the lightest, smallest bags. This reduces problems at every transfer point. Traveling light also provides added safety through the ability to move quickly. If you are not dependent on taxi drivers and porters, you can remove yourself from problem situations without assistance. You should be able to carry all your travel gear at once, and still have one hand free to open doors or dig out a ticket. (See "Choosing Luggage" in Chapter VII.)

Learn Basic Self-Defense Techniques

Before I went to Spain as a high school exchange student my father encouraged me to enroll in a self-defense course. I never did flip anyone over my shoulder, but just knowing how to handle myself really increased my confidence. Register for a self-defense class or read books on self-defense for women to learn useful skills and help you feel more secure about traveling alone.

While Traveling

Use Culturally Accepted Behavior

Augment your advance reading with some on-the-spot research on the interactions between women and men. Every culture has clearly defined boundaries between acceptable and unacceptable behavior.

Play detective and try to find out where those invisible lines are. Remember that a woman traveling alone is already operating outside the boundaries of normal behavior in many cultures. That's why it's critical to act within the boundaries in other ways.

Women travelers who think they've done nothing to invite the unwanted attention of men may be inadvertently sending the wrong signals. Aside from language differences, each culture has its own nonverbal cues. Just looking a man directly in the eyes is considered a sexual invitation in some conservative countries. Take some time to observe:

- How do men and women greet each other when they meet? Do they smile, shake hands, bow, or embrace?

- Are strangers treated more formally than close friends and relatives?

- Do women converse with seemingly unfamiliar men? Look at them directly?

The fact that you are a woman traveling alone can put you in the social category of a prostitute. In parts of Africa and Asia, for example, it is culturally unknown for women to venture forth alone; an assumption may be made that you have been thrown out by your family for doing "something wrong." Your behavior will be carefully observed for more clues to your status and reason for being there.

Plan Ahead

I organize my schedule to arrive in a new town at midday or in the early afternoon, leaving several daylight hours to find lodging and get situated before nightfall. If transit schedules require a night arrival, I do some extra homework, researching the name of a reputable hotel, close to the station if possible.

Even if the cost exceeds my usual budget, it's worth having the security of a definite destination when arriving in the dark. This is the one situation when I don't hesitate to take a taxi directly from the station. If I don't know of a place in advance, I conduct my research in transit on the train, bus, or boat. I ask around until I find a local resident who can give me advice. People may offer to accompany you to the hotel or help find a taxi and establish the fare. Look for middle-aged or older women, families, or other travelers for this kind of help.

Handling Problems

In most countries, the actual threat of physical violence is very small. What you're more likely to encounter as a woman traveler are persistent, inquisitive men. I try to maintain a positive attitude and not regard every approaching man as the enemy. Yet it's hard not to generalize if most of them treat me as a potential conquest.

On my first day in a new place, I take the pulse of the situation in this way: during a day of walking alone about town—shopping in a market or sitting in a cafe—I might have short conversations with ten or so men. If one out of the ten is overbearing, I'll probably write it off. If the negative encounters number three to four, that gets tiring. And if six or more are boors, then I assume I'm in enemy camp and think about leaving town.

Even if no single encounter is overwhelming, dismissing an unceasing lineup can be exhausting and time-consuming. It helps to be assertive when shaking the predators loose. Here are some well-worn techniques:

Just Say No

One of the cultural barriers operating here is that many men translate the word *no* to mean "maybe," "perhaps later," or " you haven't asked the right question." If you want to say no with conviction, then make a special point of it. Smiling and shaking your head from side to side just won't do the trick. (Besides, a side-to-side head shake in Greece or India means *yes.*) Here are some ways to assert your position:

•Change the dynamics of the situation—*stop* walking if he has been accompanying you, or *start* walking if you've been conversing at one spot. Cross the street, step off the curb, or on to a bus—anything to denote that you are going your own way alone.

•Raise your voice so that others can overhear. Repeat *no, no, no*, several times; it is understood in many languages. Be sure to learn the translation for no in the local language, too. Don't be afraid to yell loudly.

•Use physical cues to underscore your serious attitude—scowl or cross your arms in front of you. Use your hands to shoo him away. If verbal communication is a problem, exaggerate these visual cues to get your point across.

Clearly communicating the *no* message will solve 90 percent of your problems.

Learn Local Ways to Shame Men

While riding the train in Northern India, I witnessed the following incident: A young Indian woman was sitting alone in a compartment with several men. After a while, one of the men began talking to her. Although I couldn't understand the conversation, her actions seemed very clear—she took the end of her sari from over her shoulder and brought it over her head like a scarf, partially concealing her face. She turned her head away and the man was silenced.

On another train ride, I tried a modified version for myself. I wore a large scarf over my shoulders while on the train. Whenever a man bothered me, I followed the young woman's example and brought the scarf over my head, partially covering my face as I turned away. It worked every time.

Appeal for Help

When you start to feel that almost every man is just waiting to give you trouble, remember that almost every woman may be willing to help. Women everywhere have experienced harassment from men, so you have a lot in common with women whose lives are radically different from your own.

When I encounter a local woman who speaks a language common to me, I ask her to teach me some appropriate phrases to use in difficult situations. I write them down phonetically in a small notebook that I always carry—the right words really do the trick!

If you are being harassed, appeal to any woman nearby for help, even if she can't understand a word you say. Simply point to yourself and then to the man, gesturing with your hands. Most likely, she will understand this universal situation. Ask one specific woman for help, not a crowd. Women have chased men away from me with brooms, towels, dogs, rocks, and plenty of high-spirited, rapid-fire phrases. I've met some wonderful friends that way.

Become familiar with the uniform of the local police in each country you visit. On your walks through town, make a mental note when you pass a police kiosk or station so you can return quickly if you need assistance.

Whenever I stay in a large city, I adopt a well-appointed central hotel as my drop-in "rest stop." I greet the doorman and other hotel personnel and make use of the comfortable lobby and rest rooms. At times, I've returned to this hotel to seek respite from an unrelenting "admirer." On trains, of course, you can call the conductor, unless *he* is the problem. My first appeal is always to nearby women when possible.

Recognize the Standard Types

Women who've traveled a lot recognize these standard types:

►The Inquisitor—These men initiate conversation by asking you the "standard" traveler questions. The questions vary from country to country, but generally go something like:

Who are you?

Where do you come from?

How old are you?

Are you married? Where is your husband? Your children?

How long have you been in our country? Do you like it here?

Do you pray?

These questions (including the last one, which may be asked in

Muslim countries) often represent an honest attempt to be friendly. But sometimes they move on to more intimate subjects:

How do you like the men here?

Would you like to go with me?

Have you ever had a boyfriend from here?

Have you ever made love with a man from here?

Would you like to have my baby?

I received this generous offer on a beach in Mexico. Simply stop answering questions when they turn to a subject you dislike. Or take control of the situation by asking a few questions yourself:

Why do you ask so many questions?

Where is your wife? Your family?

Why are you bothering me?

Asking in the presence of others, or in a loud voice, will usually stop the inquisition. But sometimes the best response is no response at all. In the tourist centers of southern Europe, it became so hard to end conversations that I found it better to refuse to talk at the outset.

➤The Follower—There are two kinds of followers. Some walk right beside you, making small talk in six different languages while trying to strike up a conversation. The other type will silently follow you for an hour or longer through town or along the road, which is a sign of admiration in some cultures.

To a Western woman, this can seem like a serious threat. In reality it usually is not. Still, it is best to be cautious—if you are being followed, walk toward the center of town or another populated area. Stop and confront the person in front of others. Walk directly to the police station or into a hotel and see if your shadow follows you in.

➤The Native Guide, the Gigolo—Working in hotels and businesses catering to tourists, they seek out one romance after another for fun and profit. The "beach boys" of Kuta Beach on Bali will pursue women in a way that would not likely occur elsewhere on the island. Greek *kamaki* ("harpoons") hang out at the tourist spots, looking to spear a catch. This behavior is a by-product of tourism; to get away from it, you must either go beyond the travel poster destinations or team up temporarily with someone else while visiting those areas.

➤The Language Student—These are the guys who want to converse so they can practice their English. Or they approach you at a cafe and request your help in writing a letter. Sometimes the request is legitimate; help out if you feel disposed to. Test their sincerity by determining if they understand the meaning of the word *no*.

Avoid High Risk Situations

It is difficult to generalize between urban and rural situations and across many different cultures. The same behavior would be interpreted very differently in Oslo than in Nairobi, in Buenos Aires than in a rural mountain village a hundred miles to the west. Use your judgment, be cautious, and rely on your intuition.

Establish a set of ground rules for yourself—situations that you will never allow yourself to get into no matter how innocent they may appear to be. Refer to these ground rules when you receive invitations and make plans, and don't make any exceptions. A conservative set of ground rules includes:

•Never allow yourself to be alone in a room with a man unless you know him well and trust him completely. This is a good practice even when receiving medical or other professional services.

•If you need to meet a man or accompany him, bring along a chaperone—a friend, a young person, or another traveler.

•If hotel personnel want to enter your room in a service capacity, open the door wide and step into the hall while they are inside. You don't have to act in a suspicious or hostile manner, just indicate that you want to let them do their job.

•Don't go on a boat, on an excursion to a secluded beach, or hiking into the woods or countryside alone with a man. Don't accept a free private lesson in snorkeling, sailing, or surfing. Your definition of a hike or picnic may not match his. Don't invite intimacy unless you want it.

•Even if they promise that a girlfriend, wife, or mother will be waiting at the other end, don't count on it unless you have independently verified the information ahead of time.

Remember that a key to your hotel room could fall into anyone's hands. To deter unwanted visitors, only stay in rooms that can be double locked or bolted from inside. In the "developing" world, it is common for budget hotel rooms to be equipped with a hasp-type latch. Use your own padlock to secure the door.

If your next destination is notorious as a problem area for women traveling alone, find another traveler to go along with you. For example, the southern coast of Spain is the jumping off point for travel to Morocco. Solo male travelers may offer to accompany you to ease the level of harassment you might endure, without any expectation of a physical relationship between you. Discuss the situation clearly before agreeing to travel together, then keep oriented to where you are and have enough local currency to bolt if problems arise.

Harassment of Lesbians

Lesbian travelers can encounter homophobia anywhere. It can take the form of an ice-cold reception or a serious threat to your safety. There are countries where the penalty for being a lesbian is severe. Your trip planning should include an investigation of how safe or comfortable it is for you to be an out lesbian where you plan to travel.

An easily accessible resource is *Sisterhood Is Global*, Robin Morgan's 1984 anthology of the international women's movement, which presents research on both official policy and practice towards homosexuality in seventy nations worldwide. For more up-to-date information on the situation in any country consult the following publications:

> •**The International Lesbian and Gay Association (ILGA)** publishes *The Pink Book*, a country-by-country guide to lesbian and gay rights. Contact: **ILGA, Information Secretariat, c/o Antenne Rose, 81 rue Marché-au-Charbon, 1000 Brussels, Belgium (32-2-502-2471).**

> •**The International Lesbian Information Service (ILIS)** publishes a quarterly newsletter on what lesbians are doing around the world. Contact: **ILIS, c/o COC, Rozenstraat 8, 1016 NX Amsterdam, the Netherlands (31-20-23-45-96).**

• *Out in the World* by Shelly Anderson, an excellent guide to the international lesbian movement, describes legal status, organizing efforts, and contact names for groups in over fifty countries and regions worldwide.

It is common in many Latin American, southern European, and some Middle Eastern and African societies for women friends to hold hands and walk arm-in-arm in public—in those places you can enjoy following the local custom. But don't be fooled into thinking that it represents an enlightened attitude about lesbians. Depending on your travel goals you can employ one or both of the following approaches.

When Necessary, Use Creative Methods to Overcome the Obstacles

For example, outside the U.S. (where double beds are the norm), obtaining a double bed can be problematic. It will be assumed that two women traveling together want two single beds. You can get around this by: making advance reservations and requesting the accommodations you want; having one partner sign in and get the key while the other waits outside with the bags; offering an explanation that applies to you, such as having back trouble and needing a large soft surface to do stretching exercises on; or asking for a family room with a double and single bed. In many places a room with a double bed is less expensive than one with two single beds and so you can claim the need to economize. Another approach is to ask to see the available rooms and then give a (true) reason for choosing one with a double bed: you want to be close to the bathroom, you want to be away from the street, you can't walk to the third floor, you love the view looking out over the fields, etc.

When Possible, Travel in a Lesbian-Friendly Environment

Travel to cities known to be centers of lesbian and gay culture, or seek out the lesbian or gay-owned restaurants, inns, resorts, etc., in whatever country you will be visiting. For travel to Europe, *Are You Two...Together?* is an excellent resource. Get a copy of the local lesbian or gay newspaper/newsletter/magazine, and attend the events advertised. The great advantage of this approach is that you will meet other lesbians and get a chance to experience lesbian lifestyles across cultures. A fast-growing industry catering to lesbian travelers offers resorts, cruises, and adventure trips. Consult a gay-aware travel agent (you can consult the **International Gay Travel Association, PO Box 4972, Key West, FL 33041 (303/294-5135)**, or refer to gay and lesbian travel magazines such as *Our World* and *Outing Travelogue.*

Books such as *Women Going Places* (formerly *Gaia's Guide International*), *Women's Traveller* (U.S., Canada, and the Caribbean), *International Places of Interest to Women* and *Inn Places: Gay and Lesbian Accommodations in the U.S. and Worldwide* are a treasure trove of lesbian and lesbian-friendly accommodations, restaurants, coffeehouses, tea rooms, bars, resorts, and events. Some also list health clinics, hot lines, information services, activist organizations, women's centers, women's libraries and archives, feminist bookstores, and lesbian publications. They are updated every year—get your hands on the most recent edition. If you scour these books you will come up with great leads:

- The *Homomonument,* a memorial dedicated to the approximately 250,000 lesbians and gay men exterminated in the Holocaust—near the Anne Frank House in Amsterdam.

- The Fondazione Sandro Penna in Torino, Italy, which offers conferences and classes at the university level in literature, history, art, and science and is the only European institution that deals exclusively with lesbian and homosexual culture.

- Spinnboden, a lesbian archive in Berlin.

- Les Lesbiennes se Font du Cinéma in Paris, which shows films by lesbians once a month.

- A bilingual lesbian weekend that's held once a year in Japan.

- A gay center in Stockholm housing the Cafe Timmy, the Alice B. Restaurant, and the Rosa Rummet Bookstore among other attractions.

Any woman, whether or not she is a lesbian, would find these books useful—most of them are not solely addressed to lesbians. Many women who travel alone welcome the haven of a feminist environment and, if you need help, this is the network (the feminist bookstores, hot lines, women's centers, etc.) you should turn to.

Self-Defense Tips

It is highly unlikely that you will have to fight your way out of any situation. But you should know that even if you've never studied self-defense you can temporarily disarm an assailant by hitting one of these vulnerable target areas:

- *Eyes*—Strike or poke one or both eyes; it causes both eyes to water, temporarily blinding your attacker so you can get away.
- *Nose*—Hitting the nose also causes the eyes to water.
- *Throat*—Press or hit the front of the throat (the Adam's apple), causing a suffocating sensation to distract your attacker.
- *Groin*—Striking upward between the legs with foot, knee, or fist can cause a man to double over, fall on the floor, and curl up.
- *Knees*—Striking a knee from the front or side can break, dislocate, or severely sprain it.

Women are often unpracticed at using our bodies defensively. Fists, feet, elbows, and knees can all be used effectively without much practice and don't require a lot of physical strength.

Yelling loudly—not screaming, but good strong yells—can surprise and distract an opponent, who expects only fear and submission. Call names of friends loudly; pretend someone is on their way to help you.

Read *Self Defense: The Womanly Art of Self-Care, Intuition, and Choice* by Debbie Leung, or one of many other books on the topic.

FLAT BROKE AND FEMALE IN FLORENCE

I pulled the last twenty dollar traveler's check from my money belt, exchanged it for *lire*, and bought a second-class ticket from Milan to Rome. I usually didn't let my money get so low, but I wasn't worried. I had a plan. I would get off the train in Florence, purchase my next supply of traveler's checks at the American Express office, see the sights for a day or two, and then continue south.

The train rolled across hills embroidered with vineyards, stitched in shades of gold. I checked my pack at the Santa Novella Maria train station in Florence, walked outside to the tourist information kiosk, picked up a map, and headed for town. My eyes feasted on noble facades as my errand took me across the River Arno on the Ponte Vecchio. I found via Guicciardini, tracked down the blue American Express sign, and pushed the door inward. My head bumped against unyielding glass. A hand-lettered sign stated in Italian and English that the office was closed for a holiday; it would reopen on Monday.

It was noon on Friday. I walked to the Boboli Gardens, sat on a bench, and carefully counted my assets. I had nine U.S. dollars' worth of *lire* and three tangerines to get me through the weekend. I knew that the only hotels and restaurants that would accept my credit card were high-priced places that would burst my long-term travel budget like an overripe tomato.

Italian men buzzed the bench like flies as I tried to consider my options. Young and old, elegant and silly, they invaded every quiet moment I'd had since crossing the border from Switzerland. At first they seemed funny, even charming. But their constant approaches and arrogant attitudes soon made me regard them as pests. I waved them away as I decided my course of action. I still had the train ticket; I would simply advance my schedule and hop the train to Rome that evening. All I had to do was call Signor and Signora Pagano, who had invited me to stay at their apartment in Rome, to say that I was finally on my way.

Consulting my map, I backtracked through the city and strolled to the main post office at the Piazza della Repubblica. The public telephone office was located inside. I asked carefully if I would be charged for the call if no one answered. The bemused clerk said no.

There was no answer when I called at noon. No answer at 1:30, 3:00, 4:00. By 5:00 P.M. the clerks at the phone office queried "Roma?" when I reached the head of the line. A middle-aged man who had arranged my call several times informed me that most Romans left the city for the seaside on summer weekends. He predicted the Paganos would return to Roma Sunday night or Monday.

I wandered past Renaissance *palazzos* as I pondered my situation. During the previous fifteen months of travel nothing really bad had happened to me. Through it all I'd given food and small change to the poor and made loans to other travelers, considering all of it some sort of down payment against the day when I might need help myself. I thought of going to a church or appealing to one of the well-dressed American tourists for a loan. But I trusted my instincts and felt I'd be safe. The weather was good, I could leave my backpack at the station and live on the streets for one weekend. Maybe there was something to be learned from the experience.

My only concern was the relentless hounding of the leering men who'd been sniffing my trail all day. My indecisive wanderings seemed to make them more bold. Did their radar tell them I had no place to go? I felt like bait fish in a tank full of barracudas. But I wasn't about to get caught.

Evening brought a cool breeze from the hills of Tuscany. I returned to the train station and retrieved my jacket. Student Eurailpass travelers already lined the station walls, spreading sleeping bags and compressed foam pads to claim their rent-free space for the night. Even without camping gear, I thought I could survive a night in the station.

I put on my jacket and went for a long walk, determined to get as tired as possible before returning to sleep on the stone station floor. To avoid trouble with men, I tried walking more purposefully, even though I had no real destination. I'd choose a spot on the city map and confidently stride there, then stop and choose my next goal. I remembered the homeless in my own city, perennially forced to roam.

I hopscotched the city, seeking a perfect spot for a light dinner *al fresco*. Seated on a bench in a small *piazza*, I took out a tangerine and peeled it slowly. I placed each section in my mouth, waiting as long as possible before carefully bringing my teeth together to explode the juice from the thin membrane. A man walked past and circled around, closing in on me. He sat beside me, and I ignored him, carefully finishing my meal.

He was in his late twenties, darkly handsome with a white sweater slung across his shoulders; the empty sleeves hung symmetrically in front of his chest. He began asking a familiar round of questions to determine my nationality.

"Hello, are you American?"

I didn't respond.

"Parlez-vous français?"

I ignored him. Encounters throughout the day had proven that answering even the first inane question opened a conversation nearly impossible to end.

"Sprechen zie Deutsch?"

I walked across the *piazzetta* into a church. He trailed me inside. I returned to the street. He followed behind. I crossed the plaza to the other side. He continued to stalk me.

"Spraak ye Holans?"

I returned instinctively to my most familiar corner of the city. In front of the telephone office was a sidewalk *frulatte* stand; two young guys in punk haircuts served up fruit shakes, breads, and snacks to passers-by.

"Another phone call?" the shorter one asked. They'd nodded at my migrations all day.

"No, can I sit down?" I asked, looking over my shoulder.

"Sure."

I perched on a low stone step behind them, using the cart to shield me from the man who'd been dogging me. He hovered in the distance for several minutes and then left.

The young entrepreneurs introduced themselves. The taller guy was named Stefano, and the shorter one with the ponytail was named…Stefano. We communicated in a jumble of English, Italian, and Spanish.

"Giving up on your phone call?"

"The family I'm trying to reach in Roma hasn't answered the phone. Since I don't have any money, I was thinking of just getting on the train anyway, hoping that they'd be home by the time I reached the *stazione* in Roma," I ventured.

"No, no. Don't go to Roma without money! They will eat you up!" both Stefanos implored.

I didn't ask who "they" were, I already had a pretty good idea.

"Stay in Firenze, it's a kind place. No one will hurt you here."

The conversation stopped and started as they served their evening customers, mostly young couples strolling arm in arm. I watched intently as the shorter Stefano eased some yogurt into an aluminum container, sliced a banana, pitched in some strawberries, set it to blend, and poured the thick shake into a tall glass. He turned and caught my intense stare.

"Would you like something? Are you hungry?"

"No, I have some fruit." I pulled another tangerine from my pack, embarrassed by my hunger. I hadn't planned to eat the second piece of fruit until the next day, but I needed it now to keep my hunger at bay. I rotated it slowly in my hand as we talked, keenly aware of its scent.

"Where are you staying? Do you need a place?"

Men had been offering me things all day. These two seemed nice, but I just didn't know if I could trust them. "I'm sleeping at the station tonight," I said. "I'll be okay. Some people are waiting for me there," I lied.

I walked quickly back to the station along dark streets; the echo of footsteps behind propelled me forward. At the baggage-holding window, I pulled a few things from my backpack. I laid my towel down as a mat, rolled my jacket into a pillow and used my Indian shawl as a blanket. The stone station floor was cold and unyielding. It seemed like hours before I fell asleep, and just minutes later that someone kicked my feet.

I woke in the pre-dawn to see women throwing water from their pails onto the floor, using their mops to push the water around and prod the station sleepers. I grumbled awake with the rest of the crowd, stiff and cold. I retired to a bench outside, rearranged my covers and dozed until the sun heated my creaking joints.

My second wake-up was much cheerier than the first. I washed in the station bathroom, paid for another day's storage on my pack, and headed back into town. It was a splendid day in Florence. I headed straight for the Uffizi Gallery, the "big rock candy mountain" of Italian art. I paced up and down outside the gallery, trying to decide whether to spend almost half my cash to get in. A flock of street artists roosted outside the front gate. *Signorina, signorina!* Paint your portrait! Very nice! *Bella! Bella!* I turned an empty pocket inside out in response.

Two artists at the end of the row shook their heads and muttered, "Business is very bad, no Americans this year." I stood for a while and talked with them—within ten minutes we had analyzed international terrorism, its effect on the European economy, why American tourists wanted their portraits painted more than most others, and the political situation in the Middle East.

I looked up at the long building with its red-tiled roof and thought, "Here I am outside the very gates of the Uffizi. One day soon I'll get over my hunger, but I may never have another chance to see this incredible collection of art." I went to the window and bought a ticket. I traversed the long hallways for hours until I couldn't distinguish one madonna from another. I emerged squinting into tawny sunlight.

"There she is! *Signorina!*" The two artists at the end of the row beckoned animatedly for me to return. I walked over and they introduced me to several of their comrades sitting nearby. "We told our friends that we met an American who could intelligently discuss politics! Everyone was so amazed that we decided to invite you for a cup of coffee."

If this was a come-on it certainly was different. But I felt safe drinking coffee with a crew of underemployed artists. Four of them closed their paint boxes, folded wooden chairs, and left them in the care of neighboring painters. We walked to a cafe, drank *cappucini*, ate *biscotti*, and waved our arms vehemently as we argued politics for an hour or more.

I returned to the telephone office to try my calls. The Stefanos clucked in stereophonic sympathy, no luck again. I had to agree with the kind man behind the desk that the Paganos probably wouldn't return until the next day. I consulted my map, looking for the Mercato Centrale the artists had told me about. I could spend some of my dwindling *lire* on bread and cheese there. I walked north and entered the market. Dewy zucchinis, lustrous miniature eggplants, the scent of ripe melons, oranges, and figs drew me forward. I purchased two rolls and a few hundred grams of cheese. The woman behind the counter eyed me counting out the exact change; she threw on an extra lump of Bel Paese before wrapping it in paper.

I walked a few blocks and sat in yet another small *piazza*. Having no money and no place to live made me appreciate the public amenities. The city of the Medicis was a good place to be out on the street. A tall man wearing a leather jacket approached the bench and sat at its other end. After a moment's silence, he leaned toward me and said in a low voice, "Excuse me, did you speak English?"

I rolled my eyes involuntarily, and he immediately interjected, "Sorry to bother you, I just needed a small favor."

Perhaps I've overreacted, I thought. I really have met some nice people here. I turned toward the man, "Yes?" I inquired noncommittally.

"You see, I have a friend in the United States. I want to write a letter to him but I am ashamed of my English, it is so very bad."

"You speak quite well," I assured him.

"Do you have the time to help me write a short letter? Or are you in a hurry?"

"No, it's okay. I have time."

"Shall we go drink a coffee? Perhaps it's better to write the letter on a table."

"No, this is fine. Do you have some paper?"

He drew an envelope from his pocket and unfolded the blank writing paper tucked inside. *Dear David,* we started. The Italian would pronounce a sentence or two, I'd help him clean up the grammar and then write it on the paper. We composed a letter that went like this: *Dear David, I hope you are feeling very well and happy. Everything is fine here in Florence. The summer is here, the weather is beautiful, and I am in love.*

His conversation strayed and wandered; he smiled and asked me questions. Beginning to doubt his sincerity, I urged him to complete the letter. *I have fallen madly in love with a tall, beautiful woman. She has dark eyes.* I looked at him. *A beautiful smile.* I frowned. *In fact, the woman I love is the one writing this letter at this very moment.*

I was disgusted with myself for being taken in, and angry with this man for playing with me. I stood up, letter in hand. "Really, now. How many times a day do you do this?" I tore up the letter, and started to leave.

"No, please, it is true. I am crazy for you!" I picked up my daypack and he stood and quickly grabbed his jacket. "Don't you dare follow me!" I hissed at him. He smiled foolishly, and held his hands palms up.

I walked hurriedly for several blocks, willing myself not to look back. I blended in with a large group of tourists and followed them into the entrance of a public building. It was the Academia, the home of Michelangelo's *David*. Between the money I'd spent at the Uffizi and the *mercato* and the cost of keeping my backpack in storage, I didn't have enough to pay the price of admission.

I hovered in the front entrance hall, craning my neck to get a glimpse of the treasures inside. "Ticket, *signorina?*" I turned to face the guard, a short bald man in his sixties dignified by a dark uniform with gold buttons.

"I don't have a ticket."

"You can buy one at the window, there." He pointed across the marble lobby.

"I don't have enough money to buy a ticket."

"Well, don't ask me to let you in for free. It's absolutely against the rules."

"I understand."

I stood silently beside him for a few minutes. He took tickets while I watched the crowd. Then he tilted his head toward me, and muttered in heavily accented English, "I could lose my job if I let you go in for free."

"I understand," I said, nodding sympathetically.

I took the last tangerine from my backpack. I peeled it slowly, split it and gave half to the guard. We ate the sections in silence.

"Is the *David* very beautiful?" I asked. "More beautiful than the copy in Piazza della Signoria?"

"*Bello, bello.* The most beautiful statue. The copy is nothing. I work here for many years, and still every day it seems more perfect, more beautiful to me."

We both nodded, standing silently again as he took more tickets. The rush of tourists entering the museum subsided for a moment.

"Go on inside!" he whispered urgently. "Just don't tell anyone!" I flashed a thankful smile, slipped in the entrance and went to see just how perfect Michelangelo's statue was.

Back out on the streets of Firenze, I wandered. I carefully ate the last crumbs of bread and cheese and contemplated a hungry future. I'd never really known hunger before—it put a sharp edge on everything. I became acutely aware of every pizza shop, coffee house, and *gelateria* that I passed. Dinnertime scents of garlic and olive oil wove down the narrow streets, wafting around me and leading me on. Maybe it was time to try another phone call.

The ponytailed Stefano was at the *frulatte* stand. "Where've you been?" he asked, waving his hand. I want you to meet my girl-friend. She'll be here at six o'clock. Will you hurry back out?"

The telephone man raised his eyebrows when I placed the call to Roma. "They won't be there," he said, shaking his head. "How was your sleep at the train station?"

"Okay...," I said slowly, "not too bad."

"I was thinking," the telephone man said, dropping his voice, "you can stay here tonight, in the back office. You'll be more comfortable." I wasn't enthusiastic about another night on the stone floor, but I really didn't know how to judge this offer.

"You can lock the office from the inside...," he added. "I'll be here to make sure you are safe."

"I don't know," I said. "Maybe. I'll come back later."

Out front, I met Stefano's girlfriend, Tiziana. I liked her wild dark hair, her giant hoop earrings, and her husky voice. "Listen," she said. "Stefano told me about your bad luck. I told him to bring you over to my place, but I knew you probably wouldn't trust him so I came to invite you myself. You can sleep on the couch. It's a small place, but you'll be safe."

"Great," I said, smiling. I let out a huge sigh of relief. "That will be great."

She and I sat on the step by the *frulatte* stand and shared a special strawberry concoction made by Stefano. He closed the stand and hopped on his red Vespa; we followed in her yellow Fiat. In the car, we talked about how badly Italian men treated women on the street. I immediately asked Tiziana how *she* got rid of them. She showed me a gesture and spit out some words that were guaranteed to send them away. We laughed in the car, practicing the phrase over and over. I took a shower at her place and sank into sleep on the couch.

We slept late the next morning, and Tiziana dropped me off at the telephone office after noon. Signora Pagano answered the phone on the second ring. "*Si, si,*" she told me, "come to Roma right away, this afternoon. We'll have dinner together."

I rushed outside and told the Stefanos. "*Cosi bella!*" We hugged farewell. "Be careful in Roma! It's very dangerous there! The men are terrible."

I checked the train schedule and made a quick dash to say my goodbyes. I rushed to the Academia, ducked my head in and said "*Ciao, signor. Molto grazie.*" Down at the Uffizi, I waved my train ticket at the artists. "Roma, Roma, I'm going to Roma."

I settled happily on to the afternoon train and started to eat one of the bananas Stefano had given me for the trip. A fifty-year-old man sitting opposite me in the compartment leaned forward, wiggled the tip of his tongue suggestively between his lips, placed his hand on his crotch and asked if I wanted to peel his banana, too.

Automatically, I spat the word and made the gesture Tiziana had taught me. The man sat back slowly, his face turning red as the other passengers around us laughed. He stood up, quickly gathered his jacket and parcels, and left.

Watch out, Roma, here I come!

Avoiding Theft

As you pack for your trip, consider carefully—just what *can* you afford to lose? Don't take Aunt Elma's garnet ring, if it's irreplaceable—or any other valuable or sentimental item that you can't live without. Pack lightly and keep essential items with you at all times.

> *My backpack was passed hand to hand, up to the rooftop luggage rack while the battered green school bus revved its tired motor for the twenty-two-hour journey from Kathmandu, Nepal, to Varanasi, India. I clambered to my seat and considered my choices: either I could risk losing my seat by climbing off the bus to check for my pack at each small village stop throughout the night, or I could snatch some sleep and hope that when I arrived, my gear would, too.*

My travels forced me to come to grips with a stark reality—the cash value of the essential items I carried with me while traveling "light" represented more wealth than many of our world's citizens will accumulate in a lifetime. My camera, film, portable cassette player with headphones, running shoes and clothes, all strapped into a nifty backpack, could provide an almost irresistible temptation to someone living in extreme poverty. While riding on that bus from Kathmandu I realized that if my travel pack was stolen it would be a depressing loss and a huge inconvenience. But it would not mean the end of my trip.

Tales of tourist rip-offs cover ground faster than a fourteen-day European tour. One in particular stays with me—that of a Japanese student whose pack disappeared en route to his trek in Nepal. He completed the trek anyway, carrying his guitar case, with a pair of socks, a sweater and other donated clothing jammed around the guitar.

The only thing I've ever lost during my travels was a purple T-shirt left hanging on a clothesline for two days. The secret of my success? A combination of good luck, careful planning, and trusting my instincts. Attitude is important—try to be cautious without letting paranoia reign.

Accept that some situations are completely outside your control, and try not to worry about them. But more importantly, recognize those factors within your control, and take precautions to protect against needless losses.

Before Leaving Home

Check your homeowner's or renter's insurance policy to determine if your luggage is already covered by existing policies while traveling. For short-term travel, insure your belongings with one of the policies designed for travelers—ask your travel agent for their brochures, or in the U.S. call:

Access America: 800/284-8300

Travel Guard International: 800/826-1300

Tele-Trip Company: 800/228-9792.

Long-term travelers should talk to an insurance agent, then compare the cost of coverage with replacement cost for your pack and gear.

Avoid carrying large amounts of cash. Photocopy your passport, airline ticket, train pass, traveler's checks, vaccination records, and credit card numbers in case they get lost or stolen. Take one set of copies with you; leave another at home with a relative or friend. Tuck an extra passport photo (or the negative) into your luggage to expedite replacing your passport. Store copies separately from the originals.

Safe Packing

No matter what your packing style, you'll probably divide your possessions among three distinct items:

1. a larger bag (a backpack or suitcase);

2. a small one (a daypack, shoulder bag, or purse); and

3. a money belt.

Ideally, you should be able to carry your luggage, fully packed, and still have a hand free to open doors and transact business. The ability to carry your gear without assistance allows you to maintain better control over your belongings. If you cannot carry your own luggage, or just don't want to, then consider limiting your stops or signing on to an organized tour which will transport your bags for you.

Suitcase Safety

The larger pack or suitcase will get the farthest from your control. During your travels it may be checked on airplanes, deposited in storage rooms, left behind at the hotel, rolled away on carts, and hefted on to out-of-sight luggage racks. So it's appropriate to pack your clothing, toiletries, and other replaceable items in that bag. It should be lockable. Test suitcase locks to determine if they can be easily opened with a paper clip or piece of wire. Buy small brass locks to secure your backpack or travel pack; keep the keys attached to a pocketknife, with an extra set in your money belt. Better yet, buy combination locks.

Locked luggage keeps temptation from those working around it, but serious thieves will not be deterred by anything. If nothing else, they can pick up the whole bag and carry it away.

Shoulder Bag / Daypack / Purse

The shoulder bag, daypack, or purse should stay with you at most times. A bag with a shoulder strap is likely to stay closer to your body. You'll carry it on sightseeing days around town, with just enough cash for the day, a map, camera, sunglasses, or other necessities.

Don't bring your wallet from home or carry your full supply of traveler's checks in your travel bag or purse. This eliminates extra weight as well as extra worries. Never rest your purse on the floor of a restaurant, or on a hotel or car rental counter; these are likely places for purse snatchings.

On travel days, (when relocating from one place to another) carry the items you'll want handy for the journey (a book to read, some food to eat) as well as any valuables that won't fit in your money belt. Jewelry and irreplaceable items (like prescription drugs, your journal, and exposed rolls of film) should be kept in this bag. If your irreplaceable possessions don't easily fit into your shoulder bag, reconsider what you are packing.

"Slash and grab" robberies, where a thief slices through the strap and grabs the bag away from its owner, are common travel rip-offs. Choose a shoulder bag with a strong, difficult-to-cut strap to foil such attempts. Wear the strap diagonally across your body so the bag is not easy to grab. Get into the habit of holding on to the bag, not the strap. (A small flat shoulder purse can fit under your jacket or sweater, making it almost invisible.)

A daypack is a comfortable alternative but can make you easy prey in a crowd. As you head into markets and other crowded situations, try wearing the straps on opposite shoulders so the pack hangs in front, instead of behind you.

Money Belt

Your best protection against theft is to *always* keep your passport, traveler's checks, cash, credit cards, and critical documents zipped into a money belt worn under your clothes. Even if all else is lost or stolen, you'll have the essentials you need to regroup. Leave your wallet at home with library and other unneeded cards—your passport is sufficient for identification.

Many variations of the money pouch or belt are available. Some travelers hang a pouch from their neck, tucked inside their shirt. To me, this only adds the prospect of strangulation to that of robbery. For that reason, I recommend the old-fashioned zippered pouch that straps around the waist underneath your clothes.

Alternatively, try one of the new versions that wrap around your ankle or leg, to wear under pants. A shoulder-holster style adjusts to fit under one arm, with a waist strap to secure it to the body. It is less bulky at the waist and easily accessed through an open-necked dress or shirt. A new option that will appeal to those who wear slips is called **Hidden Assets**. It is a half-slip with three zippered pockets hidden in the lace hem. To order, contact: **Hidden Assets, 1539 First Avenue, Box 20056, New York, NY 10028 (212/439-0693).**

Thanks to lightweight, breathable fabrics, the money belt can be comfortable to wear. Because it's not used as a wallet, you don't need constant access to it. You should dip into it every few days, when getting out a traveler's check to change money.

Do-It-Yourself Money Belt

You can make an "inside pocket" at home that serves as a functional, low-cost alternative. Sew a cloth envelope a bit wider than your passport, a bit longer than your traveler's checks. This long pouch will hang inside your clothes and rest against your leg, like an extra pocket. Sew a strip of Velcro across the top of the pouch. Then sew matching Velcro strips inside the waistband of two or three garments you have chosen for the trip—a pair of pants, a skirt or shorts, if appropriate. For a long trip, take some extra Velcro along, to customize new clothes you purchase along the way. Or fasten the inside pocket with a safety pin.

A fannypack worn outside your waist provides a handy carrier for a small camera or the day's pocket money, but it should *not* be used to replace the money belt worn inside your clothing.

But what about those times when you can't wear a money belt— while you are swimming, or in the shower (if it's down the hall)? Depending on how secure your lodgings are, you have a couple of choices: temporarily lock your money belt inside your luggage or pack, or ask the proprietor if they have a "lock-up" box for valuables.

In budget accommodations, the lock-up box can range from an old safe to a dingy metal trunk under grandma's bed. Some people carry their money belt with them to the shower; I lock mine inside my pack for short periods of time. Cascade Designs, an outdoor sports outfitter, manufactures a waterproof waist pack, called the **Seal Pak**, to fit wallet and passport. You can go swimming and still keep your valuables dry. (Call **800/ 531-9531** for information or to order a Seal Pak.)

In uncertain circumstances, some travelers sleep wearing their money belt or hide it under their pillow (not recommended for the absent-minded, however). Virginia Urrutia, in *Two Wheels and a Taxi*, describes how fear was the stimulus for creative new safety procedures one night in Ecuador:

> *Back in my hotel room I was the one who had no*
> *confidence. I started to chain my door shut, but the chain*
> *had been broken. I reached down to double-lock the door,*
> *but the lock had been yanked apart. One remaining lock*
> *still locked, but feebly. I pushed a large desk up against*
> *the door, tied my camera to my ankles, hung my purse*
> *around my neck, turned the noisy air conditioner low,*
> *crawled into bed and slept.*[10]

Train and Bus Safety

Train and bus stations present special problems for the solo traveler. When traveling alone, it's much more difficult to leave your baggage momentarily to ask a question, verify information, buy some food, or find a bathroom. (Of course, if you are truly traveling light, you can carry it all with you and eliminate this problem.)

Check out the station in advance, either when buying your ticket or when passing by on your travels around town. Are lockers or a baggage room available for short-term use? If so, take advantage of the service—just be sure that you can retrieve your bag in time for your departure.

If no luggage-holding service is available, you may need to find someone to watch your baggage. When I want to leave a pack or suitcase behind, I look for a large family group sitting in a highly visible area. I ask them clearly to watch my bag—if we don't speak a common language, I resort to sign language. I point to my eye, then to theirs, then to my bag. I show that I will walk away in a certain direction for a small (using my fingers to indicate "a little bit") of time. Sometimes I exaggerate this request, asking a few people seated near each other simultaneously. That sets up a check system, where everybody is watching everyone else watch my bag. (I figure that everyone probably won't agree to abscond with my stuff in a short few minutes.) I've made this request repeatedly, all over the globe, with great success.

In the station, I keep my shoulder bag or daypack with me and of course have my money belt on under my clothes.

If I don't have a preassigned seat on the bus or train, I always sit beside other women or a family group. I look for the last available seat in a compartment or section to avoid troublemakers who want to sit next to me, for whatever reason. (If you don't pursue the people *you* want to meet, you may be pursued by hustlers who want to meet you.)

While riding on the bus or train, I feel more secure with my baggage in sight. That usually means placing my pack on the luggage rack opposite, where I can see it from my seat, rather than over my head. (If your paranoia level runs high, it is difficult to sit still while someone rummages around for several minutes overhead where your bag, and theirs, are both stashed.)

Some travelers want to secure their belongings while sleeping on the train or bus during the night, and carry a chain and lock their bag to the luggage rack. Others just throw it up there and hope for good karma. I have used the karma method with good results and supplemented it on rare occasions in this way: I untied the straps that cinch my pack, laced them through or around the bars of the luggage rack, and reattached them to my bag—just to detain the snatch-and-run thief for a moment and give me a chance to wake up.

If I have a berth on the train (not a lockable private compartment), I sleep leaning on my pack. This led to the habit of always packing one end of my bag with soft contents to make it comfortable to lean on.

When traveling by bus in the "Third World," you may have to put your pack or suitcase on the roof of the bus, along with everyone else's belongings. You can appeal to the driver's helper, who secures the luggage, to keep a watchful eye on your stuff; offer him a cigarette or some chewing gum to help him with the task.

Hitchhiking

In some parts of the world, hitching is still safe and a good way to meet people. But no matter where you are, don't hitchhike alone. I've hitched (with travel partners) across Ireland, up and down the British Isles, through Europe, in Mexico, and up the Malaysian peninsula. Ireland and New Zealand share reputations as safe, delightful places for women hitchhikers. This can take some getting used to, as Mary Zinkin describes:

> *A man I met on the plane flying to the South Island offered to give me a ride to the hostel. I accepted, but was on my guard the whole way, wondering if he would take me down a dark road and rape me. But no, he delivered me to the door, shook my hand and said, "Have a nice holiday."*
>
> *Coming from the United States, it was hard to orient myself to a place where I was really safe—I wasn't used to that. But in New Zealand people are accustomed to seeing women travel alone, and hitchhiking is very common. (They call anyone traveling alone a hitchhiker, no matter how they are traveling.)*

Before setting out, investigate the advisability of hitchhiking with several sources of information. Make sure you carry a supply of water, in case you get stuck waiting a long time for a ride, and always have a map so you can independently verify your route.

Camping Out

Camping is a popular low-cost travel option, especially in Europe. Theft or harassment of women in campgrounds is virtually unknown, according to Lenore Baken, author of *Camp Europe by Train*.

Occasionally you might find a women's camping area such as **Camping des Femmes**, in the Dordogne region of southwestern France, **St. Aubin de Rabirat, 24250 Domme (53-28-50-28)**. On the Greek island of Lesbos near the village of Skala Eressos there is an unofficial women-only camping area.

Camping is common in rural parts of Central America and Africa but less prevalent in towns where lodging costs are low. When searching for a nonofficial camping spot, seek out women for permission and advice at local farms or villages. Make sure your campsite is safe from harassment, natural perils (animals or flash floods), and in a respectful location (away from cemeteries or other sacred places).

Around Town

Review a map of the town with your hotel clerk to find out if there are dangerous areas to avoid. A woman traveling alone, or two women traveling together, will want to ask about nighttime safety. Just as at home, walking purposefully with confidence will make you a less likely robbery target.

Instant Friends

Lots of people make money from tourists. Some are just more obvious than others. Be aware that people may seek out your friendship hoping for gifts, free meals, or even marriage. It may be difficult to discern the motives of an overly friendly stranger; maintain an attitude that is cautious but friendly. Traveling is a good time to exercise your intuition; tune in your radar and rely on it.

Is someone who appears out of the dark offering to help carry your luggage trying to help you or take advantage of you? If your intuition is broadcasting a mixed message, play it safe by making a joke about being a strong woman and carry the bags yourself.

The further you stray from the beaten path, the more curiosity you will attract. People may approach you for the sheer joy of cross-cultural interaction. They'll ask if by chance you know their cousin who lives in Chicago. Or tell you about an American friend from Santa Barbara. They may simply want to practice their English or enjoy the status of having a Western friend to show off to the neighbors.

Vendors

Ronna Neuenschwander, who has traveled extensively in Western Africa, says:

> *In Senegal, vendors will follow you for a long time. Treat them kindly—don't ignore or dismiss them out of hand. Look at what they have to offer, and say no firmly if there's nothing you want. If they are very persistent— and they can be—turn the tables by asking for something you do want. Perhaps they can find it or direct you to another vendor who has it. In remote places, their persistence may simply be because they want to meet and talk with you.*

In major tourist destinations, skillful vendors engage a traveler in conversation by greeting her in several languages, trying one after another until they get a response. Kay Grasing described the strategy she developed in Egypt: "The hawkers drove me crazy until I finally told them I spoke Icelandic. Then I looked straight ahead as if I didn't understand English or was hard of hearing."

Touts, Tour Guides and Taxi Drivers

Most con artists you will meet come in the guise of "helpful friends" who offer you a special discount at their cousin's shop, a good price on a hotel room, or "hard to get" tickets to local cultural exhibitions.

In reality, these touts are working for a commission on the business they deliver. They can be boorish leeches who are difficult to shake off, or lively and charming companions with fascinating tales full of local history, well worth the hidden "commission" you pay for their help.

Touts earn money by delivering paying customers to a hotel, shop, performance, or tour. Their commission is rarely paid in front of you, the customer. They can be taxi, rickshaw, or camel drivers, work at the hotel desk, or just happen to chat you up at a bank or sitting at a cafe. Sometimes they are children sent to the train station to draw customers to a family inn, or guides who offer to take you to a relative's shop where you can get a bargain price.

In Southern Europe, the Middle East, South America, and Asia, touts can be incredibly persistent. They will try to ingratiate themselves to make you feel beholden to them. Women especially are targets because we often feel obligated to be polite. Martha Banyas describes what she encountered in Turkey:

> *They suck you in by getting you involved in a conversation, then pull you in the shop and try to sell you something. The longer they can keep you talking and keep you there, the better their chances are of making a sale. They'll serve you tea and give you things, and obligate you so that you feel that pressure.... I don't want to spend my time sitting around a shop I have no interest in, being manipulated.*

Martha recommends a firm refusal to enter the shop in the first place. "I'm not afraid of taking a strong stand if they start to pressure me. I won't be pushed into going somewhere I don't want to go. If they cross that line, I don't have qualms about being rude to them."

Avoid giving strangers money to buy you a ticket unless the price of the performance is clearly posted and you are giving exact change. Take a chance if there is only a small amount of money at stake. And, be sure there really *is* a charge for the performance.

Is there a positive side to dealing with touts? Yes, at times. Competition between touts can help you, the customer. Get price quotes for rooms from several people at the ferry dock or train station before you comply with their inevitable request to "come see the room." They may gladly point out the shortcomings of the competition.

In a large city or crowded marketplace, a guide can help you shop quickly and efficiently if they are not obligated to one store:

> Jaipur, India, seemed to be the dhurrie rug capital of the world, and I decided to buy three small cotton dhurries to ship home. I hired a rickshaw for a morning of shopping after the eager driver displayed his "references," a small notebook filled with testimonials in many languages.
>
> We visited perhaps a dozen rug shops—many of them impossible to find without his help. I sketched the rugs I liked, making notes on the prices. After three hours, I'd seen hundreds of rugs. The rickshaw driver was obviously dismayed when I returned home without any purchases.
>
> That evening I decided which rugs to buy and mulled over my bargaining strategy. I had planned to return without the driver, intent on not paying any commission. But two of the shops were beyond walking distance. If I needed a rickshaw for the return trip, wouldn't it be fair to let the original driver collect the commission?
>
> I bargained fiercely the next morning, relishing each hard-won prize as I brought it back to the rickshaw. I was well satisfied with the prices I paid; if the driver was slipped a few rupees on the deal, I felt he had earned them.

It's important to keep things in perspective—the commission they make may be equivalent to the price of a soda back home and sometimes can be a worthwhile investment. Besides, showing up without a "guide" is no guarantee of a lower price.

Tour guides can be touts as well. It's a sure sign when they hurry through the tour in order to show you the "best shop" before the crowds get there. If you are negotiating privately to hire a guide, ask specifically how long the tour will last and what it will cover. If you are not interested in shopping, state so clearly as soon as the subject is brought up.

Taxi drivers are in a class by themselves. They can save your life, become your instant "best friend," and serve as an impromptu tour guide. Some are also maestros at bilking travelers.

Always agree on the fare before you get into a taxi, unless it has a properly working meter. If necessary, ask a local person to help you establish the fare—it could be a bystander on the street, someone you met on the train or plane, a doorman of a nearby hotel, or a local police officer. Ask specifically if there will be extra charges for baggage, traveling at night, the return trip, or whatever. Virginia Urrutia describes a lesson learned in the Andes:

> Foolishly I had not agreed upon a price before we set out. I still had the unbroken 1000 sucre note and he claimed to be utterly lacking in sucres. My knee was smarting and so was my temper. We quibbled a while and then he snatched the 1000 sucre note from my hand and said that this would pay for what I owed him, as well as the trip to the Middle of the World. Off he drove. I was defeated.[11]

Lack of proper change is universally claimed; occasionally is it true. Try to have the fare ready in exact change. Once you hand over too much money, you may be engaged in a battle of wills to get any cash back.

Pickpockets

Guidebooks and other travelers will warn you about the most common local scams—Rome is famous for its youthful pickpockets; in Jakarta, several teens may distract you on the bus while a compatriot uses a razor to slit open the bottom of your backpack, fannypack or purse. The contents come pouring out just in time for the thieves' quick getaway at the next stop. In Barcelona, pickpockets around the Plaza Cataluña are well-dressed women and men carrying briefcases.

Pickpockets create and take advantage of distractions and crowds to jostle against you. Your first reaction to any distracting scene should be to secure your belongings. Be cautious in crowds; don't carry much money or a large bag to the marketplace. Use a string bag or other local shopping bag for your food purchases. Carry your pack or purse in front of you if you are likely to get jostled on public transport or at the market. If you are carrying a conspicuous camera, hold onto the body of the camera rather than the strap.

Thieves

Watch out for fake "bucket shops" in cities like Athens or Bangkok. Bucket shops market unsold airline tickets for greatly discounted prices, advertising by word of mouth on the budget travel circuit. Legitimate bucket shops will be listed in your guidebook and can provide a real service. Fly-by-night alternatives open their doors, collect deposits of $100 to $200 from dozens of travelers, then close down before customers can return to pick up their tickets.

Most thieves prefer more mundane work, lifting valuables from your hotel room, checked baggage, or car, or picking your pocket in a crowd. Some observers claim that hotel-room thefts are more likely to occur within a day of departure—either due to inside knowledge on the part of the thief or decreased vigilance of a tourist turning her thoughts toward home.

Rental cars are a common target for thieves in Europe. The car license plate may indicate that it's a rental. When renting a car, always get a vehicle with a separate trunk, rather than a hatchback, which keeps luggage visible. Don't leave your possessions on display in the passenger seats. Keep in mind that even locked cars and trunks are easily broken into. Again, don't carry things you hate to lose. Insure your belongings, or carry an old suitcase filled with used clothes to lower your risk of loss.

Your chances of getting robbed with a weapon are much lower outside the U.S. Although the prospect of physical danger is truly remote, if it should arise, you should hand over the goods without a fight. Carrying a weapon of your own is ill-advised.

Many countries that rely on tourism for foreign exchange heavily penalize thieves and vigorously prosecute those who prey on tourists. Thailand has a special Tourist Police Force designed for that very purpose; tourist theft is rare there.

Safe Traveling Suggestions

•Insure your belongings.

•Pack light, and leave irreplaceable items at home.

•Keep control of your belongings; wear a money belt at all times.

•Have copies of critical documents to aid in quick replacement.

•Secure your baggage in stations and on the train or bus.

•Be cautious in crowds, hold on to your bags securely.

•Keep rental cars locked; place belongings in trunk and out of sight.

•Be aware of con artists and touts.

•Don't get pressured into making purchases you don't want.

•Only hitchhike where safe, never alone.

•Camp where others can see you.

•Cultivate your intuition and learn to rely on it.

Bribes

Bribes are commonplace in many cultures. Be aware of their cultural significance before you enter a country. Try to get local advice from residents or other travelers about how to deal with the situation before it comes up—find out about appropriate amounts of money and ways to pass it along. You may not like paying a bribe, but it may be necessary. If you are directly asked to pay a specific amount, try to bargain it down.

At some airports and border crossings, "expediters" hire themselves out to get travelers' paperwork done efficiently. They charge one lump sum and pay the appropriate bribes to officials at every step of the way.

Changing Money

You'll need to decide the best way to gain access to your money while traveling. Many travelers purchase traveler's checks amounting to the full budget for their trip and change them to local currency as needed. Others use credit card advances and automatic teller machine (ATM) withdrawals, already converted to local currency, to augment their traveler's checks.

Credit Card Advances and ATM Cards

In most major cities and an increasing number of small towns of the world, you can now obtain local currency by using your bank cards in two different ways: you can use your ATM card, or you can get a cash advance against a major credit card.

Consumer Reports Travel Letter reports the big news: using your ATM card may provide the best foreign exchange rate because your withdrawal is converted at a wholesale currency exchange rate (only available to banks in large-scale transactions) and no transaction fee is charged. Your total savings may be 5 to 8 percent over the retail cost of cashing traveler's checks.

If your ATM card works in the Cirrus or Plus networks at home, theoretically you can use it at ATMs in foreign banks connected to the same network. ATMs overseas should be programmed in multiple languages and are available twenty-four hours a day. But before you plan your finances on an ATM strategy, make sure you will have sufficient access to the machines. Ask your bank for an updated list of locations worldwide so you can compare the list to your itinerary. (Cirrus and Plus claim nearly 100,000 ATMs in 10,000 cities around the world. Plus is concentrated on the United Kingdom and Canada, Cirrus in Continental Europe and Asia. Neither has much coverage in South America or Africa yet.)

Check out the official exchange rates where you will be headed, as some Eastern European countries with two-tier exchange rates may make traveler's checks more advantageous. And be sure to ask your bank if you will have to change your personal identification number (PIN) code before going overseas, or if you need to predesignate which account your card will draw from. Carry the name and telephone number of a representative from your hometown bank to call in case a machine eats your card and keep a back-up supply of traveler's checks to keep from getting stranded.

You won't have to look for ATMs to get a credit card advance; simply go into any bank that displays a VISA or MasterCard sign. Cash advances on credit cards may be slightly more costly due to interest charges on the advance and a percentage or transaction fee. (Check with your bank to determine what the fees will be before you travel.) But the opportunities for getting cash should be widespread.

Traveler's Checks

Consider your anticipated rate of spending before choosing denominations of traveler's checks. It's wise to get a mixture—small bills to cover last-minute expenses before leaving the country; larger bills to cover hotel and large purchases. Thick wads of small denomination traveler's checks can be hot and bulky in your money belt. While traveler's checks are available in many foreign currencies, most travelers carry checks in U.S. dollars or British pounds sterling. That necessitates changing money to the local currency, which can be a complex or confusing transaction.

Some travelers purchase a day's worth of foreign currency at their local commercial bank before departure. They are willing to pay the higher fees (and receive a less-favorable exchange rate) for the convenience of having cash when they arrive. I recommend, however, that you wait and change a small amount of money immediately upon arrival at a foreign airport or train station. Because you may not know how that rate compares to the rate in town, change just enough to get you into town and checked into a hotel room. (If arriving at night, on a weekend, or holiday, you may want to change more.) Find out what a taxi or other transport will cost to get you into town; when you change money, be sure to get some small bills so you won't have to hassle with the driver. This also serves as a control against confusion; if you changed $20 and know that the taxi ride to town should cost you the equivalent of $5, you won't get easily overcharged, no matter how confusing that new currency initially seems.

Procedures and options for changing money vary widely from country to country, and even within countries. Take notice of differing exchange rates listed at hotels, banks, and special money-changing shops or stalls. The best rates are usually offered at banks, but at times the bank lines can be long. For the ease of changing money at the hotel desk and avoiding a line at the bank, you may have to pay dearly—as much as 15 percent more.

Be prepared to show your passport when changing money. Watch out for bad exchange rates at high-priced tourist spots. Rates may differ slightly for cash and traveler's checks (the traveler's checks usually command a better rate), and your cost of changing money will probably include a transaction fee.

Ask if the fee will be charged as a percentage or as a flat fee, and adjust your transaction accordingly. (A flat fee equivalent to 50¢, for example, would amount to a 5 percent fee when exchanging $10, but only a .5 percent fee when exchanging $100. Such a fee makes exchanging large amounts worthwhile, while a percentage fee won't penalize you for returning to change small checks again and again.) Compare fees for cashing traveler's checks and currency—sometimes there will be a significant difference.

Request some small bills when changing money. Large bills may be difficult to change in small towns. In some countries, old or torn bills are suspect and should be avoided. You'll know because merchants will keep giving them to you but will not accept them from you.

Money changing is one of many areas where each traveler has to find the balance between convenience and cost. To the budget traveler on an extended trip, it may be worthwhile to wait an hour or longer at the bank for the best exchange rate in town. Others may be willing to spend a bit more on the transaction in exchange for saving time. Make a quick mental calculation of the difference between the higher and lower rate, and decide if the wait is justified.

Foreign Money Anxiety

I arrived in Israel the day the government devalued their currency. After a period of rampant inflation, the treasury printed new money and lopped three zeroes off the end—1,000 *shekels* became one *shekel* overnight. Everything in the stores had "old" and "new" prices, people carried "old" and "new" money in different pockets, and I wandered dazed for days.

Perhaps foreign money anxiety is a corollary to math anxiety. When faced with mentally calculating an exchange rate, or making transactions in a currency where it costs over 3,000 *whatevers* just for lunch, any traveler can easily feel overwhelmed. Here are some strategies for easing the conversion:

•Do not leave the money-changing window until you understand the transaction clearly and are sure you received the right amount of cash. Any legitimate money changer should provide an adding machine tape or written receipt to verify their calculations.

•Resist the temptation to convert every price you see to your home currency in your head. This practice only maintains confusion, especially for those who dislike mental calculations.

•Try to start thinking in the foreign currency. Focus on the price of some basic items—a loaf of bread, the cost of a bus ride, last night's dinner, a night in your hotel. Then, compare other prices to those. ("This bracelet costs as much as a night in my hotel; that seems expensive.") Study the ads for food and other goods in a local newspaper; this can also help imprint the new money system in your head.

•If you still feel nervous and must know how much everything costs in "real money," make a small chart and carry it in your pocket or purse for referral when necessary. Here's an example using Danish *kroner*, at an exchange rate of .1653 to the U.S. dollar.

Kroner	Dollars	Dollars	Kroner
1	.1653 (17¢)	1	6.05
10	1.65	10	60.50
100	16.530	100	605.00

Moving the decimal point gives you an easy way to convert money. Round off numbers if it helps (one *krone* is about 17¢). Don't try to make an exact calculation—just get the basic relationship between the two currencies established in your brain: each *krone* is worth about 17¢; it takes just over 6 *kroner* to equal one dollar.

Whenever you can, do the conversion in the direction it's simplest. In this situation, it's much easier to calculate from dollars to *kroner* (multiply by 6) than from *kroner* to dollars (multiply by .17)

Carry a pocket calculator or a computerized converter calculator if you find it helpful as backup, or to verify major transactions.

Changing Money on the Black Market

In countries with internal currency control and high inflation, a black market often exists for foreign exchange. People will approach you on the street, in museums, or at archaeological sites, restaurants, and hotels and offer you two, three, or even ten times the official exchange rate for your desirable Western currency.

Black market money-changing is always illegal. In some countries it is highly visible and not prosecuted. In others, the penalties can be severe, including detention and deportation. Socially conscious travelers may want to bypass black market transactions, which benefit a few profiteers to the detriment of the overall economy.

If you can't resist the temptation to multiply your spending power, ask several experienced travelers and local people who work with tourists about the dangers involved. You may be required to show bank receipts when leaving a country to prove that you changed money legally while there. This requires changing at least some of your money legally.

Black market rip-offs are legendary and range from the grab-and-run thief to the single good bill placed on a stack of blank paper. Avoid changing money outside on the street or in any dark place. The most reliable people for "unofficial" money-changing seem to be restaurant and hotel proprietors—people you can come back and find if needed and who have some standing in the community.

A Final Note

Avoid overexchanging currency before you leave a country; plan your activities and expenses so that you won't have to change back more than a minimal amount of money (because usually each time you change money, you pay a fee). Give away or spend all your coins before crossing the border, or save them for mementos, as they may be difficult or impossible to change on the other side.

Clean out your pockets of leftover foreign currencies by making a purchase at an airport duty-free shop. Or donate your leftover foreign coins to fund programs that allow inner-city youth to spend time with international travelers in youth hostels. Send coins to **American Youth Hostels Kids' Program, PO Box 28607, Washington DC 20038**.

Food and Water Precautions

Culinary adventures can be memorable for more than one reason. The pleasures of eating and drinking are tempered by the threat of food- and water-borne illness.

I've seen cautious travelers who get sick despite a strict health regimen; others eat with abandon and never seem affected. Above all, *know thyself*. Do you possess an iron stomach, able to withstand many bacteriological assaults? Or does your delicate nature require a bit more pampering? Do you worry a lot about your health, or does it rarely cross your mind? All these factors should influence just how cautious you should be.

Preventing Problems

Diarrhea, the most common travelers' ailment, is a body's attempt to flush out hostile bacteria. Outside your home environment, bacteria that may be harmless to local people can trigger your body's defense mechanisms simply because you are unaccustomed to them.

Build Up Your Internal Defenses

One strategy for avoiding diarrhea is to boost your body's ability to handle a wider range of bacteria. I'm convinced that acidophilus (natural yogurt culture) provides added health protection by generating more flora in the intestines. I buy it at a health food store and ask for the type that doesn't require refrigeration. I take two to four acidophilus tablets daily, starting a week or two before departure, and continue taking one per day while traveling. I up my intake at the slightest suspicion of an upset stomach.

One tour operator suggests that travelers drink only nonchlorinated water for two weeks to a month before departure, on the theory that chlorine inhibits the body's immune system. They claim that not one of a hundred people who've followed this regimen has gotten diarrhea.

Some travelers swear by preventative use of Pepto-Bismol (two ounces liquid or two tablets four times daily) to coat the stomach and thereby stave off digestive problems. This isn't recommended for long-term travelers. I prefer acclimating my stomach to fortifying it in this way, but those with a delicate system may find this helpful. (Be aware that ulcer, stomach medications, and antacids weaken your internal defenses by reducing stomach acids that control diarrhea-causing bacteria.)

Some believe that vitamin C can help maintain your health and guard against colds and respiratory infections and that vitamin E is useful in countering the effects of environmental toxins, particularly in urban areas. Also recommended by some is regular consumption of freshly prepared yogurt (sold in covered containers) and fresh garlic.

Monitor Consumption

The second strategy is to closely monitor and control what you ingest to minimize the intake of bacteria. Start off by being cautious. If you decide to relax your restrictions, do so carefully, one step at a time. Don't be bullied by others traveling with you; find your own comfort level and stick to it. If you want to get adventurous, choose a day when you'll be staying in town, instead of just before boarding a bus for a long-distance ride.

Water

You can safely drink tap water in about a third of the world's nations (half of which are in North America and Europe), but most travelers and the Europeans themselves drink bottled water. Flat or fizzy, it is available at most restaurants and in stores. (The U.S. Centers for Disease Control recommends you drink carbonated water because it is harder to tamper with and its slightly acidic nature helps inhibit bacterial growth.) The plastic bottles are handy to carry on trains or buses for long journeys. In restaurants, make sure the bottle arrives sealed and is opened in your presence.

Assume that all tap or well water is unsafe unless you have proof otherwise (a chlorine taste isn't proof enough). The local population can develop immunity with long-term exposure to bacteria that will make you sick, so you can't necessarily "do as the Romans do." Do not brush your teeth with tap water, and avoid swallowing water while showering. Your host may assure you that drinking water is filtered; check it out for yourself. After drinking the "filtered water" for a week at a guesthouse on the beach in Oaxaca, I got up early one morning to witness the filtration process. A young woman held a dirty dishrag over the end of the garden hose to fill the container. It did catch the pebbles and insects, and maybe that was enough, because I didn't get sick.

Fear of drinking contaminated water can easily lead to dehydration, especially in hot climates. In order to maintain your fluid consumption, you may have to drink more soda pop than you ever imagined. Never a soda drinker at home, I consume several a day when traveling. Try the local varieties; some, like grapefruit soda or apple soda, are less sweet.

Drinking beverages over ice is a particularly North American mania. You can always spot American tourists—they're the ones asking for ice in their drink. Making ice from filtered water is too expensive for most restaurants. You may be assured that ice is made from good water, but don't trust it. The best course is to leave your ice-mania back home; get accustomed to non-iced drinks.

Boiled tea and coffee are safe to drink and are ideal choices when accepting hospitality in a home. When patronizing street vendors, use a splash of hot tea or coffee to rinse out your cup before drinking. The English say that hot tea cools the body faster than any cold drink, and I have to agree. Beer and wine are almost always safe, but they will make you more thirsty. Adding alcohol does not make a drink "safer," and high alcohol consumption can exacerbate travelers' diarrhea.

When traveling to remote regions, carry your own water bottle and equipment for water purification. All water from lakes, rivers, and streams should be treated before drinking, no matter how pure and clean it appears to be. You can use either purifying tablets (put one or two tablets in a one-liter bottle, and wait for ten minutes after they are dissolved) or tincture of iodine solution. Iodine is the cheapest and is easy to carry in an eyedropper bottle. Put two drops in a glass of water (four drops in a liter of clear water), wait ten minutes, and try to get accustomed to the taste. For cold or cloudy water, use ten drops per liter and wait thirty minutes.

Portable water filters are available at camping stores; they are expensive and can be bulky cargo. A lightweight and low-cost alternative is a filtration cup, which will filter several hundred glasses of water. The cup works slowly, so you need one per person. (In the U.S., contact **Magellan's** at **800/ 962-4943** to buy a water purifier cup if they aren't available in your local stores.) When lacking other equipment, you can always boil water for twenty minutes. In an emergency, uncomfortably hot tap water (if you can find it) is usually safe.

Food

Eat at restaurants that are clean; the cooks should appear clean and healthy. Frequent restaurants patronized by others; everyone can't be there for the first time! Request dishes that must be made to order rather than ones that can sit around for a while. High temperature kills bacteria, so any hot dish just cooked from fresh ingredients should be safe. (That's why stir-fried noodles from a street vendor can be a safer bet than the lasagna in a fancy Asian restaurant.) Locally popular foods turn over much more quickly than rare or foreign dishes, which wind up sitting around waiting for the right gringo.

In tropical climates, skip dishes made with milk, milk-based sauces, and cream desserts unless you are confident of local pasteurization and refrigeration. Many travelers avoid eating raw salads, unpeeled fruit, or raw ingredients used to garnish cooked foods (like chopped onions). Others squeeze lemon or lime on salads and other foods, because citric acid helps control bacteria. Rich and fatty foods should be avoided.

Bacteria flourish in a moist environment. For that reason, many travelers won't eat from a wet plate. Dry foods, such as breads, are almost always safe and can be staples for picnic lunches or dinners.

When preparing food, peel your own fruits and vegetables, or boil or wash them in pure water. Fruits that cannot be peeled, like strawberries, should be soaked in a mild iodine solution. (Soak for fifteen minutes in ten drops of iodine per liter of water. Drain, but don't rinse.) Or, put two tablespoonfuls of bleach in a sinkful of water, soak the fruits and vegetables and then dry them on paper towels—they don't retain the bleach odor.

If you feel you've made a culinary error or fear that you may be a victim of food poisoning, take Pepto-Bismol or swallow some charcoal tablets. The charcoal will quickly soak up whatever you regretfully just consumed. Just remember that charcoal comes out black, too. Don't let it frighten you.

Handling Digestive Problems

Digestive problems can arise even after careful intake of food and water. A change in diet or increase in spicy food can be the simple cause of a stomach upset. The best thing to do is to stay calm—start with an analysis of the problem. If the diarrhea is accompanied by a fever, or if you see blood and/or mucus in your stool, you could have dysentery. Seek medical attention immediately.

The First Twenty-Four Hours

Wait it out for the first twenty-four hours. Rest and drink fluids like water, tea, and clear soups. As diarrhea eases, eat bland foods like bananas, bread, white rice, or porridge. By fighting it off the first time you will build up natural immunity that will protect you later on.

Try the local cures, such as fresh coconut milk or special tea, if you wish. Mint tea will help—carry your own tea bags or purchase it in local markets. The Chinese fifteen herb combination known as "pill curing" treats nausea and dysentery (and it also works for hangovers and jet lag). Or, reach for the old standbys, Pepto-Bismol or a kaolin-pectin mixture such as Kaopectate. Some travelers take antibiotics immediately (the usual Western medical advice). I avoid taking antibiotics as long as possible since they decrease normal intestinal flora and may therefore leave one in a more vulnerable state. My approach is to try to let the body's own defense system expel the bacteria.

During this period, it is critical to maintain your fluid intake. To avoid dehydration, fluid intake must be equal to outflow (three quarts or liters a day for adults). Some recommend rehydration drink rather than plain water. (See "Handling the Heat" in this chapter for recipes.) Be especially careful of your hygiene; wash your hands fastidiously after each toilet visit and before eating or drinking. Most travelers' diarrhea will resolve itself within a day or two with proper care.

For Severe Cases

If your diarrhea lasts for more than a couple of days or if you need to travel, you should consider taking antidiarrheal and antibacterial drugs. Antidiarrheal drugs such as Lomotil or Imodium will plug up your system. They don't cure the problem, they just shut down your intestinal tract, and they actually prevent your body from flushing out the harmful bacteria. Don't use them for longer than forty-eight hours or if you have fever or severe abdominal pain. I've heard travelers swear by Wakefield Blackberry Root Tincture, a natural remedy that will also plug you up temporarily.

Cipro or Noroxin, two new (and expensive) antibiotics, are said to be very effective against diarrhea. Bactrim, an older (and much cheaper) antibiotic, is equally as effective (but should be avoided if you are allergic to sulfa). Discuss these remedies with your physician and get supplies needed before you leave home. Beware of self-medicating; these drugs are powerful and some have side effects such as increased sensitivity to sunlight.

Be sure to keep up your fluid intake. Alter your travel plans if at all possible to allow for rest and recovery. After a bout of sickness, stay away from caffeine and spicy foods for a few days. Something bland and familiar, like pancakes, can help get your stomach back in good working order.

Staying Healthy

Health hazards vary according to destination. Read the health section of your guidebook to anticipate possible problems. If you are traveling to a remote or "Third World" location, take a travelers' health book along. I recommend *The Pocket Doctor* by Stephen Bezruchka, M.D., and *Staying Healthy in Asia, Africa, and Latin America* by Dirk Schroeder. *The Traveller's Guide to Homeopathy* by Phyllis Speight provides effective alternatives to Western drug therapies.

Predeparture Preparation

Health Insurance

Check your own health insurance policy or government program to find out exactly what is covered while you are traveling. Medical costs of minor injuries and ailments may be cheaper overseas than they are at home. You may want to consider purchasing coverage against serious illness, accident, or death.

Comprehensive travel policies are "bundled," which means they combine trip interruption, baggage loss/damage, medical expenses, and other coverage. The *Consumer Reports Travel Letter* analyzes coverage from nine major providers including Access America, American Express, Travel Guard, and Health Care Abroad. Your travel agent or insurance agent should be able to provide a variety of options—check carefully to make sure you're paying only for what you need.

•Frequent travelers should buy annual coverage instead of insuring each trip.

•Consider emergency evacuation insurance, which will reimburse you for helicopter or other special transport from a remote area or even a special flight home, if you plan to go trekking or pursue other strenuous or risky back-country travel.

•Trip cancellation insurance is a high-cost option that should only be purchased by travelers who have prepaid significant deposits for cruises or tours.

•Check carefully for wording about preexisting medical conditions when buying insurance.

•Students can get reduced-rate coverage through their school or by contacting **TravMed-Student Overseas Medical Coverage (800/732-5309).**

Vaccinations

Your guidebook should list vaccinations required or advised for your destination; the Lonely Planet and Moon Publications Guidebooks are the best I've seen (and used) for "Third World" travels. Typical vaccinations that may be required are: yellow fever, typhoid, polio, and gamma globulin for infectious hepatitis.

Call your health care provider, county health department, or a local travelers' health clinic for updated vaccination requirements—they change frequently. Cholera vaccinations are no longer required for travel to many areas as they have been judged to be ineffective. The malaria parasite has become resistant to chloroquine, the preferred treatment in Central and South America, Africa, and Asia. New treatments for chloroquine-resistant areas are constantly being developed.

Americans and Canadians can call the **International Travelers Hotline** at the U.S. Centers for Disease Control in Atlanta, Georgia, for updates on health conditions and vaccinations needed for specific countries. Call **404/332-4559** from a touch-tone phone.

Allow yourself *at least* one month before departure for vaccinations, as some require two or more injections with a time lag in between. And, you don't want to be flying overseas with a sore arm or flu-like after effects. (Gamma globulin, with a short protective span, should be obtained at the last possible moment.)

Your physician will issue and stamp a yellow vaccination card, which is as valuable as your passport. You present that card at borders to prove that you're not bringing unwanted disease into the country. Losing your yellow vaccination card or allowing vaccine periods to expire may tempt local officials to vaccinate you on the spot. Reuse of needles and nonsanitary conditions at airports and borders put you in danger of contracting serum hepatitis or worse.

See your homeopathic physician for remedies to prevent specific epidemic diseases such as hepatitis, typhoid, and malaria. Homeopathic remedies don't guarantee immunity but may lessen your chances of contracting disease without the risk of side effects. Check to see which remedies qualify as required vaccinations for your destination.

Dental Work

I'll never forget the dentist's stall one market day in Rajasthan—a large glass jar full of extracted teeth served as the signpost of a successful practice. Extraction is standard for tooth infections in many parts of the "Third World." Get your teeth checked if you want to keep them, especially before traveling off the beaten path.

Conversely, low-cost medical and dental care is available in Mexico and many other countries; some travelers wait to get problems treated there. But don't expect identical treatment to that at home.

Medications / Prescriptions

Bring along any prescription medications you use regularly, in clearly marked original bottles. Bring an extra pair of eyeglasses, and your eyeglass prescription as well. (You may be able to stock up on extra medications and eyeglasses overseas—you'll discover significant savings in many countries.)

Carry extra contact lenses, along with plenty of cleaning solution, which can be hard to find and very expensive.

Research Local Care

If you are likely to need medical care while traveling, or are very concerned about finding doctors who speak English, research the availability of local doctors, or join **IAMAT**, the nonprofit **International Association for Medical Assistance to Travellers**. For a voluntary contribution, you can obtain lists of doctors ready to assist travelers worldwide. In the U.S., contact IAMAT at **417 Center Street, Lewiston NY 14092 (716/754-4883)**; in Canada, **1287 St. Clair Avenue West, Toronto, M6E 1B8 (416/652-0137)**; in New Zealand, **PO Box 5049, Christchurch 5**; in Switzerland, **57 Voirets, 1212 Grand-Lancy, Geneva**.

As an IAMAT member, you will receive a directory of Western-trained English- and French-speaking doctors worldwide who are on call twenty-four hours daily. Participating doctors charge a fee that's prearranged by IAMAT. IAMAT also provides very useful immunization and malaria-risk charts. Their charts list climatic conditions, seasonal clothing, and sanitary conditions of water, milk, and food.

Your national embassy should also provide information and medical referrals for medical emergencies.

While Traveling

Abortion

If you need to terminate a pregnancy, first determine the local politics of abortion. (In countries such as India and China where family planning is widely practiced and encouraged, low-cost abortions may be routinely available.) If abortion is illegal, check with a local feminist organization or the doctor at the American embassy for advice. You may have to relocate, but stay calm, and take the time you need to make clear decisions.

Seek out Western doctors if it will make you feel more comfortable. Ask about the availability of RU 486, the French "abortion pill." Remember that church-sponsored and missionary hospitals may have anti-abortion policies that differ from state policy.

Abortion can be accomplished with acupuncture, although you may have a difficult time finding an acupuncturist willing to admit the fact or perform the procedure. An experienced herbalist can provide a natural abortifacient (although many consider this alternative to be very risky).

AIDS Prevention

The risk of infection can be eliminated by avoiding infected blood products, dirty intravenous needles, and unprotected sexual encounters. Heterosexual transmission of AIDS is now more common than homosexual transmission in many parts of the world.

Most hospitals in major cities routinely screen blood products for HIV. Check with the Red Cross or your local embassy to be sure about blood supplies.

Avoid injections unless absolutely necessary. If needed, purchase your own sterilized syringes. Be assured about sterilization procedures before getting ears pierced, dental work, tattoos or acupuncture.

Avoid sex with strangers. Carry condoms or dental dams, and make their use a condition of sexual contact. In addition, use contraceptive foams, jellies and creams that contain the spermicide nonoxynol 9 (which kills the HIV virus on contact). If necessary, seek educational information about safe sex before leaving on your trip.

Bladder and Urinary Tract Infections

Changes in your diet or environment may make you more susceptible to these infections. Dehydration from extreme heat can lead to urinary tract infections. The infection begins as frequent passing of urine with burning pain. If you are prone to such infections, bring antibiotics along. Preventative measures include: wearing cotton underpants and cotton skirts or dresses, rather than pants; always wiping from front to back after a bowel movement or urinating; drinking plenty of fluids; and urinating frequently (including before and after sexual activity).

Try to stave off possible infection by drinking a pint of water each hour and eliminating caffeine and alcohol. Cranberry or other acidic, noncitrus juices (try pomegranate) can help fight infection by changing the pH of the urinary tract. Cranberry capsules (to be taken orally) are available from health food stores. Herbal remedies include cantheris, uva ursi, and equisetum (horsetail).

If symptoms persist or worsen you should get a urine test and appropriate medication from a physician. Don't self-prescribe; the type of medication needed will depend on the particular bacteria causing the infection. To prevent a secondary yeast infection caused by taking antibiotics try yogurt (without sugar or honey) douches or acidophilus capsules inserted vaginally.

Breast Self-Exams

Maintain monthly breast self-examinations while traveling. Seek immediate advice or treatment if you discover a lump or anything unusual.

Constipation

Digestive extremes are common to travelers. Eat a high-fiber diet, add fruit, decrease consumption of animal products, exercise, and drink plenty of water. Some recommend lemon juice in hot water taken thirty minutes before breakfast.

Contraception

If you rely on birth control pills for contraception, be cautious if you get diarrhea for more than one day. The pill may not be absorbed so you should assume that you are unprotected for that cycle. Carry enough to last your entire trip or write down the specific hormone doses in the pills you take. Brand names may not match up overseas.

Diaphragm and cervical cap users should carry an adequate supply of contraceptive jelly; it can be difficult to find outside large cities.

Hygiene

Maintain a high standard of hygiene to avoid infection. Wash hands as often as possible and be sure to wash before eating, especially where the local custom requires eating with the hands.

Insomnia

Changing schedules and environments may induce insomnia in some travelers. Hyland's Homeopathic Calms or Calms Forté are gentle and effective sleep aids. Valerian, skullcap, and hops are herbal remedies to promote sleep. You might try earplugs or an eyeshade, particularly to assist sleep on trains and buses.

Menopause

Dress in layers to help compensate for temperature changes due to hot flashes. Keep yourself out of high stress situations if mood swings are a problem. The single most useful herb for many gynecological problems is vitex. Others that are helpful in evening out hormonal changes are dioscorea, angelica senesis, arctium lappa and licorice. Vitamin B complex, vitamin C, and vitamin E are also useful in curbing symptoms of menopause.

Menstruation

It is common for menstruation to become irregular or stop temporarily while traveling, especially in temperature extremes. This does not require medical attention but may cause stress for sexually active heterosexual women. Be prepared for your period to arrive quite early or late by carrying basic supplies with you at all times.

Menstrual supplies (especially tampons) may be expensive or difficult to find. Carry a good supply and restock from drugstores in large cities. Long-term travelers may want to experiment with using a menstrual sponge before leaving home. In considering the menstrual sponge, you should weigh the advantage of not having to buy or carry supplies against the disadvantage of having to keep the sponge sanitary, which may be hard to do in some parts of the world.

Bring your customary remedies for menstrual cramps such as ibuprofen, lobelia tincture, or *dong quai*. Ask women you meet to recommend local treatments for cramps. You might find something that works better than what you're currently using.

If you have a debilitating period, you are probably in the habit of planning around it. This might prove difficult to do while traveling since periods often go off their cycle. Naturopathic remedies which bring on your period may be helpful in severe cases, particularly if you will be doing something unusually strenuous.

Mosquito Bites

Wear long-sleeved shirts and long pants in the evening when mosquitos come out. Use natural mosquito repellants such as chrysanthemum extract, citronella, and lemon eucalyptus oil. A daily dose of Vitamin B_1 acts as a natural mosquito repellant by slightly altering your body odor (and helps reduce stress, too). Nutritional yeast, taken with water or food, is a good source of B vitamins.

Synthetic compounds such as diethyl-meta-toluamide ("deet") may be necessary in malaria-infested areas. I prefer the roll-on repellants (like Cutter's) as their use doesn't cover your hands with chemicals prior to eating.

Motion Sickness

Seek out the most stable seats available—front seats in cars and buses and middle sections of boats and planes. Keep your eyes on the horizon, and don't read if you feel queasy.

Skin patches (placed behind the ear) are said to be highly effective in preventing motion sickness. You should bring these with you as they may not be widely available outside the West. Or try powdered ginger in capsules (two capsules thirty minutes before departure).

Pregnancy

Maureen Wheeler devotes an entire chapter in *Travel with Children* to traveling while pregnant. She describes it as a safe time to travel, despite warnings from all sides: if you feel well and confident, you can travel. The second trimester is the best time for a pregnant woman to travel. It is wise to minimize travel during the final month of pregnancy. And airline regulations make it extremely difficult to fly beyond thirty-five weeks gestation without a doctor's note.

Special care must be taken: some vaccinations and medications are contra-indicated for pregnancy; you will need to conserve energy and make frequent bathroom stops. Wheeler recommends which vitamins to take along. Pregnant women need to be especially careful about food and water. Avoid iodine and other chemical water purifiers; boil water instead. Carry a small inflatable back pillow for comfort during travel. Bring along a letter from your obstetrician with your medical history and details of your pregnancy. Take the list of IAMAT doctors with you (see above), and see a doctor for anything more than mild diarrhea.

Bring along a book detailing health issues relating to pregnancy so you can monitor developments and watch for problems. Learn foreign phrases related to your pregnancy and delivery date to answer the many questions you may be asked.

If considering sea travel, look for a calm water crossing. Pregnancy tends to increase the probability and intensity of sea sickness.

Stress

Emotional problems can arise while traveling or can stow away in your suitcase as baggage you hoped to leave at home. Exhausting travel days, the need to adjust to radically different cultures, fear, loneliness, and sickness all create stress. So does the pressure of having a "perfect vacation."

If you can't sleep, have a poor appetite, or feel buffeted by a never-ending series of accidents and minor illnesses, there may be an emotional cause to the problem.

Seek out ways to reduce stress on your trip. Find ways to make your trip easier, spending more money if necessary. Seek out a travel partner, or take time to be alone. Eat well, rest, and excuse yourself from the task of seeing and doing all there is to see and do. (Even travelers need days off!) Walk, get plenty of exercise, and follow your favorite relaxation routine. Treat yourself to some new clothes, a nice meal, or a better hotel. Avoid drugs and alcohol.

Traditional Chinese herbs such as chrysanthemum, pearl, and ginseng are a natural way to ease stress (as well as counteract skin and health problems associated with traveling). Chamomile, passionflower, and avena are also useful.

If you need to talk with someone, look for a women's organization, a feminist bookstore, a tour group leader, or another traveler. Or spend the money to call a friend at home.

Sunburn

Exposure to direct sun is linked to both benign and malignant skin cancers. While suntanning has long been recognized as unhealthy, new research shows that a sunburn can greatly increase your chances of developing malignant melanoma. Melanomas are now the most common form of cancer in women under age thirty-five.

Radiation is more intense during the two hours before and after noon, closer to the equator, and at higher altitudes. Harmful rays reflect off city streets and sand at the beach and penetrate water as deep as thirty feet. Sunlight reflecting off snow is especially strong and harmful. The deeper blue the sky, the more intense the ultraviolet radiation. Experts recommend use of a sunblock rated SPF 15. Depending on your skin type, SPF 15 will protect you for three hours (very fair skin) to over eleven hours (very dark skin) with five and a half hours of protection for average skin types. Apply sun block while you are in the airplane if you will arrive in strong light. Snow reflects 85 percent of the sun's UVB rays, so sunscreen isn't just for hot weather travel. Wear sunglasses to protect eyes from harmful rays.

If you want to look tan, try self-tanning cream instead of baking in the sun. To treat sunburn or burns, use vitamin E, aloe vera gel or the

Chinese herb *ching wan hung*. Califlora Gel by Boericke and Taffel is useful for many sorts of burns, cuts, bug bites, and rashes. It is antiseptic and very healing to the skin.

Yeast Infections

Hot weather, nonventilated or wet clothing, use of antibiotics, and changes of diet can all instigate vaginal yeast infections. Self-treatment includes ingesting acidophilus tablets or yogurt. Yogurt (with no sugar or honey) or diluted white vinegar can be used as a douche, and acidophilus tablets can be used vaginally (insert before going to sleep). Or, fill gelatin capsules with boric acid; insert one each night for four to six days to change the vagina's pH and make it less hospitable to yeast. Decrease or eliminate sugar and alcohol consumption; eat more citrus fruit.

If you are prone to yeast infections and prefer the Western medical approach, pack a tube of Miconazole (not for pregnant women) or Monistat 7 in your medical kit.

Climate

Changes in climate can produce unusual health complications. Familiarize yourself with symptoms of climate and altitude sickness before traveling.

Handling the Heat

Moderate your activity in the desert or tropics, especially during the first few days of your trip. There's a good reason why people take siestas during the hottest part of the day—follow their lead. Older travelers, those with fair complexions, and those with heart disease are more subject to the effects of hot weather.

Loss of salt and water due to sweating and extreme heat can lead to dehydration and exhaustion. Keep up your intake of liquids; drink before you feel thirsty. Salt your food in hot climes—about a teaspoon a day in extreme conditions. Heat exhaustion will double you over with cramps. (I thought I was having an appendicitis attack during a case of heat exhaustion in the Thar desert.) Headache, an inability to walk, dizziness, and a rapid heartbeat can be signs of dehydration. Your urine is a good indicator of water levels in your system—if it turns a dark color, or if you are urinating infrequently, start drinking serious amounts of liquid.

Bring along packets of a rehydration drink (like Recharge or Emergen-C) to replace essential sugar, salt, and electrolytes. Local varieties may be available in powdered form, which you can mix with clean water or juice. Buy canned fruit juice and add some salt in an emergency (avoid fruit juice if suffering from diarrhea). Or mix canned tomato juice half and half with canned sauerkraut juice.

It's easy to make your own rehydration fluid. The World Health Organization recommends adding the following ingredients to one quart of boiled water: 1/4 teaspoon (3.5 g.) table salt; 1/2 teaspoon (2.5 g.) baking soda (sodium bicarbonate); 4 tablespoons (20 g.) sugar or honey. (If you can't find baking soda, increase table salt to 1/2 teaspoon.) The formula should be no saltier than tears.

High temperatures can lead to irritability and impatience. Slow down, stop for a drink, and realize what is happening. Reduce alcohol and caffeine consumption in the heat; they both dehydrate. Belladonna is a homeopathic remedy for sunstroke.

Before departure, acclimate your body to higher temperatures by taking saunas or steam baths or using a hot tub. While traveling, treat dry hair and skin with a local coconut or other oil. Loose-fitting cotton clothing reduces sweating and allows for evaporation. Wear a hat to control your body temperature and reduce the possibility of sunstroke. Clean cuts and scrapes properly, and use antiseptic cream to avoid infections from open sores.

Coping with Extreme Cold

Keeping hydrated is as important in cold weather as in hot weather. Hot drinks and warming foods are important. A strong cup of fresh ginger tea will warm a person quickly. Wear natural fiber clothing in layers and keep dry. For cold feet, sprinkle cayenne pepper in your socks before walking or skiing.

Adjusting to High Altitude

Lower oxygen levels at high altitudes can induce fatigue, nausea, palpitations, loss of appetite, and severe headache. Adapt to high altitude by taking two days to reach 8,000 feet and stay at that altitude until symptoms decrease. Begin increasing fluid intake at about 8,000 feet; drink as much as two gallons of water a day at 12,000 feet. If you have more than a mild headache at high altitude, descend 1,000 feet and stay overnight or come back up slowly. Over 12,000 feet, guard against a net gain of more than 1,500 feet per day. Take Siberian ginseng to help adjust to high altitudes; coca tea is used for the same purpose in Peru and Ecuador.

If you plan to be at greater than 8,000 feet for more than one or two days (particularly if you will be ascending to higher altitudes), ask your physician about the advisability of taking supplies of acetazolamide (used for preventing altitude sickness) and dexamethasone (used to treat symptoms of severe altitude sickness). Shortness of breath, cough, severe headache, drowsiness, or loss of consciousness should be treated with oxygen and a rapid descent to lower altitudes.

But What If...??

Most traveler's ailments really are minor—a day or two of stomach upset, a cold, or the flu. Take recommended precautions, be careful, but don't live in constant fear. A good attitude is your best ally.

If you feel comfortable doing so, go ahead and take advantage of local remedies. In Oaxaca, I sliced my foot open while climbing a rocky slope. Fearing the deep wound would keep me off my feet for a week or more, I willingly agreed to soak the injury in a solution made from *cuachalala*—the bark of a local tree. The healing was so rapid it looked like time-lapse photography. After two days, just a slight scar remained.

After suffering amoebic dysentery for weeks and finding no success with Western remedies, friends brought me to a woman who had natural healing powers. She scanned my body with her hand until she came to my lower back. "There's something alive here that keeps running away," she told me. "Do you want to get rid of it?" I nodded "yes" and she held her hand above that spot, generating intense heat for about fifteen seconds. She then told me to go home and rest the following day, warning that it would be a difficult one. It was—my insides emptied out completely. But after that, it was gone.

I've heard many stories of travelers making good use of local cures like this one from Mary Zinkin:

> I took off for a couple of days on a rented motorbike near the Burmese border, along with a Scottish traveler who wanted to do the same. I got in a little accident in a remote village. My elbow and knee got cut up pretty bad, and I was worried about the abrasions in the tropical climate. Neosporin just kept it oozing.
>
> The next morning I went for a walk. After a few minutes I turned a corner and saw a sign that said "FOREIGNER, COME IN FOR A CUP OF HERBAL MEDICINAL TEA." So I went in, and there was a Chinese herbalist—just like Dr. Yang in Woody Allen's movie Alice. He gave me a cup of tea, and I sat down and drank it. Then the doctor saw my abrasions and gave me a little tube—I have no idea what it was, but it cleared it right up.

Very few travelers get seriously ill. Still, the prospect is scary, especially to those traveling alone. You will find it is not difficult to find someone to take care of you; tell others what you need, and ask for their help. Innkeepers, travelers, and local medical or religious staff are all likely to help. You won't be alone.

And remember, if you do get sick you can almost always fly home. Air travel makes most parts of the globe less than twenty-four hours away. (But keep in mind that for tropical diseases, you may be much better off staying where the experts are.) The American, British, New

Zealand, Australian, and Canadian embassies will all assist their citizens. Americans can call the **U.S. State Department Citizens Emergency Center** at **202/647-5225** from anywhere in the world for emergency assistance. Citizens of other countries should check before leaving home to find out if similar assistance is available.

Suggested Medical Kit

Start with this suggested list; add and delete items based on your medical history, healing philosophy, and country of destination.

- Adhesive bandages or gauze and tape
- Antibiotic cream for scrapes and burns (buy the ophthalmic kind—it can also be used for eye infections)
- Antibiotics and prescription drugs—clearly marked in original bottles with instructions for use
- Diarrhea remedy—Pepto-Bismol or other tablets or liquid; acidophilus capsules; and Lomotil or Wakefield Blackberry Tincture
- Earplugs and eyeshade to assist sleep on trains, buses, and noisy hotel rooms
- Iodine or water treatment tablets
- Over-the-counter remedies—aspirin or other pain reliever, antacids, antihistamines for colds and mild allergies, laxatives
- Moleskin to pad feet and relieve blisters
- Sunscreen
- Insect repellant

If needed:

- Support bandage for persistent injuries (knee or ankle)
- Motion sickness preventative (patch-style to place behind ear) or ginger capsules
- Extra eyeglasses or contact lenses and cleaning solution along with lens prescription

Homeopathic Medical Kit

Meet with a homeopath to review potential problems associated with your itinerary, and put together a small kit of remedies. Kit may include calendula or comfrey gel, goldenseal and nux vomica. Cinchona, for example, is the homeopathic remedy against malaria. Some essentials are:

• Arnica oil or various creams for topical use on bruises or strained muscles

• Echinacea tincture or tablets for early stages of colds or flu

• Califora Gel for burns, cuts, bug bites, and rashes

How Not to Get Lost

Even though *you* know where you are all the time when traveling, your loved ones don't. Every news report of earthquake, typhoon, or airplane crash can set them on edge and a family or personal emergency can make them desperate to find you.

Keep in Touch

Although it's fun to disappear down a crooked trail into oblivion, it is a kind and good practice to let others know something of your itinerary. One solution is a weekly postcard—every Saturday you could send a card to the person or household who is your main contact. Dispense with the romantic descriptions of last night's sunset, and stick to the facts: "I'm in Valencia, taking tomorrow's train to Cartagena, where I plan to stay at a hotel on the beach for four or five days." In some places, letters will travel much faster than postcards, so it's wise to inquire. Receiving these cards or letters on a weekly basis can calm most fears and can provide helpful clues if you need to be located in an emergency.

Don't commit to phoning unless you know you can do so. I've waited eight hours at a telephone office in India, had to crawl under a table in order to hear the conversation, and had the line cut after less than a minute. (However, in many parts of the world, less than an hour's wait delivers you to a private phone booth in a government telephone office.)

EurAide offers a message service for travelers in Europe called **Overseas Access**. Family or friends can leave messages for you; you call in to a local European number to check for your calls. Other services include mail forwarding and travel assistance from their Munich office. Contact: **EurAide, PO Box 2375, Naperville, IL 60567 (708/420-2343)**. In an emergency, holders of an International Student or Teacher Identity Card can utilize their twenty-four hour international toll-free hot line; some travel insurance companies offer a similar hot line service.

If you don't have an organized contact plan and someone needs to track you down, in a true emergency they should contact your embassy and ask for assistance from the local police. The more specific information they can provide, the more likely they are to receive help.

Leave a Trail

Caution is the sister of adventure. The more remote my destination, the more cautious I am in making preparations. When I know that my trail will be difficult to follow, I leave information behind.

One reason I recommend staying at small family-run inns and guest-houses is that you have, at least temporarily, someone watching your comings and goings. When preparing to go off to more rural, less traveled places, ask these people to watch for your return. (Often, I would leave my travel pack behind, taking only my daypack. Or, I'd unload things I wouldn't need and leave them in a package.)

Leave a note clearly stating : your name, nationality, passport number, a brief description of yourself, where you are going and for how long, the name of the person taking you there (if any), or the name of people you will be visiting (if you know). Be careful about stating your date of return—is it exact or flexible? You don't want to call out the police unnecessarily because you decided to stay on an extra week.

Ask your innkeepers to hold on to the note and deliver it to the local police or embassy of your country if you haven't returned by a specific day. If you're lying in a hut somewhere with a broken leg, you'll probably be glad to see help arrive.

Another good precaution is to solicit advice from several local people before heading out of town. This not only provides you with helpful information, it leaves more people who've met you and know of your plans. When looking for feedback on your plans, just remember the self-interest of those you are asking. Guides for hire may tell you that it is "dangerous" or "impossible" for you to travel alone. A taxi driver will tell you why the bus is "out of the question," you should hire a car, etc. Try to ask people without a vested interest in how you spend your time or money.

Always Look Back

Develop this habit and don't forget it: look over your shoulder. When getting up from a park bench, look behind to see what you've left. When leaving a room where you've stayed, look under the bed, in the bathroom, and in the corners. Getting off the train, double-check your seat and luggage shelf overhead. Count the number of items you are carrying, and recount them every time you move.

On your first day's walk in a new town, look behind to note landmarks so you can find your way back. Make a mental note: the green water tower, the building with the clock, any landmark to help you get back.

Take a Card

Once I arrived in an Indian town exhausted after a long train ride. I found a cheap, nondescript place to stay, slept soundly for twelve hours, woke up, showered, and went exploring. Hours later, when it was time to head back, I couldn't remember the name of the hotel or where it was!

After months of staying in inns named after Lakshmi, Durga, and all the Indian gods, guest houses named Rose and Daffodil and every flower in a bouquet, and hotels named to reassure the wary traveler— Honest, Friendly, Clean Hotel, I simply blanked out. I had to return to the train station and retrace my steps, false starts and all.

That experience led to a simple new routine: each time I sign in at a new hotel, I take their business card and slip it into my pocket. I carry it with me on my first few outings, until my new home is easy to find from any direction. It comes in handy when I ask for directions, especially if the name is written in more than one language. And, if I like the place, I tuck the card into my journal or pack to recommend to someone else.

Write It Down

Veteran travelers without mastery of the language or alphabet start each day with a small notebook in hand. On one side of the page, they list in English the names of all the places they plan to visit that day. Then, they ask a hotel clerk or local friend to write the corresponding name for each place in a second column. In that way, they have a customized "point and ask" guidebook for the day.

VII

Traveling Smart
and Light

What to Take and How to Pack It

I once shared a room with a Finnish woman named Kristina whom I met on a late-night ferryboat. As we unpacked our bags, she lectured me on the necessity of packing light. When she was almost finished she turned to me and said, "Of course, everyone's allowed to spoil themselves a little bit, so I've brought along a few things I just can't live without." From the bottom of her backpack, she pulled out two final items—a large cut-glass bottle filled with enough perfume to last well over a year and a pair of bright red spike-heeled shoes!

Each traveler has her unique list of what's essential. In *Spinsters Abroad*, Dea Birkett reveals that Victorian traveler Alexandra David-Neel carried with her a folding bathtub. (Of course, *she* didn't carry it. Like most Victorian women who ventured forth "alone" she was, in fact, accompanied by hired bearers who carried tables and chairs, bedding, cushions, rugs, and typewriters.)

Dervla Murphy—like other twentieth-century adventurers who truly traveled alone—traveled light. The "list of kit" for her overland bicycle journey from Ireland to Afghanistan included no more than one change of clothes, toilet articles, medical supplies, two books, one .25 automatic pistol, four rounds of ammunition, spare tires and parts for her bicycle.

Clothing

Get accustomed to the idea that a three-, four-, six- or even twelve-week trip can best be enjoyed with just one week's worth of clothing. Now consider that enough clothes for a week is just a bit more than you'd take for a weekend. Hopefully you won't be too surprised when I recommend that any trip (even one several months long) can be handled efficiently by taking only *carry-on* luggage.

Traveling light means freedom and independence. Porters aren't always available or affordable. Who cares if someone sees you wear the same thing twice? Traveling light in weight makes you light in spirit; it's easier to pick up and go or change plans.

The key to light packing is careful planning.

Everyone's closet has a few "losers"—clothes you put on and take off again before ever leaving the house. They never seem quite right for the occasion or the day. Other clothes are simply "winners"—you just love to wear them because they always look and make you feel good. Your ideal travel wardrobe will consist of seven carefully chosen "winners"—three "bottoms" (skirts and/or pants) and four "tops" (three casual and one more formal).

Colors

Decide on a basic color scheme—black/white, beige/brown, or navy/tan—so that everything you carry can be worn with everything else. These colors may be determined by a couple of favorite items you already plan to take with you. Once you choose a color scheme, don't deviate from it.

Color coordination lets you create twelve separate outfits from your three bottoms and four tops. While all your items could be solid colors, they don't have to be. You could choose prints for either tops or bottoms. I've found that prints work well as bottoms because they hide dirt and stains and don't need washing as often. I often travel with prints on the bottom (a cotton plaid skirt, a cotton flowered skirt, and print pants), using solids for all the tops.

A matching top and bottom outfit (such as a two-piece dress) will provide a dressier option, suitable for border crossings and applying for visas at embassies. Use the two-piece outfit as the base and build your wardrobe around it. Check out the multipiece clothing "systems," which offer dozens of coordinated tops and bottoms that mix and match. Often made of cotton knit, they pack and travel well.

Plan to layer clothes to accommodate changes of temperature. Buy tops that will fit over one another, and try them on to see how many layers you can wear at once.

Fabrics

Choose simple styles that wash and dry easily; don't bring any clothes that require dry cleaning or ironing. Natural fibers, like cotton or wool knits, feel good and travel well. Test for wrinkling by bunching the fabric in your hand—do the wrinkles relax easily after a moment or does it retain a crushed look? No-wrinkle synthetic clothes don't breathe well and can make you overheat in tropical climates.

Accessories

Use accessories to dress up and add variety to your wardrobe. Tie a large scarf with metallic threads around your neck or waist, or wear it as a shawl to turn a daytime dress into evening wear. Bring along some bright-colored earrings or an easy-to-pack belt.

Packing List

Make a packing list and stick to it. Assemble your travel wardrobe on a chair or in a corner of your closet; revise and refine it over time until your selection is just right. Here are two sample packing lists from my trips:

Europe / Big City / Beach

1 pair comfortable pants

1 blue jean skirt, straight

2 short-sleeve tops

1 bathing suit, any style

1 lightweight long-sleeved shirt

1 pair shorts (for beach only)

1 sarong for beach cover-up

1 pair beach/shower thongs

1 pair comfortable walking shoes

1 sweater or jacket

1 cotton skirt

1 tank top

2 bras

2 – 4 pairs socks

4 pairs underpants

1 towel

Non-Western Countries / Hot Weather

1 pair baggy pants with cargo pockets   2 bras

2 loose skirts, below-knee length   2 pairs socks

3 short-sleeved tops   4 pairs underpants

1 lightweight long-sleeved shirt   1 towel

1 bathing suit, one-piece

1 pair walking/sturdy sandals

1 pair beach/shower thongs

1 pair running shoes, if trekking

1 sarong for beach cover-up

1 sweater or jacket

Cold Weather Adjustments

If your itinerary includes radical climate changes, make wardrobe adjustments along the way rather than carrying the extra clothes when you don't need them. If the cold weather travel comes first, bring old clothes and give them away, or mail home the heavy gear you won't be needing. When traveling from warm to cold, pack a jacket. Then buy a heavy sweater when you reach colder temperatures. Add a pair of leggings for a thermal underlayer, or switch your cotton pants to wool.

Tips for Choosing Clothes

➤Pack lightly and plan to buy clothes during the trip. It's fun to shop, and the clothes carry memories with them. But don't take a chance on finding the right size shoes or underwear unless you match the average size of women at your destination.

➤If you have to conduct business at just one point during your trip, mail clothes ahead, or buy formal clothes when you get there.

➤To add variety, try wearing clothes backwards—a V-back T-shirt can be turned around for evening wear; button your cardigan sweater in the back for a change.

►Call it a *sarong*, a *pareo*, or a *sulu*, it's all the same: a bright-colored piece of fabric you can wrap around your body many different ways to use as a skirt or dress. Also useful as a shawl, a turban in the desert, a beach blanket or coverlet for a nighttime train ride.

Double-check your packing list by imagining all your planned activities—what will you wear to the theater? on a sightseeing day around town? to the beach? Fill gaps by adding accessories instead of more clothes.

Shoes

Your basic pair of walking shoes should be very comfortable and already broken in. For summer wear, sandals with wide straps, good soles and proper support are ideal. In Asia, slip-on sandals are best to allow for frequent need to leave shoes at doorways of temples or homes.

Rubber shower thongs are lightweight and double as bedroom slippers and beach thongs. Running shoes are a heavy addition, and should be packed only if you are planning significant hiking or walking on rough terrain.

Nonclothing Items

Organize these in small pouches, side pockets, and zippered bags to keep them from jumbling around and creating chaos in your pack. Choose items from this list that make sense for the length of your trip and your destination. For a long trip, or when traveling in the "Third World," nonclothing items can comprise as much as 50 percent of all you carry.

•*Toiletries*—These are easier to access in a see-through plastic or net pouch. Shampoo and toothpaste are heavy and are available everywhere. Don't take more than twelve ounces of shampoo; even that lasts for over a month. A trial size of toothpaste (.85 oz.) lasts for three weeks of twice daily usage. A three ounce tube of toothpaste lasts for nine weeks. Buy trial sizes of lotions and toiletries. Dental floss comes in handy for many emergencies. A plastic cover to fit over the end of your toothbrush works better than a travel toothbrush that snaps together from two pieces. Always pack your toiletry kit inside a plastic or zip-lock bag to avoid damage to your clothes from accidental spillage.

•*Camera and film*—See "Choosing a Camera" in this chapter.

•*Tiny sewing kit*—Use a hotel giveaway sewing kit, or make your own by winding one or two basic colors of thread (I take heavy-duty white and black) around a two-inch section of thin wood (like part of a chopstick). Add two to three sewing needles and a couple of safety pins and buttons and pack it all into a film canister.

•*Pocketknife*—I'd never travel without my Swiss army knife. I cut my hair with the tiny scissors, use the blades, corkscrew, and can opener for picnic lunches and the screwdrivers to fix broken plumbing!

•*Laundry bag*—Find a plastic bag with a string closure for your laundry (the kind that comes with your purchases from some clothing stores), and stock it with a braided rubber travel clothesline and a flat sink stopper. Or, buy a zippered pouch for your laundry, and use it as a pillow at night or on long train rides. Buy your laundry soap while traveling (solid bars or small bags of laundry powder are readily available). Throw in your dirty clothes, and your portable laundromat is ready for operation.

•*Emergency kit*—I keep a small zippered pouch in my daypack or shoulder bag at all times for emergencies. In it are: one or two tampons, a set of foam earplugs, a few Pepto-Bismol tablets, my pocketknife, and a couple of Band-Aids.

•*Gifts*—Look around your house or shop for small mementos and knickknacks to use as gifts for hosts and new friends. Good ideas for gifts in developing countries include: sample sizes of perfumes and toiletries; small toys; pocket-size mirrors; balloons; lapel pins and postcards; tiny games and shiny stickers for kids.

•*"Talking book"*—Put together a small photo album for show and tell. Include photos of your home, family, and friends (different generations generate a lot of interest), postcards from your home city or state, photos of yourself skiing, gardening, or cooking. This book will provide openings for many interactions, especially when you don't know the language.

•*Portable cassette player and tapes*—These are optional items. Before you decide if you want to carry them, take a luggage hike. If you decide the cassette player is too heavy, just bring two or three of your favorite tapes along. Ask to play the tapes in small cafes, or borrow a tape player from another traveler.

•*Writing kit*—Buy a plastic school pencil pouch and pack some pens, a small spiral notebook for daily notes and lists, a glue stick, a small amount of strong string (which can be used in emergencies as a clothesline, shoelace, to tie up your suitcase or pack if a zipper breaks), a few paper clips and rubber bands. Keep your journal separate. If you have difficulty reading maps, a small flat magnifying glass (the Read Easy is as thin as a piece of paper) can help.

•*Calling cards*—Use your business card or print some simple cards with your name and address for introductions and exchanging; they will save you the effort of endlessly writing down that information.

•*Bandanna*—This can be a portable tablecloth for picnics, a napkin, a headband or kerchief, a bandage, or a carry-bag for fruit or nuts. I once used a bandana to repair a large hole in a screen in San Blas, with a pair of earrings to clip it on.

•*Medical kit*—Pack medicines appropriate to yourself and your destination in a separate bag so they don't get wet with your toiletries. See "Staying Healthy" in Chapter VI for a suggested medical kit.

How to Pack Your Bags

After what may be a time of hectic preparation, it is important to pack calmly, by yourself. Avoid distractions and last-minute advice from observers. Get out your packing list and stick to it. Test-pack your bag several days before departure to leave time for necessary corrections.

Assemble everything on the bed or floor. Put your clothes in one stack, and nonclothing items in a separate stack. First, improve internal organization by combining like objects in stuff sacks. I put all my underwear, bras, and socks in a small net bag. Once organized, you should have a stack of clothes and a series of small zippered pouches or net bags.

First, pack your money belt with passport, traveler's checks, cash, and airplane tickets.

Then put aside the clothes you plan to wear when leaving on the trip. Try to wear your heaviest shoes and clothes and pack the lighter ones.

Next, take your most valuable items and pack them in your shoulder bag or daypack. These may include your camera, film, and journal. Add anything you want to be accessible during the trip—your guidebook, medications, an extra shirt or sweater.

Whether you are packing the remainder into a suitcase or travel-pack, the same basic principles apply. Stand the bag with handles or straps up, the way it will be carried most of the time. Note which end is the bottom of the bag, and pack shoes and other heavy weight at the bottom to lessen shifting loads when carrying.

Your clothes can now be packed by folding, rolling or stuffing:

•*Fold* your shirts, skirts, and pants and lay them as flat as possible.

•*Roll* your towel, bathing suit, and anything else that won't wrinkle and place the rolled items around the edges of the bag.

•*Stuff* small items into vacant spaces inside shoes and into corners.

Position stuff sacks so they help even the load. Your goal is not a mountain with a peak in the center but an even stack with corners adequately filled. Put toiletry kit into a plastic bag, and place it so that the tops of bottles will stand upright when the bag is being carried.

On a long trip, get into the routine of always packing your bag the same way. Eventually, you'll be able to open a zipper halfway and pull out the precise item you want on a completely dark train in the middle of the night.

Five Things to Leave Behind on Your Next Trip

1. *Anything electrical*

Travel irons, clothes steamers, and hair dryers are heavy and bulky. Add an adapter plug and you're asking for trouble. Try to get along without them.

2. *Your address book*

Your address book may not weigh much, but the responsibility of sending all those postcards can drag you down. (Besides, buying and mailing a single postcard can cost over a dollar in many countries.) For any trip less than six weeks, free yourself of the responsibility of sending postcards; you'll get home before they do, anyway. Do take a short list of addresses and phone numbers for emergency contacts; don't rely on memory.

If you're duty-bound to send postcards, bring preaddressed peel-off labels from home. Stick each label on a postcard so you'll know when you're done.

3. *Extra books*

To an avid reader, a two-week vacation can mean packing a book a day. Knock that stack over and try a new strategy. Bring your guide-book (or photocopies of relevant sections) and no more than two other paperbacks. Rotate reading and trading those two books. (Buy used books if that will make trading less painful.) Many small hotels have a bookshelf for free exchanges. If you are planning to read the classics of the region or a locally renowned author, you'll find others are, too. Many opportunities will arise for trading books. (And be assured,

English-language newspapers are available worldwide.)

As an alternative, you might consider giving up reading altogether. There's plenty of life to observe while sitting in stations and streetside cafes, and your pack will be more comfortable to carry.

4. Special clothes for a single occasion

Beware of the last-minute addition, and don't carry a special item to wear at one particular event. Unless you have an audience with the Queen, you can get away with wearing something else.

5. Hair products and makeup

Tomorrow morning, count the number of products and appliances you use to prepare yourself for the world. Can you cull just two or three critical items for your trip and leave the rest behind? Would a haircut or permanent create a wash-and-wear hairstyle alternative? Start in advance to simplify your style.

Choosing Luggage

Hopefully, I've convinced you to travel with less than you ever thought possible. Now the question remains—what type of luggage should you use?

Distributing your belongings into a two-piece system (the third piece is your money belt), makes your luggage easy to carry. Having two separate pieces also provides flexible options for side trips.

Even for a six-month trip around the world (or especially for such a long trip) take no more than carry-on luggage, with a total weight of twenty-five pounds. Carry-on bags (20 x 19 x 9 inches maximum) allow you to get in and out of airports more quickly, make you immune to luggage-handling strikes or slowdowns, and offer increased security with fewer people handling your luggage. Most airlines allow two carry-on items per person.

Choose one of these systems to fit your travel style and plans:

System 1: **The Convertible Travel Pack + Daypack**

Convertible travel packs aren't just for college students and trekkers in Nepal. Neat and handsome pieces of soft-sided luggage, they make perfect sense for any independent traveler and can prevent aching joints and back pain by distributing the load evenly.

Most travel packs can be carried in three different ways: with a standard hand grip, with a shoulder strap, or with pull-out backpack straps. The capacity of travel packs ranges from 2,800 to 4,900 cubic inches. The larger packs must be checked as baggage. Airlines don't like to check standard backpacks because the straps and buckles catch easily on conveyor belts and cause damage. With this pack, you can tuck the straps in before checking it on a plane to avoid problems. On the ground, strap on the bag to leave your hands free to handle tickets and guidebooks.

Features to Look for:

➤Smaller-capacity packs may offer only shoulder straps in a fixed suspension system. If you are shorter or taller than average and plan on carrying the pack a lot, look for an adjustable suspension system that will fit your body correctly.

➤A chest strap and padded waist strap help distribute weight evenly across your body, making the load very light on your shoulders.

➤An expandable travel pack starts out as a piece of carry-on luggage. As your needs grow, unzip the expansion compartment and add an extra 1,000 cubic inches of space for extra clothes and souvenirs.

I highly recommend the detachable daypack. For day trips, stock it with camera, guidebook, and journal, add an extra shirt and sweater for overnight or weekend side trips. Simplify travel days by zipping it onto the backpack.

System 2: Soft-Sided Carry-On + Shoulder Bag

If you won't be toting your luggage around much, this system offers a slightly more formal look and a bit less wrinkling of your clothes. Divide your gear into two bags—one fits under the airplane seat, the other overhead.

Soft-sided bags travel best and protect your clothes better when fairly full. The shoulder bag can range from purse-size to luggage-size.

Features to Look for:

➤If physical limitations keep you from lifting weight, consider a soft- or hard-sided case with built-in wheels, or add a lightweight luggage trolley like flight attendants use.

➤Some soft-sided carry-ons have multiple compartments separated by partitions to help organize your clothes and keep them neat.

System 3: Garment Bag + Carry-On

For the business-minded or more formally dressed traveler with few destinations, a garment bag is a good option. But outside the city and in any back-country or bus travel, the garment bag can be awkward to handle.

Features to Look for:

➤Choose a garment bag with built-in pockets.

➤Look for one that has hangers that easily transfer from garment bag to closet.

➤Make sure the garment bag has straps to cinch it closed when folded over.

Other Luggage Options

For that shopping trip to Hong Kong, Florence, or anywhere, pack a lightweight folding tote bag or duffel bag inside your luggage to help bring home the goods. Look for expanding bags with multiple zippers, which provide several different size options when open.

Wilderness or sports travelers may consider cargo gear bags for carrying equipment like ski boots, but their boxy shape makes them uncomfortable to carry for any length of time. Waterproof bags are available for kayaking and sailing trips.

Tips for Choosing Luggage

When buying luggage, your major considerations will be construction of the bag and ease of carrying.

Before you go luggage shopping, collect everything you plan to take on the trip (or an equivalent amount of clothing). Include several small pouches to represent toiletries and camera gear. Bring it all to the store and pack it in the bags. A reputable luggage store should allow you to buy a bag and take it home for the same test.

Everything you plan to take should fit into the bag, in a well-organized way. The fully packed bag should have a bit of extra space, enough for an extra sweater or small gifts you may buy during the trip. Resist the temptation to buy oversized bags; they encourage last-minute additions that result in unneeded weight.

As a final test, take a "luggage hike." Carry your fully packed bag for two to four blocks, then up and down two flights of stairs. Are you still sure you can't get away with a smaller bag?

Once you've found the size of luggage you need, check the construction by examining these features:

•Check for strong fabric by discreetly poking the bag with a ballpoint pen. Densely woven fabrics (which measure 1,000 denier) hold up well; one excellent brand of fabric is Cordura nylon. Avoid leather; it's strong but very heavy.

•Zippers can be the first stress point to give way. Metal zippers should be heavy duty and sewn in with strong thread. The zipper pull should snap down to prevent accidental unzipping. A good nylon zipper is equally as strong as a metal zipper and may work more easily. Make sure it is self-retracting (it will go back on track if it splits open). A new type of zipper can be locked shut with a tiny key, avoiding the need for separate locks.

•All handles and straps should be securely attached and comfortable to carry. Straps should be reinforced, doubly secured with leather pads. Take a good pull on the strap and see how it handles the stress. Double-handled bags should strap together to prevent excessive stress created by pulling the bag solely with one handle.

•Outside cinch straps reduce stress on zippers and add to the life of the bag. A cloth flap over the zipper protects the contents of the bag from rain.

•Locks should not be flimsy. Whether built-in or attached to zipper hasps, combination locks are preferable, but a bit more expensive.

Identifying Your Luggage

Once you've purchased your bag, strap a luggage tag inside with your permanent address. Outside luggage tags should have a covered flap which prevents passers-by from learning your name and address. Before each trip, write your itinerary on a piece of paper and leave it inside the bag, in case it gets lost. That increases the chances of your luggage catching up with you before you get back home.

If you will be checking luggage, tie a distinctive ribbon or make a design with tape on the outside as an easy spotting device to help you recover luggage in crowded airports.

Choosing a Camera

Your afternoon stroll to the town square delivers you to the pulsing heart of a colorful festival. You reach for your camera and snap several photographs to record the scene. Which photographer are you?

- An avid photographer armed with two 35mm single lens reflex cameras, you've loaded your camera bag with wide angle, zoom lenses, and plenty of film. You're glad you left that extra skirt at home and brought your telescoping tripod instead. You screw the polarizer filter on top of the skylight filter as you crouch in the center of the street to position yourself for the best angle on the approaching procession.

- A bit shy when it comes to photographing people, you'd sure like to get some pictures of those dancers. You grab the lightweight camera from your shoulder bag, slide back the cover, push the zoom button and shoot several photos without moving from your spot on the sidelines.

Each photographer knows herself and what she wants. Each will bring home memorable photos because she is familiar with her equipment and its operation.

If your fantasy trip includes taking dramatic photos with a single lens reflex (SLR) camera, buy it several months in advance. Because the SLR may be fully manual, you will need more time to teach yourself how to use it. Or sign up for a class at your local community college.

If you prefer to travel light and are more interested in good snapshots than the technicalities of good photography, consider buying one of the new "point and shoot" generation of automatic 35mm cameras for your next trip. They are easy to use, inconspicuous, and take uniformly good pictures. The built-in flash and optional zoom lens are ideal features for most travelers. Auto-focus technology eliminates time spent struggling with the camera and is a great asset to the shy or inexperienced photographer.

You can buy a new or used compact camera; used cameras are quite a bit more economical but may not have all of the features of the latest models. When shopping, be prepared to discuss these major camera features:

Lenses

The lens is the most essential component of the camera. The more money you spend, the better lens you will get. The "mm" designations on a camera denote the millimeter size of the lens. A basic 35mm lens compact camera with built-in flash will serve adequately as a travel camera.

By spending a bit more, you can also get a zoom lens for close-up pictures. Two zoom lens options are generally available—the dual lens and the adjustable zoom lens.

•A *dual lens* provides two separate focal lengths, 35mm and 70mm, for example. Switching from 35mm to 70mm brings your subject twice as close without moving a step.

•An *adjustable zoom lens* lets you choose any focal length between 35mm and 70 or 105mm or longer. You can zoom in even closer and have many more choices of settings.

Extras

Other optional features are available on automatic cameras. Consider which of these are important to you:

•Most automatic cameras now have built-in flash features that fire automatically in low light. This is a major advantage over SLR cameras for travel. Automatic or button activated "fill flash" helps fill in shadows on subjects that are strongly backlit.

•A self-timer will give you ten seconds to put yourself into the picture. Great for solo travelers.

•Many cameras automatically set the correct film speed each time you load a cartridge of DX-coated film into the camera.

•Water- or weather-proof cameras are useful in humid and tropical areas.

When buying a camera, look for simple, durable (rather than flashy) models. Don't pay extra for a carrying case if you plan to carry the camera in your shoulder bag or daypack.

Instant photo cameras (like Polaroids) are a big hit when traveling abroad. Photo subjects enjoy seeing themselves and usually want a photo souvenir. I recommend these cameras only as a second camera; pack *lots* of film and don't expect to bring home many photos.

With any new or borrowed camera, shoot a practice roll of film at home before you leave. Find out what kind of batteries the camera uses and bring extras along, especially if they are an unusual size. Protect your camera from sand and dust, which are ruinous.

Film

Buy plenty of film before leaving unless you are certain it will be available at a reasonable cost at your destination. As a general guideline, buy one or two rolls of thirty-six exposures, per week of your trip. Professional photojournalist Barbara Gundle suggests that you label each film can with its roll number, and place the exposed film in a second zip-lock bag. Bring the exposed rolls home for processing—it will usually save money. Exposed film can be safely carried until its expiration date, if kept out of direct sunlight and extreme heat. If traveling for an extended period of time, buy prepaid film processing mailers and mail your film home. (Barbara advises that you be cautious about mailing film; wait to send mailers from major post offices in big cities or send it with other travelers to help ensure its safe arrival.)

Protecting Your Film from X Rays

You should protect your film from harmful X rays at airport security gates, especially if you'll be passing through multiple airport security checks; X-ray damage is cumulative. Barbara recommends this method: buy film in clear film cans (Fuji film) or get your friends to save clear cans for you. Unbox the film, place all the rolls in clear zip-lock plastic bags, and pack it at the top of your daypack or shoulder bag. As you approach the security gate, pull out the plastic bag, hand it around the gate and request a visual inspection. Empty the film from your camera and send the empty camera through the X-ray machine. Don't accept assurances that the radiation level is set low; politely insist on a visual inspection. Lead-lined film protection bags are available, but not recommended; often the security attendants just crank up the X-ray power to get a look inside the bag.

Prints versus Slides

Prints usually cost about twice as much to develop but are easy to carry and fun to share with one or two people at a time.

Slides are cheaper to process but require a slide projector for viewing. Although expensive, a slide projector may be a worthwhile investment if you are planning to travel a lot, take many photographs over time, or want to share your slides with larger groups of people. Slide projectors can be borrowed or rented for a low fee. Prints can easily be made from slides.

What, No Camera?

Consider the freedom of leaving your camera at home. Capture memories in your mind. Paint watercolors or make pencil sketches to prompt your memory. Keep a journal. Buy professionally prepared slides or postcards. Ask new friends for a photo, or find a street photographer to take your picture.

Don't Get Framed by Your Camera

We've all seen, or even presented, some slide shows we'd rather forget. For many travelers, photos of the trip can be a disappointing collection of barely recognizable landmarks.

Like other amateur photographers, I want to bring home great pictures to help me remember and share my experiences. But travel photography presents some special challenges, especially when you're venturing outside your own culture.

Through years of wandering with my camera, I've learned a few key adjustments both to my attitude and my technique to help me capture a photo record of my journey.

Attitude

As a winter resident of a small Mexican town, I saw tourists acting like walking, talking camera tripods. They came, they shot, they left. Their cameras came between them and everything and everyone else. They photographed local people as if they were part of the scenery.

Cris Miller suggests that travel photographers imagine the following scene: you are at home, working in your yard. A Land Rover pulls up and eight people get out, speaking a foreign language. Without much of an introduction, they circle around and start snapping pictures of you in your dirty overalls and mud-streaked face. Then they start to bargain for your old trowel. How would you feel in that situation?

Your camera can alienate you from people or it can bring you closer to them; it's all in how you use it. These methods can help you use a camera as a tool for initiating contact and making lasting friends on the road:

•Carry your camera in an inconspicuous way. Let people meet *you* before they meet a machine. Use a shoulder bag to hold your camera and other daytime essentials—it is less attractive to thieves looking for camera bags stuffed with equipment.

•See a place and its people through your own eyes before peering through the lens of a camera. Whether planning to stay for three hours, three days, or three weeks, I keep my camera in its case for a good long orientation period. I don't reach for the camera until I'm almost ready to leave. Then I record my favorite scenes. While the mission church and town hall were most impressive on my first days in the Mexican town, a week later I had some truly special spots: *Mi Jacalito* restaurant, where Ana and her little brother Omar waited tables after school, and the place on the beach where the local fishermen chatted while cleaning their catch each afternoon. Of course, a festival or market day must be captured on the spot.

•Establish a rapport with people you wish to photograph. In rural Mexico, as in many countries, it is customary to greet those you pass on the street. Even if you've just arrived in town, that greeting can be the opening for a direct personal contact. Take a few minutes to discuss the weather or admire a flower along the road. Sit together on a park bench and watch the birds for a short while. Then, slowly take out your camera and ask permission to use it. Whether or not you speak their language, it is possible to point to the camera and then to them, with a questioning look that will be universally understood. A respectful request is usually granted with a smile and a nod. But be prepared to accept a refusal to be photographed without argument (in some cultures or religions, photography is considered dangerous or offensive). In that case, immediately put your camera away in order to help put the situation again at ease.

•Remember that your camera is a fascinating piece of technology—try letting a new friend look through the lens. Give a brief lesson so *they* can photograph *you* (a great help to solo travelers). Then, reverse roles and snap some photos of them.

•In places where cameras are uncommon, your subjects may

pose stiffly with arms glued to their sides, serious expressions on their faces (much as our great-grandparents posed for their once-in-a-lifetime portrait). Don't fight the serious pose, just be prepared to snap another picture right afterwards, when smiles of relief and more natural poses emerge.

•Learning at least a few conversational phrases in the local language will go far to demonstrate your respect for the culture and will, in turn, help you in photographing the people you meet.

Technique

Take a tip from professional photographers: shoot lots of film and then edit the results to glean the best images. Don't be afraid to shoot multiple frames of each subject, varying each one with a slight change in distance, angle, or exposure (especially in tricky light conditions). Buy extra rolls of film and give yourself a chance to upgrade the general quality of your work.

The best color photographs can be taken early in the morning (from just before dawn and for the next two hours) and late in the afternoon, two hours before sunset. Spend the middle part of the day on other activities—doing laundry, shopping, or visiting museums. Days start early—before dawn—in most non-Western countries; start your day when the locals do, and take your camera along during your morning stroll.

People make more interesting subjects than buildings or scenic views. When you do photograph a building or a wide vista, add depth and interest to the photo by including something in the foreground—a person, flower or tree, a vehicle or a sign. My picture of the Star Ferry Terminal in Hong Kong is also a portrait of a rickshaw driver asleep in his cab parked out front.

Photograph scenes from everyday life—the crowd waiting for the bus, a busy day at the market, children returning from school with matching book bags and uniforms. Include the more mundane aspects of your travel day; show how you get from one historic location to another. Asking directions with map in hand, jostling for position on a crowded bus, eating lunch at a food stall in the train station—these scenes make a place more real and invite lively discussion of your travels.

I've never paid for the right to photograph anyone. I've sometimes offered a small gift, like a piece of fruit, but I decline requests to photograph someone for a fee. Don't agree to send someone a copy of a picture unless you truly will follow through on the task.

Avoid photographing bridges, police stations, or army camps, especially in developing countries. Such pictures may be prohibited.

Add variety to your photographs by framing your subjects in interesting ways. I photographed a turbaned man crossing the town square of Jaiselmeer, India, from inside a building so the dark silhouette of the arched window contrasted dramatically with the hot desert light outside. Don't be afraid to fill the frame of your photos with colorful close-ups of striking images—intricately woven cloth in the markets of Antigua, Guatemala; stunning glass mosaic tiles at Wat Pra Keo in Bangkok; a basket overflowing with glorious red tomatoes in southern Italy; or the bright smile of a young friend anywhere in the world.

Find themes to create unusual series of photos. One friend's portrait series of Hill Tribe elders in northern Thailand captured each one smoking a distinctive homemade pipe. Shoot a series of picturesque Irish pubs, or intricately decorated truck cabs in Pakistan. Take portraits of children, or do a series on flowers. In Greece one summer, I shot the most spectacular beaches while lying flat on the sand so that my tanned feet framed each photo.

Have fun with your camera. At major tourist attractions I like to photograph other people taking photos. At the Forbidden City in Beijing, foreign tourists snap each other in front of the giant banner of Chairman Mao, while Chinese tourists pay to be photographed sitting behind the wheel of a handsome sedan. A favorite photo from Athens is of a middle-aged tourist snapping a shot of her plump husband slouching beside a tall, trim Greek *evzone* soldier standing at stony attention. Study the work of other photographers, and look for travel photography books in the library. Then relax and experiment on your own.

Remember, people are people everywhere. If you can demonstrate your humanity *behind* the camera, theirs will emerge on film.

Seven Ways to Spice Up Your Slide Show

1. Edit your slides.

It's much better to present fewer, high-quality slides than to let inferior slides drag down your work. If there's any doubt, take it out!

2. Arrange your slides in an interesting, thematic order.

Don't be bound to chronology; do include a brief account of your itinerary in your introduction, if you like. Group the slides by topic— everyday life, religion, historic sights, etc. Separate groups with "headline" slides (open with a sign saying "Welcome to Tunisia" or use a sunset to end a section).

3. Preview your slide show at least once.

Think about your commentary for each slide. Find ways to alter the pace, moving quickly at some point to stimulate interest. Some slides have greater impact without narration.

4. Provide background music.

Purchase a cassette of indigenous instrumental music on your trip. Let the music create ambience as your guests arrive; lower the volume to a barely audible level as background to your slide narration.

5. Serve a food or beverage authentic to your destination.

You don't have to prepare a five-course meal; a snack will add flavor to the experience.

6. Share some artifacts.

Pass around a small container of spices to accompany a slide of spices in the marketplace. The added sense of smell will bring the visuals to life. Small carvings or other items easy to distinguish in semidarkness also work well.

7. Keep your slide show to one hour, maximum.

Leave your friends asking for more!

Selecting Guidebooks

It would be foolish to sail into unknown waters without a nautical chart; it's just as foolish to head for a new destination without a guidebook.

A guidebook is invaluable for the concentrated information it provides. I couldn't hope to understand the history, geography, economy, and culture of a place by simply making surface observations. And they're handy for finding a hotel at night after a long train ride. But don't let a guidebook rule your life; use it as a starting point for information and exploration.

At times I've buried my guidebook, preferring to make my own discoveries. It's given me a wonderful sense of freedom and spontaneity, but I've missed seeing things I really would have enjoyed. (For two months in Holland I lived just twenty-minutes from the Rijksmuseum in Arnhem, one of Europe's finest modern art museums, with over two hundred paintings by van Gogh. But I didn't discover that until I was long gone.)

Finding the One That's Right for You

There are over a thousand guidebooks currently available in the English language. Each book or series is designed and researched with a particular audience in mind. If you asked a business person, a student, a culture buff, and an outdoor enthusiast about their favorite things to do and see in any particular region, you'd likely get widely divergent answers. A guidebook can be written from any of these (or other) perspectives. That makes it an influential travel partner.

The intended audience isn't always described on the book cover, so how can you figure out which one is right for you? I suggest that you shop for guidebooks with a short list of questions in hand (or mind). Think of three questions you're likely to ask on your trip, such as:

What are my options for getting to Machú Picchú?

What is the historical and cultural background of Machú Picchú?

How much will a hotel cost me in Cuzco?

Now, compare several travel guides for your destination and rate their responses to your three questions. Which ones list hotels within your budget that sound acceptable to you? Which one is organized in the most useful way? Which one feels like it is speaking to the kind of traveler you are?

Another strategy is to check out what several guidebook series say about your hometown, or a place you've already visited. Which one agrees with your own opinions? Do they publish a guide to your next destination? Ask your friends for recommendations, or familiarize yourself with several guidebooks from the library.

Other clues to look for:

•Urban/rural emphasis—does the book only list major cities in each country (like *Europe on $40 a Day*) or does it include smaller towns in the countryside?

•What special insights or information does the guide have to offer you as a woman traveler?

•Do you expect your guidebook to provide background information on history and culture, or will you seek it from other sources?

•How much relative space is devoted to restaurants, lodging, shopping, and museum and cultural activities?

•Does the book actually deliver all that the title promises?

•When was the book published? Guidebooks can become outdated by the time the ink dries. If you're interested in current prices for food and lodging, buy an updated guide. If historical features are more your interest, consider a used guidebook or borrow an older version.

Ask a knowledgeable bookseller for a recommendation. A growing number of bookstores specialize in travel books and offer an unusually large selection. Many do mail order business. To locate one near you, look in your phone directory or search for ads in travel magazines.

Major Names in Guidebooks

For Upper- to Mid-Range Travelers

Fielding's Guides—John McPhee said Fielding's travel guides "did not tell people what to see. It told them what to spend, and where." These guides cover resort destinations and contain a toll-free number for updates and questions.

Fodor's Guides—These all-purpose guides are preferred by main-stream and business travelers; *Fodor's Wall Street Journal Business Travel Guides* are bound in small stapled sections to allow frequent travelers to carry only the relevant sections on each trip.

Berlitz Travellers' Guides—The pocket travel guides give a solid general overview and are small and handy to carry. Recommended for people traveling on tours as a good source of background infor-mation. The phrase books are well-organized with phrases geared to-ward a mainstream traveler. Cover Australia, Canada, Mexico, Caribbean, Turkey, parts of Europe.

Birnbaum Travel Guides—Excellent, family-oriented guides with lots of information on shopping and restaurants in Europe, South America, Mexico, Caribbean, and Eastern Europe.

Frommer's Guides—Comprehensive guides cover a wide price range, from deluxe to inexpensive, while the Dollar a Day series is written for those who expect to pay the designated amount ($40, or whatever amount, per person) daily for accommodations and meals at "non-standard, less pretentious places." A solid source of good in-formation.

Rick Steves' Europe through the Back Door—Steves' books offer common-sense advice to help develop your travel smarts. His "itin-erary guides" (*Spain in Twenty-Two Days*) are helpful if you're in a hurry—train routes are planned to maximize efficiency. These books have a loyal following. His popular European museum guide is called *Mona Winks*.

For Budget and Adventurous Travelers

Lonely Planet—*On a Shoestring Guides* and *Travel Survival Kits* are loaded with useful information for travelers bound for Asia, Africa, South America, and Oceania. They publish an excellent series on Polynesia. Lonely Planet phrase books are easy to carry and well-organized with phrases useful to shoestring travelers.

Moon Publications Travel Handbooks—Very thorough on cultural and historical information. Current titles cover Southeast Asia and the Pacific; their upcoming *India Handbook* promises to be an excellent decoder of a complex culture. The *Indonesia Handbook* is a classic—it's banned there due to its honest political analysis. Hawaii books are recommended.

Real Guides—Published as **Rough Guides** in Britain, these culturally and socially sensitive books include more than the usual information for women and lesbian travelers in Europe, Eastern Europe, Morocco, and Peru and offer good insights for campers.

Let's Go—This series is written by students and aimed at the traveler on a daily budget of $10 to $40 (in Europe and Britain). Even if you don't imagine yourself hitchhiking, you may want to take advantage of their cost-conscious lodging and excellent restaurant recommendations, which are thoroughly updated annually.

John Muir—Outstanding among their many excellent travel books is *A People's Guide to Mexico*, which is by far the best guidebook for Mexico.

Berkeley Guides—This ambitious new series, published by Fodor and written by students at U.C. Berkeley for budget travelers, offers special resource sections for women, gays and lesbians, and disabled readers. Their inaugural titles cover Eastern Europe, Mexico, the Pacific Northwest and Alaska, and California (with Baja, Las Vegas, and the Grand Canyon thrown in), with more on the way.

People to People Guides—Aimed at solo travelers to Poland and Romania, these new guides list over a thousand people eager to meet visitors and show them around.

General Guides

Insight Guides—Stocked with photos, good cultural information and background reading for many regions of the world, these guides can help you narrow down your destinations while planning your itinerary, but they are too heavy to carry along on your trip.

Michelin—*Green Guides* are packed with art, historical, and cultural information, if you can get through the dense text and small print. *Red Guides* rate restaurants and hotels in Western Europe, in a wider price range than you might imagine.

Blue Guides—Unrelated to the Michelin Guides, these extremely comprehensive British guides are tops for historical and cultural background information for Europe and the Middle East.

Bet You Can't Take Just One

It's difficult to find just one book that will suit all your needs, especially if you're traveling to more than one place. But the combined weight of several guidebooks can be prohibitive (unless you buy a guidebook on diskette to use on your laptop computer). Lighten your load by crafting your own, personalized guidebook:

•Photocopy or cut out relevant pages from more than one guidebook and insert in a folder or binder. (To economize, buy last year's guide from a used-book store or public library book sale.) Destroying any book goes against my grain too, but the truth is that after you return from your trip you won't have much use for that guidebook—you'll want an updated version for your next trip.

•Add notes or clippings from travel articles found in magazines or the newspaper.

•Make a list of names and phone numbers of local contacts you plan to seek out.

•Spend an afternoon at the library doing historical or cultural research. Look for videos, magazines and special newsletters; record the information in your travel journal.

Guidebooks, like restaurants, tend to attract their own following. By using several different guidebooks, you can mingle with a variety of traveler cultures. Kay Grasing observed that "Lonely Planet's top of the line is my moderate level; but the people I meet are more interesting than those who use Fodor's."

Guidebooks that cover multiple countries must limit their discussion of every topic and place. Start out with a good comprehensive guide, then consider buying a second guidebook while traveling, trading with a traveler crossing the border in the opposite direction, or mail yourself a second guidebook or photocopied pages so you can pick them up when you'll need them later on.

How to Find the Cheapest Airline Tickets

Travelers who want to stretch their budget and are willing to spend the extra effort to save money should consider all the angles before purchasing a standard airline ticket.

Become an Air Courier

If you are flexible, over twenty-one years of age, and can give up your baggage allowance and travel with only carry-on luggage, you can become an air courier. Courier firms book flights from major U.S. cities (New York, Chicago, Los Angeles, San Francisco) to major European and Asian destinations. A representative of the air-freight courier firm meets you at the airport with the baggage you will check for them (consisting of completely legal small parcels and documents); another relieves you of the baggage on the other end.

The period of stay is prearranged, (although it may not be guaranteed). Fares vary and usually decrease as the departure date nears if no one has been found to take the flight.

Look in your telephone directory under "air courier" (if you live in a small town, go to the library and look in telephone directories of major cities) and call for specific terms and conditions. Several books are available such as *Air Courier's Handbook* by Jennifer Bayse or the *Courier Air Travel Handbook* by Mark I. Field.

Buy an International Student Identity Card (ISIC)

If you are a full-time student or teacher, this card entitles you to substantial savings in air fares, rail passes, and entrance fees to museums and cultural events in sixty-five countries. Special rates as well as opportunities to work and study abroad apply to students under twenty-six years of age. The international network of travel agencies associated with ISIC offers low fares and good advice. The card provides basic sickness and accident insurance and access to the Traveler's Assistance Hotline for help with medical, financial, or legal emergencies. It's well worth checking out. Contact the **Council on International Educational Exchange.** In the U.S.: **205 E. Forty-second Street, New York, NY 10017 (212/661-1450)**; in the United Kingdom: **28A Poland Street, London W1V 3DB (071/437-7767)**; in Australia: **222-224 Faraday Street, Carolton, Melbourne, Victoria 3053 (03/347-6911).**

Look for Bucket Shops

These travel agencies market unsold airline seats at discount prices (and differ from distress merchants, which sell last-minute tickets at low prices). Bucket shops may book you on smaller airlines (Middle Eastern or East European) or routes that involve backtracking. They probably won't arrange rental cars or perform other services of mainstream travel agencies. If you have more time than money, use a bucket shop to get the best deal.

Read your Sunday newspaper travel section; look for simple ads listing low prices in small print. Then make your phone calls and ask plenty of questions. These tickets are often nonrefundable and nonexchangeable; travel dates may be difficult or impossible to change.

By buying tickets at bucket shops around the world, you can save money and maximize flexibility. But be cautious. Fake bucket shops can rip you off. Don't hand over your money until you get a ticket. Ask other travelers and proprietors of hotels for directions to bucket shops and recommendations on which ones are trustworthy.

Athens bucket shops sell bargain tickets to Asia and Africa. New Delhi bucket shops have the cheapest fares from India back to London. Bangkok bucket shops often have terrific deals to Indonesia, Australia, and Europe. London's bucket shops specialize in low fares to Africa and India and across Europe. Americans can save money by flying to London and booking ongoing tickets from there. Look in magazines such as *Time Out* in London for bucket shop ads.

Patronize Ethnic Travel Agencies

Cheap fares accompany a high volume of travel. When seeking bargain fares to any part of the world, talk to travel agencies that service the overseas community of immigrants from that region.

For example, travel agencies operating out of Chinatown in San Francisco offer unbeatable fares to China. You may be able to take advantage of charter or group rates. (Look through newspapers or phone books from large cities to find names and phone numbers of these travel agencies.)

Research Air Passes

Air passes offer unlimited travel for a specified period of time in a designated area and are an especially good value when you want to traverse a large geographical area. Like rail passes, most air passes must be purchased before you leave home.

An "All-Australia Air-Pass" offers terrific savings for crisscrossing that continent. The "Pacific Air Pass" links Samoa, Fiji, and the Soloman Islands. LIAT airlines' "Super Caribbean Explorer Pass" is good for thirty days of unlimited forward stops (no backtracking allowed) on twenty-one islands.

Other passes include: "Visit U.S.A. Pass" (marketed in Europe only), "Visit Scandinavia Pass" (travel within Denmark, Norway, and Sweden), the "France Pass," the "Holiday Ticket for Finland," "Visit Norway Pass," "Visit Spain Pass," "U.K. Air Pass," "Polypas for Eight Destinations in the South Pacific," "Discover Pacific Pass," "Discover India Air Pass" (can be purchased in India with foreign currency), "Discover Thailand," "Visit South America," "Visit Argentina," "Brazil Airpass," "Visit Chile," "Discover Colombia," "Vimex for Mexico," "Peruvian Airpass," and "Avensa" (Venezuela air pass).

Instead of offering special passes, some airlines, such as Air New Zealand, offer visitors a substantial discount on *any* ticket for domestic flights. This works well for travelers not planning multiple flights within a country. Another interesting ticket is the "Circle Pacific," which allows multiple stops in East Asia and the South Pacific.

Send for tourist information brochures from national tourist offices, look in travel magazines, or inquire with the national airline of a specific country to get updated information on air passes.

Check Out the Package Deals

You don't fancy yourself as a package tourist? You don't want air fare plus eight nights at a hotel? What if the package is cheaper than the lowest-priced round-trip air fare you've been able to find?

Buying the package doesn't mean you have to stay at the hotel. You may be able to use the vouchers at other hotels or buy the package without the contents (the lodging, I mean). Ask your travel agent.

Weigh Round-the-World Fares versus Pay-As-You-Go Fares

For extended travelers making a round-the-world trip, this can be a tricky decision. Round-the-world tickets require that you complete the trip in six months or one year. Two or three airlines often join together to offer the fare, and your destinations may be limited by their service areas. Once your itinerary is established, most tickets allow you to change the date you travel from one point to another but do not permit you to change the itinerary (you cannot add a stop to your route, or change the order of your stops).

In exchange for accepting these limitations, you avoid the task of researching and buying tickets in foreign countries under possibly confusing conditions. As long as the airline stays in business, and you don't lose your ticket, you have the security of a prepaid ticket for your whole journey. Depending on your itinerary and dates of travel, the round-the-world ticket can be more or less costly than individually purchased tickets.

If you don't want to be hedged in by a time limit and prefer the flexibility of adding destinations and changing your itinerary, consider paying as you go. There are several keys to successful pay-as-you-go travel:

- Utilize cheap overland options, like trains, ferries and boats. Express buses are a cheap and fast way to cross Europe, for example.

- Plan to buy tickets in the worldwide travel bargain centers (bucket shops in Bangkok, Athens, Amsterdam, and Hong Kong), and avoid purchasing tickets in expensive places.

Consult guidebooks for inexpensive travel options. Lonely Planet's *Africa Guidebook* lists two travel clubs that offer very low fares from Europe to Africa. Newspapers from foreign cities, available at large newsstands worldwide, offer additional clues.

Even when traveling one-way around the world, it may be cheaper to buy a series of round-trip tickets. Give away or sell the return coupon, or trade it if you can. (But remember that the need to present passports for international flights can make it difficult to trade or sell tickets.)

Make sure you contact a ticket consolidator, who can combine several one-way discount tickets to match your itinerary and thereby beat the price of a round-the-world ticket.

Beware—You May Need That MCO

Some Shangri-las want assurance that you can leave as easily as you arrived. Countries that witnessed "hippie invasions" in the sixties and seventies now require that visitors show an outbound ticket before they will let you in.

There are several ways to deal with the problem if you are not planning to fly out. If you are traveling overland or by boat but have an ongoing ticket for a later flight elsewhere in the region, ask the travel agent to list your complete itinerary, and the "open leg" (nonflight portion) may be overlooked.

You can try flashing a wad of traveler's checks, but that leaves you at the whim of the border official. If he or she is feeling strict that day and won't accept any explanation, you could be forced to buy an outbound ticket on the spot. If you find yourself in that predicament, buy the least expensive ticket you can and make sure it is refundable. Ask specifically about refund policies, and get them in writing. (Airlines can make you wait as long as a year for ticket refunds.)

You can avoid the whole situation by carrying an MCO (Miscellaneous Charge Order) from an airline. An MCO is simply a blank airline ticket; it looks like a standard ticket but has no destination or date filled in. If you're planning a lot of overland travel, the MCO can help you through many border crossings. You can exchange it for a regular ticket at some point if you decide to fly on the airline that issued the MCO, but don't count on other airlines accepting it. When purchasing an MCO it's best to verify that it is refundable *on demand* so you don't get caught in a lengthy wait for the refund.

Remember, prices and conditions change rapidly in the travel industry. Conduct independent research and talk to knowledgeable travel agents before purchasing an MCO.

Get the Most Out of Your Tickets

Build a relationship with a travel agent who understands and can meet your desires—whether they be for cheap tickets or creative routing. Some travel agencies specialize in certain types of travel (such as cruises) or a certain clientele (such as business travelers or students). Ask your friends for recommendations, or test several agencies with the same inquiry. Once you find an agency you feel confident in, become a regular customer, and your requests should receive extra attention.

Always inquire about free stopovers when purchasing an airline ticket. You may be able to make five stops on the continent of South America for the price of a round-rip ticket to Buenos Aires by utilizing two free stopovers on the outgoing and two on the return portion of your flight. You can cover a huge continent by effectively using your free stops.

The least expensive ticket to your destination may be one that includes it as a free stopover on a highly discounted ticket to a point further away. Ask your travel agent about "hidden city" tickets.

Seasonal and Weather Planning

The most underresearched aspect of most trips is the weather. Travelers who spend months reading about culture and studying language may devote a scant five minutes to inquiring about the weather at their intended destination. Yet, climate and other variations of seasonal travel can profoundly affect a trip.

Do Your Homework

A woman in the Pacific Northwest planned a trip to sunny Italy to escape the dreary December weather. Just before purchasing her tickets, she was shocked to learn that Rome was overcast and rainy in December, too.

Photographs on travel posters are taken on the best day of the year. Don't rely on pretty pictures or your own assumptions about the weather. Research the climate before deciding when to visit. You'll need to find out weather trends for planning purposes and then check the weather map or report for last-minute updates.

Consider the source of information when inquiring about the weather. A national tourist office, whose job is to promote tourism, may not provide all the details you require. It's easy to present partial information, giving statistics for temperatures but not humidity, for example. Averages can be calculated in many ways and could mask the actual maximum and minimum temperatures. Air temperature shifts faster than water temperature. How will you know when swimming season really begins?

Independent sources, like geography or weather books, newspapers, and magazines can provide the information you need. Guidebooks should have weather information, also. A typical guidebook may provide the following information:

The best season to trek Nepal is October to mid-December. That is the season of best visibility (of mountain peaks), brightest weather, and most tolerable nighttime temperatures.

What if you can't possibly go between October and December? Additional research shows that:

September is okay; January and February get very cold. Avoid the monsoon, which begins in March—rain brings poor visibility, muddy trails, and leeches.

"The Travel Planner" at the back of each month's issue of *Condé Nast Traveler* magazine, lists very specific weather planning information for a six-month period. Their chart shows that Kathmandu during August, for example, boasts an afternoon temperature of 82 degrees. Yet the precipitation for the month is 13 inches, and the chances of a dry day only 40 percent.

Contrast that with December in Kathmandu, when afternoon temperatures reach a pleasant 64 degrees, chances of a dry day are 95 percent and precipitation for the month equals less than one inch. The planner also lists area of blue sky (53 percent during August in Kathmandu compared to 86 percent in December).

Of course, if you are planning to trek into the Himalayas, you will want to remember that temperatures quickly plummet as altitude increases.

Become an Amateur Meteorologist

Pay attention to your own local weather—how do you feel at 55 degrees, at 70 or 95 degrees? At what temperature do you need a sweater to be comfortable? At what temperature does the heat reduce your energy level? At what water temperature are you comfortable swimming?

Study a map or globe. The highest temperatures year round are on the equator; temperatures tend to decrease at higher latitudes (further from the equator) and higher altitudes. On the equator, there are generally two seasons—hot and wet, and hot and dry. The equator divides the seasons, which are opposite on Northern and Southern Hemispheres.

The sea takes longer to warm than land at the beginning of each summer and longer to cool down in the autumn. Therefore, the sea is much cooler in March than it is in October (in the Northern Hemisphere).

Enclosed seas tend to be warmer than oceans at the same latitude. Swimming on the Mediterranean side of Spain will be much more comfortable than on the Atlantic side. If you are planning to go snorkeling, ask what seasons have clearest water, and if there is a season for stinging jellyfish.

Study the map as you research temperatures and weather. What happens during monsoon season? An hour of refreshing rain each day, or five hours of downpour? Monsoons travel too—which way do they go and how fast do they travel? (You may want to follow a month behind the monsoon as it travels through Southeast Asia.)

Maps can provide clues to understanding cyclones and tornados. (Bangladesh is the natural strike zone for every storm pitched up by the Bay of Bengal.) Remember that rainy season equals stormy seas; if you're planning to travel by boat or ferry, be prepared.

Weather can vary drastically from one side of an island to another. On Hawaii, the south and west (leeward) coasts enjoy over 300 days of sunshine annually, while the east and north (windward) coasts get more than a 100 inches of rain, creating green forests and waterfalls.

Look for the Shoulder

Seasons are created by people, too. Because most tourists want to visit a place during ideal temperatures and climate, they create an excessive demand for services that has been dubbed "high season." High season is equivalent to rush hour anywhere on the globe. It means higher prices and bigger crowds. (Some year-round destinations, such as Hawaii, have no high and low season; prices remain virtually the same year round.)

High season is also a product of travelers' vacation schedules. School holidays release American teachers, students, and families during July and August; Germans in July; the French in August. May and August school holidays in Australia make Bali a crowded destination during those months and at Christmas.

Low season means low tourist demand and lower prices. It may also be the least desirable season weather-wise. Luckily, shoulder season comes in between. In Europe, the shoulder season is at either end of the busy summer, from April to May and from September to October. These are times when crowds are gone, prices go down, and the weather is still quite good. Since most tourists are flying in one direction, cheap air fares will deliver you the opposite way. Experienced travelers often prefer to travel during shoulder season.

Be Aware of Religious Seasons

Religious observances can be a highlight or hindrance to your travels. Find out about dominant religious and cultural holidays before you travel, and be prepared for difficulties in finding a room or making other tourist arrangements if you arrive during a holiday.

Ramadan, a Muslim holiday, is a month of fasting when the observant do not eat from sunup to sundown. In Muslim countries, meals may be hard to find and food service disrupted during this period.

Mardi Gras, or Carnival, is a Christian celebration, ending on Fat Tuesday, the last day before the fasting season of Lent. Celebrated carnivals are held in New Orleans, Rio de Janeiro, Nice, and Cologne, smaller festivals in the Caribbean and Central and South America. In Latin America, many families go to the beach during Easter week.

Jewish holidays will especially impact your travels to Israel, and *fiestas* are sprinkled throughout the year in Spain. India, with its hundreds of deities, has a religious festival almost every month. Major Hindu festivals can attract thousands of Indian pilgrims to small towns. Make sure you're consulting a calendar that shows the holidays relevant to your trip. Even Christian holidays take place on different days in different parts of the world.

Nonreligious local festivals and customs are worth knowing about, as well. In mid-August, many Romans and Parisians clear out of their cities. Depending on your interests, the vacant streets can be a disappointment or a delight.

There's nothing you can do to guarantee good weather or the absence of noisy crowds, but thorough research can prepare you for almost anything that might come your way.

VIII

Extended Travel

How Long Is Long Enough?

Once in a while, maybe once in a lifetime, it happens. You look around and realize that there's nothing holding you back. You have the flexibility, the freedom, and the money to travel for an extended period of time.

So, how long is long enough? That can be an enigma. It's easy to recognize when a trip is too short; you've barely quit waking up to the alarm clock left at home. You've finally learned how to read the menu and order what you want without pointing to it. You've just established your regular table at a seaside cafe and it's time to go home. Too soon.

Two weeks is not long enough—an American anomaly in the industrialized world. Even if you're not European, perhaps you can organize a vacation like the Europeans enjoy—four, five, or six weeks.

Stretch the Possibilities

How about three months, six months, or a year? When I initially conceived of an extended trip, I couldn't imagine traveling for longer than six months. Where would I go? How would I spend my time?

The first three months are just a warm-up. Beginning in the fourth month, you begin to figure out what it is you're looking for, or forget what it was you left behind.

Round about six months, you start to find the groove. You're really comfortable. You discover the key to your own private journey. There's magic in your backpack and a lucky star overhead.

By then you're having so much fun you won't ever want to stop.

You travel more slowly, staying longer in each place. You spend hours sitting under an ancient tree, watching the landscape take a slow bath in golden light; weeks ambling down a back road the bus traversed in a day, finding adventure all along the way. You've learned to feel at home wherever you are.

You start to feel that you could just keep traveling forever. After all it took to put your life on hold, you decide to keep going as long as you can.

Finally, one morning you'll wake to a fresh chill in the air, the breathy hint of another season turning the page, and wish for your own bed. You turn at the sound of a certain voice. It reminds you of a close friend you haven't seen in a year.

It's nice to travel until you yourself decide when to go home. Not the calendar, not your bank book, your child or employer or partner calling your name. The best way to end a trip is just to decide one day that it is over.

Change Gears

Guidebooks abound with strategies to "See Europe in Twenty-One Days." On an extended trip, you will likely move much more slowly. Consider these guidelines, but plan your own trip to fit your goals and travel style.

•List the countries you plan to visit.

•Start out by budgeting at least a month in each country. (Based on your rate of travel, adjust from two weeks to several months.)

•Talk to travel agents, read guidebooks, and interview other travelers who've been there. Adjust your plan as you get new information. Start attaching cost estimates to your plan. (Remember that slowing your rate of travel often reduces expenditures.)

•Build in a re-evaluation point after one-quarter or one-third of your trip. Does your original plan still make sense?

Putting Your Life on Hold

Our lives are interconnected webs, woven of daily and weekly tasks, responsibilities at work and at home, relationships with family and friends. At times I feel like the spider, spinning my web, creating my nest. I'm in control, constructing a place and a life of my own design. At other times, I've felt like the fly, hopelessly trapped, incapable of escape.

Does thinking about putting your life on hold, stepping away from it for several months or a year, make you feel more like the fly than the spider—overwhelmed, rather than in control? If so, take a deep breath and read to the end of this section. It's easy to slide from thinking "I'd like to go because..." to "I can't leave because...." First, separate the "big D" from the "little D's."

Decisions, Decisions

The "big D" is the the big decision—shall I go on an extended trip? To answer this question, consider these issues:

- Do I have the financial resources to support myself while traveling? How much can I spend, and how much money will I come home to? Do I have a reasonable chance to earn money while traveling?

- Is there a family or personal situation that absolutely requires my presence? (A grave illness, for example).

- Is this a good time for me to leave my work, home, and personal relationships? Will I miss out on anything critical to my personal growth?

In making the "big D," focus first on what you want. Do you really want to go away for three months, six months, or a year? If the answer is "yes"—a clear "yes"—an unarguable "yes"—and no financial or personal obstacles prevent your leaving, then all the other decisions you have to make become the "little D's," the little decisions you will make in order to prepare your departure and get free.

The list of "little D's" is long and may take a while to resolve. Leaving your family and friends, house or apartment, job, car, and pets requires planning and perseverance. It takes time to untangle what you've carefully woven. But once you have decided to go, don't let logistical details stand in your way.

Allow four to six months to prepare for an extended trip; the higher your motivation and the fewer complications, the more quickly you can prepare. The time-line that follows can be condensed as necessary.

Be creative when faced with the tasks before you. Brainstorm each possible angle, every potential solution. For example, depending on your situation and the length of your planned trip, you might have several options for dealing with your residence:

•Sell your house or give up your apartment, and put your possessions in long-term storage for a low cost.

•Rent or sublet your place for several months or a year. (Visiting professors and medical interns are a good source of potential tenants.)

•Find a house-sitter to live there for free or at a reduced rent in exchange for caring for your things. Someone you already know might be right for the task.

•Take advantage of a "home vacation exchange" and temporarily trade your home for one to use overseas.

In each scenario, start with thinking how it might work, not why it won't. Ask one or two friends to help in brainstorming; they may think of possibilities that elude you.

Valuables

What will you do with your jewelry and other precious possessions? Can you leave a box or two with a trusted friend or family member, or will you rent a safety deposit box?

Car

Ask your mechanic about the advantages and disadvantages of storing your car. Would you feel comfortable lending it to a friend? Could you sell it, put the money in a special account, and buy another when you return?

Job

Is it possible to take an unpaid leave of absence? How can you leave on good terms? If you quit, is there any chance of getting your job back later? Do you want to return to the same work, or use this break as a chance to try something different? Will you seek work while traveling?

A TIME-LINE FOR PREPARATION

4 to 6 MONTHS BEFORE:

Make basic decisions about destination, length of trip.

Brainstorm housing options.

Consider job options.

Cut expenses, save all money.

Start language study.

3 MONTHS BEFORE:

Apply for credit cards (before leaving job).

Apply for passport—request extra pages for extended travel.

Get full medical exam.

Research immunizations needed, set up timetable.

Get dental checkup and necessary work done.

Read books, keep files on places to visit.

Increase physical activity; get in shape.

Purchase camera, start using it.

Research plane fares, watch for sales.

2 MONTHS BEFORE:	Make car arrangements.
	Research health/travel insurance.
	Purchase backpack or luggage.
	Start assembling clothing and supplies.
	Make dietary adjustments.
	If moving house, start sorting and packing. Arrange temporary housing if necessary.
	Update address book.
	Submit job resignation; train replacement.
	Recruit a "home secretary."
1 MONTH BEFORE:	Finish getting inoculations.
	Pack, store, or sell everything.
	Cancel subscriptionss.
	Buy travel insurance.
	Buy airplane ticket(s).
	Organize vertical file for the home secretary.
	Organize bank accounts and finances.
	Decide how to get money while traveling.

Make or update a will.

Pack gear and test weight; make adjustments.

Apply for visas if necessary.

Start saying good-byes.

Cancel/notify unneeded credit cards; services.

Buy/collect small gifts.

FINAL COUNTDOWN: Vacate house; move to temporary quarters.

Store/sell/lend car.

Buy film.

Buy traveler's checks.

Transfer documents to the home secretary.

Forward mail to your "home secretary." Pack and leave!

Predeparture Tips

Cancel Your Mail

One of the great benefits of leaving the country is the opportunity to eliminate the huge tide of unnecessary mail that washes up on your doorstep.

Cut address labels from magazines and organizational newsletters and glue them to postcards informing them that you are leaving the country for an indefinite period of time. Or use toll-free phone numbers, when available, to do this.

Save natural resources by eliminating unsolicited junk mail addressed to you. Write to: **Mail Preference Service, Direct Marketing Association, 6 East Forty-third Street, New York, NY 10017**. Include your full name, address, and phone number and ask that your name be removed from all lists.

Obtain Passport and Visas

Thousands of travelers each year are shocked when they are turned away from a country's border due to the lack of a blurry stamp in their passport. It is your responsibility to find out if a visa is required for entrance to each country you plan to visit. (Visa requirements change, so relying on a friend's advice who went there several years ago could be a mistake.) Check with current government sources of information, or contact the embassy or consulate of the country directly.

Travel agents and guidebooks can help pinpoint places where visas may be easily obtained near the border. For example, getting a visa from the Chinese Consulate in the U.S. can take several weeks (especially nerve-wracking when they have your passport and your departure date is fast approaching); in Hong Kong, you can obtain a Chinese visa within twenty-four hours. Double- and triple-check your information on visas. Believe it or not, you can be forced to get back on the plane without ever leaving the airport.

If you will be needing multiple visas during your trip, carry a dozen or more passport photos, or better yet, bring the negative along for quick reprints.

Get your passport early if you plan to mail it off with visa applications. Photocopy it and keep the copy in your luggage to aid rapid replacement if necessary.

Begin Physical Conditioning

Make early dietary adjustments to help your body ease into its new environment. Add foods to your diet that are typical of your destination, such as spicy food if you're going to Ethiopia or hot food if you're going to Korea.

Increase your level of physical exercise: walk an hour or two more each day, go hiking or backpacking, or lift weights to increase upper body strength for carrying luggage. Initiate a more serious training program for overland trekking or bicycle travel.

Start taking acidophilus tablets to build intestinal flora and fortitude. Try cutting out consumption of all chlorinated water two weeks before departure to do the same. Don't forget to start taking malaria pills a week or two before departure, if needed.

Start Saying Your Good-byes

Saying farewell to the many people in your life is a time-consuming and emotional task. Start early to avoid a crush of visitors during your final hectic days of preparation. Make dates with people, let them cook you a meal, or invite them along on your errands or daily walk.

Your Home Secretary

Although it sounds like a high-level post in the British Cabinet, the "home secretary" is simply the person you recruit to take care of your financial life while on extended travel.

Finding the Right Person

Depending on complications involved, this person could be an accountant, a lawyer, a local bookkeeper, a friend, or a relative. Sometimes a team works well, such as a paid bookkeeper to transact your business, making decisions in consultation with a trusted friend or family member. Since my financial empire fits easily into a shoe box, I've always recruited friends to watch over things while I'm gone and then rewarded them with a special gift upon my return.

You should appoint someone whom you trust absolutely to take care of your business in a timely manner and make decisions in your absence. She should be good with money—the kind of person who balances her checkbook and pays her bills on time. It helps to find someone who is planning a fairly stable life while you are gone. (You don't want her handing over that shoe box to someone else). It should be someone in your confidence, who will know all your financial affairs and be cosigner on your bank account(s). You should sign a notarized form giving her power of attorney to act on your behalf.

The Task

The home secretary's job is to keep the money flowing to you when you need it, and to pay your obligations in your absence. This involves tasks such as:

- Paying your credit card and other bills.
- Overseeing a storage unit or the rental of your home or apartment.
- Screening your mail for items that need immediate attention.

Set Up the Vertical File

You will want to set up a well-organized file system with clear directions and tasks for the home secretary. I use a vertical file, an accordion-pleated expanding cardboard file available from office supply stores that stands easily on a desk top. The sections within the vertical file came labeled alphabetically, but I've made my own labels to organize the sections with names like these:

- VISA card
- American Express card
- Checking account
- Savings account
- Storage unit
- Travel insurance
- Traveler's checks
- Misc. credit and I.D. cards
- Insurance policies
- Important documents
- Car
- Income taxes

The first four sections, for credit cards and bank accounts, will receive monthly attention. The storage unit and travel insurance may require quarterly payments, while other categories are used primarily as storage for important papers and keys.

I leave credit cards, library card and other identification from my wallet that I don't need or want on the trip in the "misc. credit and I.D. cards" section.

"Important documents" holds photocopies of my passport and yellow immunization record, my address book, and will.

I highlight the names, addresses, and phone numbers of family members in the address book in case they need to be contacted.

Leave Clear Written Instructions

Once you've got the sections organized, type a single sheet of paper to insert in each section that provides full information for that area of responsibility. For example:

> *My VISA card is # 0123 456 789.*
>
> *It expires 10/96.*
>
> *My credit limit is $2,000.*
>
> *If lost or stolen, report to 800-555-1212.*
>
> *I called and spoke with Jane Adams and informed her that I was authorizing you to contact them on my behalf during my absence. Attached is a copy of the letter I sent to Jane to verify the same information.*
>
> *Please pay bill in full each month when it arrives.*

Each month when the VISA bill arrives, your home secretary can simply pay the invoice and file it in the VISA section of the vertical file.

After preparing written instructions for each category of the vertical file, type a summary overview of what needs to be done, and when. For example:

> *Monthly—I plan to buy traveler's checks when needed, $1,000 at a time. I will write and inform you each time I plan to buy traveler's checks. Please transfer money from savings to maintain my checking balance at $1,200 to $1,500 at all times.*
>
> *Rent on my storage unit must be paid monthly; they will not send a bill or reminder. If rent is not paid, they will auction the contents for payment.*

*In **January**, **April**, and **July**—pay insurance on storage unit.*

*In **April**—please file for automatic extension of my federal income tax. Papers are prepared and signed by me, located in "Income taxes."*

All verbal instructions should also be in writing. Once you're gone, you want your home secretary to have a clear understanding of everything that needs to happen. You may want to prepare a wall or desk calendar reminder system, writing on the appropriate days or weeks, "storage unit rent due" or "pay car insurance."

In the inevitable rush of departure, this is one task that should not be slighted. Take plenty of time to prepare your vertical file and train your home secretary so there is no confusion about what needs to be done and when.

Finances and Record-Keeping on the Road

Finances

Purchasing Traveler's Checks Abroad

On an extended trip, it's too risky and bulky to carry all your money with you. During eighteen months of travel, from 1985 to 1987, I spent about $6,000. I left home with $1,000 in traveler's checks, and obtained additional traveler's checks $1,000 at a time from local offices of American Express.

I applied for an American Express card specifically for that purpose. It functions as a check guarantee card, so I also carried about ten personal checks to complete the transactions. This method requires just a bit of planning; carry the American Express booklet listing their offices worldwide, and make sure you get to one before you run out of money.

Wiring Money

For years, wiring money was the standard method of sending and receiving money overseas. Someone goes to their bank in Omaha and has the bank telegraph a money transfer to you in Montevideo. Even if your friend in Omaha makes the transaction right on time, somehow things often end up in a time warp. I've met travelers stranded for days or even weeks, making daily visits to the bank to see if their money has arrived. I do not recommended wiring money overseas.

In a pinch, your friends or relatives can send cash to you in major foreign cities via international couriers. Better yet, they can wire money from a local American Express office to you at almost any other AMEX office worldwide. In an emergency, the high fees may be worth paying to complete the ten-minute transaction.

Cash

Some people don't mind carrying lots of cash. As a budget traveler, I simply don't want to risk losing the rest of my trip. Small bills are handy for certain transactions, so I usually carry $25 to $50 in small bills. I replenish my supply by purchasing leftover cash from short-term travelers bound for home.

Cash and Credit—Mix and Match

See "Changing Money" in Chapter VI for a full description of Automatic Teller Machine (ATM) withdrawals and cash advances on credit cards. When financing an extended trip, those two options can leave money earning interest in your bank account for longer but may force you to carry more cash than you feel comfortable with.

Your itinerary ultimately determines which method you employ. If you'll be passing through cities where banks offer credit card and ATM services, go ahead and use those as your primary sources of money. If you plan a lot of back-country and small town travel, you're probably better off with the safety and security of traveler's checks. A combination of traveler's checks and bank cards could provide the flexibility and security you need just about anywhere.

Record-Keeping on the Road

Have you ever counted your traveler's checks halfway through your trip and sworn that one or two had disappeared? You search for the little form the company gave you to record your transactions. Just as you feared, you quit making notations after cashing the first one.

It took months of traveling to figure out what information I wanted to keep track of. Although I didn't worry about tracking daily expenses, I did want a record of larger amounts of money as they came and went. Here's the system I developed:

I carry a small calendar book that displays a week on every two pages. At the back of the calendar are a dozen or so blank pages that I use to keep personal records. Inside the same leather binder as the calendar is my address book. (I don't recommend taking your address book along for any trip less than six weeks, but you'll need it on a longer journey.) Choose a calendar or notebook system to track whatever you feel is important.

Tracking Finances

I record both incoming and outgoing money in a simple log.

Each time I buy a batch of traveler's checks, I list all the check numbers on the same page. Then I record the date I cash them, the place, and any special notes on what I purchase with the money.

My traveler's check log looks like this:

30 May—$500 from American Express, Nijmegen

$100 cash—for bicycle trip

$400 in traveler's checks, 8 @ $50 ea.

HH 119 330 485 Nijmegen, 15 June

HH 119 330 486 Nijmegen, 20 June

HH 119 330 487 Milano 25 June

Keeping a Record of Daily Events

While I keep a journal during my trips, I never force myself to record daily entries in it. Instead, I try to note two or three summary lines about each day on the small daily sections of my calendar:

9/11 Boat from Sami to Kerkyra—969 dr. Met a neat woman from Finland named Kristina; she showed me cheap place to stay.

9/12 Kristina rents a car, we drive around the island; I spot a neat beach town—Kalami; very quiet, plan to go there in a couple of days

9/13 Kristina's friend Speros takes us to a bouzouki nightclub with his friends; wild dancing, we break 2,400 plates!

Those short notations allow me to recreate my entire trip, which is helpful when giving friends advice. I note the names of favorite hotels and lodges, and sometimes their prices, providing a lot of good tips for other travelers.

Creating a Film Log

On my eighteen-month trip, I shot thirty-five rolls of film. Since I wouldn't be seeing those pictures for quite some time, I needed a way to keep track of what I photographed to help me remember names of people and places when I finally saw the slides.

I assigned a number to each roll of film as I put it in my camera. A page at the back of my calendar/notebook called "film log" contained a running list of my rolls of film along with brief notes on where I was or what I had photographed.

I had purchased prepaid film-processing mailers before leaving the U.S., and I also noted the date I mailed the film off, and from where. (I thought this would help me trace lost rolls of film, but I never did recover two rolls I mailed from India). My film notes looked like this:

Roll 31—Italy, Roma and Firenze (mailed to Mom).

Roll 32—Camping Lake Martinagno; Brindisi

To supplement the notes on my film log, I'd make small notations on the appropriate calendar pages. On July 2, I wrote "SR 31," my shorthand for "started roll 31." The next film note appears July 12 when I "started roll 32." That way, any notes written in my calendar between July 2 and July 12 could help me identify pictures on roll 31.

Your home secretary, or another friend or family member, can receive and store your returned film—whoever receives it can get a sneak preview of your trip.

Professional photographer Barbara Gundle recommends a more detailed film log:

Year & Roll	Frame	Notes
92031	*01-05*	*Bus terminal, Belo Horizonte, Brazil*
	06-11	*São Lourenço art deco bathhouse*
	12-20	*village of Cristina*
	21-25	*sunset Caxambú Parque Hidromineral*
	26-36	*my hosts, Ana, Gilberto, and Gloria*

Barbara's foolproof method takes only a minute or two each day to record. It will help you remember great details even a decade after your trip (and is just as valuable to use when shooting pictures at home).

Recording Medical History

I had an ongoing problem with bladder infections while traveling. Each time I saw a doctor, it was a different person in a different town. I quickly realized that if I didn't keep track of my symptoms and medications, no one else could. So I kept a page noting medical problems and medications prescribed.

Logging Correspondence

I wrote hundreds of letters on my round-the-world trip. After a while, it was impossible to recall—when had I last written to Beverly? Had I already told her about the package I had sent? To cut down on the confusion, I maintained a cryptic correspondence log:

2/13 Beverly, re: camel trip, Jaipur, sent package
2/14 postcard to Mom and Dad, re: camel trip, Jaipur, plans

When you're traveling for a year and a half, you're not just on vacation. Life is not suspended, it is carried out in very different ways. I was alone for much of my trip and could only rely on myself to record and remember both exquisite and mundane moments. I had no rules to obey, no schedule to follow, and very little to ground me in time or space. Now, looking back, I realize that making notes in my leather-bound black book helped me to stay centered. The calendar entries, records of letters sent, medical adventures, and film exposed, all provided a sense of order which comforted me.

Mail Call

The best way to handle mail when traveling is to forget about it. Have no expectations, and you won't be disappointed. The more mail stops you commit to, the more hurdles you have when changing plans. For any trip shorter than six weeks, don't bother with mail. Or arrange one mail stop along the way. For a lengthy trip, set up a mail stop every six to eight weeks. That leaves enough time to inform folks back home of your next destination. Don't expect to receive money in the mail, especially in "Third World" countries.

Sending Mail

If you have many people to correspond with and don't want to write virtually the same letter over and over, organize a photocopy letter system before you leave. My newsy letters were called "Thaliagrams." I wrote one every six weeks or so and mailed it to my home secretary who photocopied it and sent it to a prearranged mailing list of friends and relatives.

Each letter was several pages long and included the interesting details of my travels that I would not have described repeatedly in individual letters. Each Thaliagram listed a future mail stop where I would look for return mail. (I also responded individually to anyone who sent me a personal letter.)

You can greatly expedite outgoing mail by taking your letters to an international airport and asking someone in the ticket line to mail them when they arrive home. (It helps to have the appropriate stamps already affixed to the envelopes.) Leave the letter unsealed, so you can display the contents, in case they are suspicious.

Faxing letters can be useful for quick turnaround. Many international hotels have fax facilities; most offer their services to nonguests. Fax a letter and stop by twenty-four or forty-eight hours later for a reply.

When using regular post, remember that letters may travel much faster than postcards. Aerograms are usually the cheapest and most efficient way to write, postcards are often the most expensive. In poor countries, get your outgoing letters franked (cancelled) at the post office to avoid stamp thieves.

Receiving Mail

If you are visiting someone, have mail sent in care of them. Otherwise, you can receive mail (through General Delivery) in almost every large town and city of the world.

Poste Restante

Have your friends and family clearly print your name and address when sending letters to you (last name, followed by first name). Ask them to underline your last name, especially if it is a name uncommon in the country you'll be receiving the letter.

Poste Restante is the French equivalent of General Delivery, and is a term used widely around the world. Check a guidebook for your destination—it may have a local variation. GPO stands for

Wonderful Friend
Their Address
City, State, Zip
Country

Smythe, Emma
Poste Restante
GPO
Any City, Country

General Post Office, which is the main post office of a town. No matter how many post offices there are in a city, there is only one GPO. (That makes it a good meeting place.)

Most GPOs hold mail sent *Poste Restante* for one month, but this can vary widely. The more organized places have alphabetized cubby holes and stamp the arrival date on the letter. When your time is up, the letter is returned to the sender.

Typically, you go to the *Poste Restante* window and show your identification; a passport is best. The clerk then compares your name to those on the letters. Because my name is unusual, I print it, large and clear, on a piece of paper exactly as it will appear on the envelope.

Ask your correspondents to *print* your name and address; cursive writing may be indecipherable for a non-English speaker. Don't be surprised if there is a small charge for the service, especially in African and Southeast Asian countries.

Lista Correos

In Spanish-speaking countries, the equivalent term is *Lista Correos*, which means "mail list." There may be an actual list of those who have mail waiting that you should review. The list may be attached to a clipboard or posted on a bulletin board along one wall. Each day's mail is listed separately, so be sure to check all the available lists.

Strategies for Success

It's wise to check for mail under your first name as well as your surname. If you're having trouble finding an anticipated letter, try every possible combination, including *M* for Ms. or Miss or Mrs. (I checked repeatedly at the Athens Post Office for a letter I knew should be there; on the third successive day I located it in a separate section organized according to the Greek alphabet.) Politely peer over the counter or the clerk's shoulder, as you will be much more successful at recognizing your letters than they will.

If you plan to pick up mail repeatedly at the same post office, make an effort to build a relationship with the *Poste Restante* clerk. A candy bar, pack of cigarettes, or other small treat will bring you good service, and sweeten special requests.

If you have multiple mail stops, ask your correspondents to photocopy letters and send duplicates to various stops; that increases your chances of at least one getting through. (Dated or numbered letters avoid confusion.)

Some post offices are notorious for bad service, others famous for their efficiency. Read your guidebook for suggestions before deciding on your mail stops.

Other Mail Pickup Options

American Express holds mail for their clients for thirty days. If you carry their credit card or their traveler's checks, you can have access to this service worldwide. Before leaving on your trip call **800/528-4800** and request the *Traveler's Companion* booklet with their worldwide mailing addresses. Have your correspondents address mail clearly, write "Client Letter Service" on the envelope, and note "hold until (date)" if you wish to stretch the thirty-day limit. In smaller towns, the AMEX office is a travel agency, which may not be open on Saturdays, as the post office often is. For a fee (in Europe at least) they will forward mail to another AMEX office.

Packages

It is much better to send than to receive.

If you must receive a package, I hope you're planning to be in a well-organized place. Then you have a chance of getting it in one piece and on time. My friend Gill's mother sent her a Christmas package to Kathmandu, all the way from Australia. When she went to collect it at the post office, she was told they were a bit behind in sorting packages and shown the back room where a Himalayan mountain of parcels almost defied assault. Because she knew it was a hand-knit sweater, three of us returned and tossed parcels from one end of the room to the other for an hour until we located it.

One Christmas box sent to me eventually did arrive in India; most of the chocolates had been eaten, but a few had only one bite taken out of them. Another box never did show up—at least it hasn't yet.

Tape cassettes and film are valued prizes and are often stolen. Try to disguise these items in larger packages.

Some countries have restrictions on items that can be received. Your post office should have the list of restricted items for all countries.

Shipping packages can be blissfully easy in some places. In Bangkok and Hong Kong, just cart all the contents of a parcel to the post office, where clerks at a special window will find a box, pack it, and seal it for you. In India, specialists wait outside the post office, ready to sew your package shut in burlap and affix wax seals all over it. Finding a box there can take several hours, however.

Sending parcels by sea mail (two to three months) is considerably cheaper than by air mail (one to three weeks). If you'll soon be crossing a border, compare postal rates on the other side before mailing anything—it may be significantly cheaper to hold on to things and mail them after you cross the border. (Indonesia's postage rates are quite expensive; you'll save handily by waiting until you get to Singapore, if traveling in that direction.)

Telegrams

In places where telephones have not yet invaded every household, telegrams are widely used for communication. Compare prices for sending a telegram before making an international phone call. If you are expecting a telegram, be sure to ask whether it will be held at *Poste Restante*, or a special telegram desk or telegram office. If a telegram is sent to you c/o *Poste Restante*, you may have to check both places. Check the log book; most telegram offices keep track of incoming messages and their disposition.

Telephone Calls

If you want to communicate with someone, set a date to call them, collect. Then you can call from wherever you are (almost). Inquire about telephone charges before calling from a hotel—surcharges can add as much as 30 percent to the cost of your call. Place calls from government-operated long distance telephone centers, often located next to the main post office or a train station. If you plan to make lots of international phone calls, get an international calling card from your telephone company.

In the U.S., contact numbers for international calling cards are:

- **AT&T—USA DIRECT: 800/874-4000**
- **MCI—Call USA: 800/444-4444**
- **Sprint: 800/877-4646**

But, What If...?

The most difficult thing for friends and family to face is their inability to contact you if an emergency arises while you are traveling. EurAide offers an answering service for travelers in Europe called **Overseas Access**. Family or friends can call and leave messages for you; you call in to a local European number to check for your messages. Contact: **EurAide, PO Box 2375, Naperville, IL 60567 (708/420-2343)**.

Working Abroad

Most long-term-travel fantasies eventually include the idea of finding paid employment overseas. Although you may happen upon job openings while traveling (as many travelers do), a bit of research and preparation can greatly increase your chances of finding a job at the end of the rainbow. Be aware that most countries require a work permit for paid employment with requirements that most casual travelers cannot meet. You can get around this by working for an organization based in your home country, working illegally (in countries where the laws are not stringently enforced), or qualifying for some exception to the permit requirement. (For example, Americans of Irish heritage may be able to claim Irish citizenship under an obscure law that would qualify them to work in any of the eleven European Economic Community nations.)

Temporary Jobs

Casual Labor

If you are willing to pick fruit, harvest grapes, work on a ranch, in a fish factory, restaurant, or inn, you can find casual labor for money, or trade your work for food and lodging. In *Work Your Way Around the World*, Susan Griffith explains how you can follow the harvest across Europe and find jobs in tourism.

Transitions Abroad magazine publishes an annual *Directory to Overseas Employment*, which includes job leads for farm hands in Norway, summer camp counselors in Italy, teachers in East Africa, and dietitians and engineers in Papua New Guinea. Contact: **Transitions Abroad, PO Box 344, Amherst, MA 01004 (800/562-1973).**

Teaching English as a Second Language

Thousands of opportunities around the world exist for travelers who want to teach English. Teaching credentials are not always required, although a certificate from an EFL (English as a Foreign Language) or ESL (English as a Second Language) training school may be needed. *Teaching English Abroad* by Susan Griffith tells you how much training you'll need, where to find it, how to locate jobs once you're ready, and how to deal with problems that arise once you're working.

Work for Students

Full-time students are eligible to participate in the Council on International Educational Exchange's **Work Abroad** program. Work Abroad helps you obtain work permissions and organize your overseas job, provides orientation and housing leads for paying jobs in Britain, Ireland, France, Germany, New Zealand, Canada, Costa Rica, and Jamaica. (And the CIEE Education Abroad Scholarship Fund for Minority Students supports participation of minorities in any CIEE-sponsored program, including study, work, voluntary service, and internships.) Contact any Council Travel office or the CIEE **Work Abroad** program for more information: **CIEE, 205 East Forty-second Street, New York, NY 10017.**

Other options for students are described in *Time Out: Taking a Break from School to Travel, Work, and Study in the U.S. and Abroad* by Robert Gilpin and Caroline Fitzgibbons.

Permanent Jobs

Living and working for an extended period in a foreign country offers opportunities not available on a transient visit. Beware of international employment agencies advertising in classified newspaper ads that request hefty advance fees for providing work leads. Instead, subscribe to a newsletter such as *The International*

Employment Gazette, which lists hundreds of job openings worldwide in each biweekly issue **(800/882-9188)**. You might want to take a look at books such as *How to Get a Job in Europe: The Insider's Guide* by Robert Sanborn, which offers job-seeking tips for twelve countries.

Professional Positions

Many professional and technical jobs are available for bilingual workers. If you'd like to investigate the possibilities while traveling, bring a curriculum vitae written in the style used in the country where you're seeking work.

You can also conduct a job search from home by consulting trade associations, industry journals, or by letting an international recruiter conduct the search for you. International recruiters maintain files of job seekers and job listings, matching them up worldwide. For more information, read *The Directory of Jobs and Careers Abroad* by Alex Lepinski, which provides job-searching assistance in fields such as agriculture, au pair, banking, computer services, journalism, law, medicine, nursing, oil, mining and engineering, secretarial, translating and interpreting, teaching, transport, tourism and catering, voluntary work, international organizations and the United Nations. Specific contacts are listed by job and by country.

If you have management skills and can live for an extended period of time under difficult conditions and you speak or can quickly learn a second or third language, consider seeking a job managing a project for an international relief or rural development agency. Preference is given to those with Peace Corps or similar experience; turnover is low and the jobs are quite competitive. *The Almanac of International Jobs and Careers* by Ronald and Caryl Krannich contains lists of potential employers such as international organizations, associations, societies and research institutions, nonprofit corporations and foundations, private voluntary organizations and colleges and universities.

Opportunities for Teachers

For qualified English-speaking teachers, jobs may be available at one of over five hundred private international schools around the world. Recruitment fairs for teachers are held annually in the United States, Europe, Africa, and Asia. For up-to-date information, subscribe to *Overseas Academic Opportunities,* a newsletter that lists elementary and secondary school openings worldwide. Contact: **Overseas Academic Opportunities, 949 East Twenty-ninth Street, Brooklyn, NY 11210.**

The Fulbright Teacher Exchange Program provides direct classroom exchanges for U.S. educators at all levels with colleagues in thirty-four countries. Contact: **Fulbright Teacher Exchange Program, 301 Fourth Street, S.W., Washington, DC 20547.**

Opportunities for Medical Personnel

Medical educators are needed who are willing to learn a host country's language and stay from a few months to two years. Contact: **Project Hope, People to People Health Foundation, Carter Hall, Millwood, VA 22646 (703/837-2100).**

Options is a free newsletter from Project Concern, which places doctors, nurses, and health care workers in "Third World" countries and underserved areas of the United States. Contact: **Options, PO Box 85333, San Diego, CA 92138.**

Other Specialized Fields

A few hours of library and bookstore research will yield many specialized books, such as these, for job-seekers:

• *Guide to Cruise Ship Jobs* by George Reilly

• *Directory of Opportunities in International Law* by Paul Brinkman

• *Opportunities in Foreign Languages Careers* by Edwin Arnold.

The Shock of Culture

Culture shock can take many forms. After an extended overseas trip, I am horrified by simple aspects of Western culture that everyone else seems to take for granted. Of course, even when I haven't been traveling, I get horrified by simple aspects of Western culture that most people take for granted. After a trip, it just gets worse.

My journals record some of these observations:

> *I can't stand going into a supermarket. The fluorescent lights, the shelves crammed with an endless variety of products—far too many choices that make me dizzy. It seems a crass display of everything that is excessive about my country. But how long can I avoid going there?*

When away for extended periods of time, technological changes can make the traveler a modern day Rip van Winkle.

> *While I was gone, telephone answering machines took over like an alien menace. My first few days back in the U.S., I called the homes of my good friends, listening to their voices on tape, asking for my voice on tape. I just didn't have the heart to leave a message, so time after time, I just hung up. Later they asked why I hadn't called....*

After observing and adopting the unwritten rules of social behavior in other cultures, you may have to relearn the rules of your own:

> *Almost every time I come back from Mexico, I have to readjust my internal time clock. I mess up my*

friends by making too many dates, too close together.
Somehow I forget that I'm not just walking from
house to house on dusty village streets, stopping to
chat. It takes time to drive from one place to another,
with the stoplights and traffic. And people are very
busy. You can't just drop by without an appointment,
and you shouldn't keep them waiting. It's not okay to
bring one friend along on the date already planned
with another, unless you have checked it out first.

After an exhilarating trip, it's not uncommon to get depressed. You wonder why you came home, even if the reasons seemed very clear while lying on that white sandy beach. It helps to spend time with others who've experienced the same things:

When I left India, I went to Holland to stay with
Geert (just returned from one-and-a-half years in
Asia) and Pede, just back after six months in his
family's home village in Moluku (Indonesia).

The three of us created a halfway house for severe
culture shock. We closed the drapes against cloudy
skies and constant rain and treated ourselves to
nightly slide shows of Indonesia, Thailand and India.
We cooked Moluccan and Indian food, shopping at
little ethnic markets. We kept the heat on high and
wore sarongs in the house. When one had to go to the
bank or post office, the others came along for moral
support.

After traveling, you may feel that you have changed dramatically. Yet everyone treats you as if nothing has happened. It seems that no one understands how you are different or what you've experienced. You have to get used to the idea that you're not so special any more. No longer a unique voyager far from home, you're just another person who belongs.

When I start a conversation with other people on the subway in New York, they look at me like I'm crazy. You're not supposed to make conversation, you're supposed to read the Times, *the* Daily News, *or the* Wall Street Journal. *All the other passengers know everything they might want to know about you by virtue of which newspaper you are reading.*

Two young Australian women got on the subway, and everyone talked to them because they were foreigners. People told stories and gave them advice. Americans are very gracious to foreigners, you know. We're just not so nice to each other.

It's not uncommon to view your former life with a new perspective. For a short while, you opted out of the daily grind. It may be a healthy reaction to feel dismay at jumping back into the fray.

After an extended trip, you may find your values have shifted. Or you may discover the courage to start a new venture you've always dreamed of. Give yourself time to settle down before making any radical changes. In the meantime, enjoy the many things that are great to come home to. Your own bed. Hot water, with choice of shower or bath. Telephones that work. Favorite foods. And good friends.

Easing Re-Entry

The initial elation of returning home may be followed by a period of exhaustion or apathy. Allow plenty of time to readjust. The longer you've been away, the farther (culturally) you've traveled, the more time you should allow for re-entry.

•Don't schedule yourself too tightly when you get back. Allow extra "down" time for sleep, rest, and reflection.

• Ask others to be tolerant of you, your schedule, and your needs during this time.

•Depending on where you've been, the traffic back home

may seem maniacal or quite serene. Be a cautious driver and a careful pedestrian until you've readjusted to local traffic patterns.

•Ease the transition by bringing home a cassette of favorite music or some food or clothing that you enjoyed during your travels.

•Avoid lecturing friends and family on their ignorance, the shallowness of their lives, how lucky or unlucky they are, etc. They won't want to hear that, but they probably will be interested in your reflections on yourself and your own life.

•Don't make huge life decisions immediately after coming home; test them over time.

•Monitor your health; continue antimalarial medication as prescribed; watch for signs of illness or parasites you may have brought home; seek medical care from those familiar with diseases of the places you've come from.

•If upon your return you find aspects of your own culture lacking, work to make positive changes in your own life and in the life of the community in which you live.

A FINAL WORD

My life is a green pasture, bordered by a wooden fence. Each section represents one of my fears; these fears circumscribe my existence.

I regularly visit the perimeter, testing my limits. Each fear that I accept makes my world a bit smaller.

Once in a while, I gather my strength, jump the rails, and run free into a land that beckons me. These are the times I feel most alive.

You may think of the stories in this book as tales of daring. But if you met the women who told them, you'd see that they are a lot like you. If there is one thing they would all want you to know, it is this— "You'll be fine."

If I could say a final word, it would be "Go."

NOTES

Chapter II

1. Maureen Murdock, *A Heroine's Journey* (New York: Random House, 1990), 12.

Chapter V

2. In writing this book, I've found myself choosing from a list of unacceptable terms all commonly used to describe groups of countries in the world. "Underdeveloped," "Third World," and "Oriental" are biased terms that reveal Western ethnocentrism. Language shapes perception—if we are to change our thinking, we need new terminology.

3. Helen Winternitz, *A Season of Stones: Living in a Palestinian Village* (New York: Atlantic Monthly Press, 1991), 6–7.

4. Ibid., 117.

5. Mildred Widmer Marshall, *Two Oregon Schoolma'ams around the World, 1937, via Trans-Siberian Railroad* (Portland, Oregon: Widdy Publishing, 1985), 39.

6. Dervla Murphy, *Muddling Through in Madagascar* (New York: The Overlook Press, 1989), 60–61.

7. Edith Durham, *High Albania* (Boston: Beacon Press, 1987), 258.

8. Joana McIntyre Varawa, *Changes in Latitude : An Uncommon Anthropology* (New York: Atlantic Monthly Press, 1989), 72.

9. Dervla Murphy, *Full Tilt: Ireland to India with a Bicycle* (London: John Murray, 1965), 152–153.

Chapter VI

10. Virginia Urrutia, *Two Wheels & a Taxi: A Slightly Daft Adventure in the Andes* (Seattle, Washington: The Mountaineers, 1987), 177.

11. Ibid., 12.

Adventure Travel

Books and Magazines

Backpacking and Camping in the Developing World by Scott Graham, Wilderness Press, 1988, 148 pages, $11.95.

The Big Book of Adventure Travel: 500 Great Escapes by James C. Simmons, New American Library, 1990, 432 pages, $14.95.

Great Expeditions, a "Journal of Adventure and Off the Beaten Path Travel," in Canada: PO Box 8000-411, Abbotsford, BC V2S 6H1 (604/852-6170); in the U.S. and elsewhere, PO Box 18036, Raleigh, NC 27609 (800/743-3639).

Transitions Abroad Magazine, PO Box 344, Amherst, MA 01004 (800/562-1973).

The Ultimate Adventure Sourcebook: A Complete Resource for Adventure and Sports Travel by Paul McMenamin, Turner Publishing Company, 1992, 400 pages, $29.95.

Organizations

Adventure Associates, PO Box 16304, Seattle, WA 98116 (206/932-8352).

Alaska Women of the Wilderness, PO Box 775226, Eagle River, AK 99577 (907/688-2226).

Backroads Bicycle Touring, 1516 Fifth Street, Berkeley, CA 94710 (800/245-3874).

Fits Equestrian, 2011 Alamo Pintado Road, Solvang, CA 93463 (800/666-3487).

Hawk, I'm Your Sister, Box 9109, Santa Fe, NM 87504 (505/984-2268).

Her Wild Song, Wilderness Journeys for Women, PO Box 6793, Portland, ME 04101.

Lost Coast Llama Caravans, 77321 Usal Road, Whitethorn, CA 95489.

Mountain Mama Pack and Riding Company, Route 3, Box 95G, Santa Fe, NM 87505 (505/986-1924).

Off the Beaten Path, PO Box 83, Vida, OR 97488 (503/896-0222).

Outdoor Vacations for Women Over Forty, PO Box 200, Groton, MA 01450 (508/448-3331).

Paddling South, 4510 Silverado Trail, Calistoga, CA 94515 (707/942-4796 or 942-4550).

Sea Kindly Sailing Charters, 999 First Coast Highway, Box 10, Fernandina Beach, FL 32034 (904/227-3826).

Venus Adventures, PO Box 39, Peaks Island, ME 04108 (207/766-5655).

Womanship, 137 Conduit Street, Annapolis, MD 21401 (301/269-0784).

Womantrek, 1411 East Olive Way, PO Box 20643, Seattle, WA 98102 (800/477-TREK).

Women in the Wilderness, 566 Ottawa Avenue, St. Paul, MN 55107 (612/227-2284).

Woodswomen, 25 West Diamond Lake Road, Minneapolis, MN 55419 (612/822-3809).

Communication

American Express *Traveler's Companion* booklet (800/528-4800).

AT&T's Language Line (800/752-6096).

Contact numbers for obtaining international calling cards are: AT&T—USA Direct: (800/874-4000); MCI—Call USA: (800/444-4444); Sprint (800/877-4646).

Mail Preference Service, Direct Marketing Association, 6 East Forty-third Street, New York, NY 10017.

Overseas Access/EurAide, PO Box 2375, Naperville, IL 60567 (708/420-2343).

Disabled / Handicapped Travelers

Books

Easy Access to National Parks: The Sierra Club Guide for People with Disabilities, Also Useful for Seniors and Families with Young Children by Wendy Roth and Michael Tompane, Sierra Club Books, 1992, 404 pages, $16.00.

Travel for the Disabled: A Handbook of Travel Resources and 500 World Access Guides by Helen Hecker, R.N., Twin Peaks Press, 1991, 192 pages, $14.95.

A World of Options for the '90s: A Guide to International Educational Exchange, Community Service and Travel for Persons with Disabilities, Mobility International USA, 1990, 338 pages, $16.00, PO Box 3551, Eugene, OR 97403.

Organizations

Environmental Traveling Companions, Fort Mason Center Bldg, San Francisco, CA 94123 (415/474-7662).

Wilderness Inquiry, 1313 Fifth Street S.E., Suite 327, Minneapolis, MN 55414 (612/379-3858).

Educational Travel

Books

Travel and Learn, The New Guide to Educational Travel, 2nd Edition by Evelyn Kaye, Blue Penguin Publications, 1992, 346 pages, $23.95.

Organizations

Academic Travel Abroad, 3210 Grace Street N.W., Washington, DC 20007 (202/333-3355).

Elderhostel, 75 Federal Street, Boston, MA 02110 (617/426-8056).

The Flight of the Mind Summer Writing Workshops for Women, 622 S.E. 29th Avenue, Portland, OR 97214 (503/236-9862).

Folkways Institute, 14600 S.E. Aldridge Road, Portland, OR 97236 (800/225-4666).

National Registration Center for Study Abroad,(414/278-0631).

Sea Quest Cruises, 600 Corporate Drive, No. 410, Ft. Lauderdale, FL 33334 (800/223-5688).

Sierra Club, 730 Polk, San Francisco, CA 94109 (415/923-5630).

Swan Hellenic Cruises, 581 Boylston Street, Boston, MA 02116 (800/426-5492).

Health and Safety

Books

The Pocket Doctor: Your Ticket to Good Health While Traveling by Stephen Bezrushka, M.D., The Mountaineers, 1988, 96 pages, $3.95.

Self-Defense: The Womanly Art of Self-Care, Intuition, and Choice, by Debbie Leung, R & M Press, 1991, 175 pages.

Staying Healthy in Asia, Africa, and Latin America: Your Complete Health Guide to Traveling and Living in Less-Developed Regions of the World by Dirk Schroeder, Volunteers in Asia Press, 1988, 168 pages, $7.95.

The Traveller's Guide to Homeopathy by Phyllis Speight, C.W. Daniel Co., 72 pages, $12.95.

Organizations

IAMAT, the International Association for Medical Assistance to Travellers, in the U.S.: 417 Center Street, Lewiston NY 14092 (716/754-4883); in Canada: 1287 St. Clair Ave. West, Toronto, M6E 1B8 (416/652-0137); in New Zealand: PO Box 5049, Christchurch 5; in Switzerland: 57 Voirets, 1212 Grand-Lancy, Geneva.

International Travelers Hotline at the Centers for Disease Control in Atlanta, Georgia (404/332-4559).

Overseas Access/EurAide, PO Box 2375, Naperville, IL 60567 (708/420-2343).

U.S. State Department Citizens Emergency Center (202/647-5225).

Home Exchanges

Books

Trading Places: The Wonderful World of Vacation Home Exchanging by Bill and Mary Barbour, Rutledge Hill Press, 1991, 192 pages, $9.95.

The Vacation Home and Hospitality Exchange Guide by John Kimbrough, Kimco Communications, 1991, 175 pages, $14.95.

Organizations

The ACCESS Foundation for the Disabled, PO Box 356, Malverne, NY 11565 (516/887-5798).

The Invented City, 41 Sutter Street, Suite 1090, San Francisco, CA 94104 (800/788-2489 in U.S., 415/673-0347 worldwide).

Vacation Exchange Club, PO Box 820, Haleiwa, HI 96712 (800/638-3841).

Worldhomes Holiday Exchange, 1707 Platt Crescent North, Vancouver, BC V7J 1X9, Canada (604/987-3262).

Homestays

Organizations

The Experiment in International Living, Federation Office, PO Box 595, Putney, VT 05346 (802/257-7751).

Friendship Force, Suite 575, South Tower, One CNN Center, Atlanta, GA 30303 (404/522-9490).

International Homestays Foreign Language/Study Abroad Programs, Box 903, South Miami, FL 33143 (305/662-1090).

LEX Homestay in Japan, LEX America, 68 Leonard Street, Belmont, MA 02178 (617/489-5800).

Servas, in U.S.:11 John Street,New York, NY 10038 (212/267-0252); in Canada: Michael Johnson, 229 Hillcrest Avenue, Willowdale, Ontario M2N 3P3 (416/221-6434); in England, Scotland, or Wales: Ann Greenough, 55 Jackson Avenue, Leeds, Yorkshire LS8 1NS (0532/665-219); in Ireland: Luke Plunkett, 5 Priory Drive, Stillorgan, County Dublin (01/288-0567); in Australia: Desmond Harkin, 16 Cavill Court, Vermont South, Victoria 3133 (03/803-5004); in New Zealand: Ray Scott, 15 Harley Road, Takapuna (09/489-4442).

Lesbian Travelers

Books

Are You Two...Together? A Gay and Lesbian Travel Guide to Europe by Lindsy Van Gelder and Pamela Robin Brandt, Random House, 1991, 345 pages, $18.00.

Inn Places: Gay and Lesbian Accommodations in the U.S. and Worldwide by Marianne Ferrari, Ferrari Publications, 584 pages, $14.95, PO Box 37887, Phoenix, AZ 85069 (602/863-2408).

International Places of Interest to Women, published annually, Ferrari

Publications, PO Box 37887, Phoenix, AZ 85069 (602/863-2408).

Our World International Gay Travel Magazine, 1104 North Nova Road, Suite 251, Daytona Beach, FL 32117 (904/441-5367).

Out in the World by Shelley Anderson, Firebrand Books, 1991, 52 pages, $4.95, 141 The Commons, Ithaca, NY 14850.

Outing Travelogue, PO Box 4513, Portsmouth, NH 03802.

Women Going Places (formerly *Gaia's Guide International*), Business Factory, 15 Norfolk Place, London W2 1QJ, England (071/706-2434).

Women's Traveller, PO Box 422458, San Francisco, CA 94142-2458.

Organizations

International Gay Travel Association, PO Box 4972, Key West, FL 33041 (303/294-5135).

International Lesbian and Gay Association (ILGA), Information Secretariat, c/o Antenne Rose, 81 rue Marché-au-Charbon, 1000 Brussels, Belgium (32-2-502-2471).

International Lesbian Information Service (ILIS), c/o COC, Rozenstraat 8, 1016 NX Amsterdam, the Netherlands (31-20-23-45-96).

Guides for Travelers over Fifty

Books

Elderhostels: The Students' Choice by Mildred Hyman, John Muir Publications, 2nd Edition, 1991, 290 pages, $15.95.

The 50+ Travelers' Guidebook: Where to Go, Where to Stay, What to Do by Anita Williams and Merrimac Dillon, St. Martin's Press, 1991, 270 pages, $12.95.

Get Up and Go: A Guide for the Mature Traveler by Gene and Adele Malott, Gateway Books, 1989, 325 pages, $10.95.

Unbelievably Good Deals and Great Adventures That You Absolutely Can't Get Unless You're over Fifty by Joan Rattner Heilman, Contemporary Books, 1990, 261 pages, $7.95.

Organizations

Elderhostel, 75 Federal Street, Boston, MA 02110 (617/426-8056).

Partner Travel

Books

Travel for Two: The Art of Compromise by Margot S. Biestman, Pergot Press, 1986, 172 pages, $10.95.

Organizations

Partners-in-Travel, PO Box 491145, Los Angeles, CA 90049 (213/476-4869).

Travel Companion Exchange, PO Box 833, Amityville, NY 11701 (516/454-0880).

Socially, Environmentally, and Culturally Responsible Travel

Books

Alternative Tourism Resource Guide, The Center For Responsible Tourism, 2 Kensington Road, San Anselmo, CA 94960 (415/258-6594).

Cultural Etiquette: A Guide for the Well Intentioned, by Amoja Three Rivers, 1991, 28 pages, $4.95, distributed by Market Wimmin, Box 28, Indian Valley, VA 24105.

Do's and Taboos Around the World: A Guide to International Behavior by Roger Axtell, John Wiley and Sons, 1990, 200 pages, $10.95.

EarthTrips: A Guide to Nature Travel on a Fragile Planet by Dwight Holing, Living Planet Press, 1992, 209 pages, $12.95.

Gestures: Do's and Taboos of Body Language Around the World by Roger Axtell, John Wiley and Sons, 1991, 227 pages, $9.95.

Going Off the Beaten Path: An Untraditional Travel Guide to the U.S. by Mary Dymond Davis, The Noble Press, 1991, 466 pages, $15.95.

The Green Travel Sourcebook: A Guide for the Physically Active, the Intellectually Curious, and the Socially Aware by Daniel Grotta and Sally W. Grotta, John Wiley & Sons, 1992, 304 pages, $14.95.

Handle with Care: A Guide to Responsible Travel in Developing Countries by Scott Graham, Noble Press, 1992, 167 pages, $8.95.

Traveler's Guide to Asian Customs and Manners by Kevin Chambers, Meadowbrook, 1988, 375 pages, $8.95.

Traveler's Guide to European Customs and Manners by Elizabeth Devine and Nancy Braganti, Meadowbrook, 1984, 273 pages, $7.95.

Traveler's Guide to Latin American Customs and Manners by Elizabeth Devine and Nancy Braganti, St. Martin's, 1989, 240 pages, $10.95.

Traveler's Guide to Middle Eastern and North African Customs and Manners by Elizabeth Devine, St. Martin's, 1991, 244 pages, $13.95.

Organizations

American Youth Hostels Kids' Program, Box 28607, Washington DC 20038.

The Center for Global Education, Augsburg College, 731 Twenty-first Avenue South, Minneapolis, MN 55454 (612/330-1159).

The Center for Responsible Tourism, 2 Kensington Road, San Anselmo, CA 94960 (415/258-6594).

Co-op America's Travel Links, 14 Arrow Street, Cambridge, MA 02138 (800/648-2667).

Global Exchange Reality Tours, 2141 Mission Street, No. 202, San Francisco, CA 94110 (415/255-7296).

Plowshares Institute, PO Box 243, Simsbury, CT 06070. Send a self-addressed stamped envelope for information or call (213/651-4303).

Working Assets Travel Service, 230 California St., San Francisco, CA 94111 (800/332-3637).

Solo Travel

Books

Europe for One: A Complete Guide for Solo Travelers by Neil Cresanow, Dutton, 1982, 370 pages, $8.95.

People to People Guides (series includes: *Baltic States, Czechoslovakia, Hungary and Bulgaria, Poland, Romania*) by Jim Haynes, Zephyr Press, 1991, $10.95 each.

Traveling on Your Own: 250 Great Ideas for Group and Solo Vacations by Eleanor Berman, Clarkson Potter Publishers, 1990, 276 pages, $12.95.

Traveling Solo by Jennifer Cecil, Harper Perennial, 1992, 325 pages $13.00.

Newsletters and Magazines

Connecting, a newsletter for solo travelers, 1-1866 West Thirteenth Avenue, Vancouver, BC V6J 2H3, Canada (604/737-7791).

Going Solo—The Newsletter for People Traveling Alone, six issues per year, PO Box 1035, Cambridge, MA 02238.

Great Expeditions, a "Journal of Adventure and Off the Beaten Path Travel," in Canada: PO Box 8000-411 Abbotsford, BC V2S 6H1 (604/852-6170); in the U.S. and elsewhere: PO Box 18036, Raleigh, NC 27609 (800/743-3639).

Special Travel Guides

Air Courier Handbook, by Jennifer Bayse, Big City Books, $10, PO Box 19667, Sacramento, CA 95819.

Arthur Frommer's New World of Travel, Prentice Hall Press, 1991, 429 pages, $16.95.

Buddhist America: Centers, Retreats, Practices, edited by Don Morreale, John Muir Publications, 1988, 400 pages, $12.95.

Camp Europe by Train by Lenore Baken, Ariel Publications, 1991, 501 pages, $14.95.

Courier Air Travel Handbook by Mark I. Field, Thunderbird Press, 1992, 96 pages, $7.95 (800/345-0096).

Expatriate Paris: A Cultural and Literary Guide to Paris of the 1920s by Arlen J. Hansen, Arcade Publishing, 1990, 320 pages, $24.95.

Exploring the West Country: A Woman's Guide by Jennifer Clarke, Virago Press, 1987, 176 pages, £5.95.

Ford's Freighter Travel Guide, by Ford's Travel Guides, 150 pages, $7.50.

Frauenkalender, a feminist calendar and guide to Germany, c/o Emma, Kolpingplatz #1A, 5000 Köln (21-02-82).

Goddess Sites in Europe: Discover Places Where the Goddess Has Been Celebrated and Worshipped Throughout Time by Anneli S. Rufus and Kristan Lawson, Harper San Francisco, 1991, 304 pages, $12.95.

Guide to Cooking Schools, edited by Lawrence Caplan and Dorlene Kaplan, Shaw Guides, 1991, 326 pages, $16.95, 625 Biltmore Way, Coral Gables, FL 33134 (305/446-8888).

Guide to Photography Workshops and Schools, edited by Lawrence Caplan and Dorlene Kaplan, Shaw Guides, 1991, 278 pages $16.95, 625

Biltmore Way, Coral Gables, FL 33134 (305/446-8888).

Guide to Writers Conferences edited by Lawrence Capland and Dorlene Shane, Shaw Guides, 304 pages, $16.95, 625 Biltmore Way, Coral Gables, FL 33134 (305/446-8888).

Gypsying after Forty: A Guide to Adventure and Self-Discovery by Robert W. Harris, John Muir Publications, 1987, 264 pages, $14.95.

In Our Grandmothers' Footsteps: A Virago Guide to London by Jennifer Clarke, Virago Press, 1984, 176 pages, £4.95.

Local Heroines: A Women's History Gazetteer to England, Scotland, and Wales by Jane Legget, Pandora Press, 1988, 382 pages, £8.95.

The Meditation Temples of Thailand: A Guide, by Joe Cummings, Wayfarer Books, 1990, 100 pages, $9.00.

Music Lover's Guide to Europe: A Compendium of Festivals, Concerts and Opera by Roberta Gottesman, John Wiley & Sons, 1992, 448 pages, $14.95.

On Foot, by Adam Nicolson, Harmony Books, 1991, 160 pages, $20.00.

Our Sisters' London : Feminist Walking Tours by Katherine Sturtevant, Chicago Review Press, 1990, 192 pages, $11.95.

The Pilgrim's Guide to the Sacred Earth by Sherrill Miller, Voyageur Press, 1991, 199 pages $14.95.

La Sal de las Doñas, a feminist guide to Spain, calle Valencia #226, 08007 Barcelona.

The Shopper's Guide to Mexico by Steve Rogers and Tina Rosa, John Muir, 1989, 206 pages, $9.95.

Shopping and Traveling in Exotic Asia, Impact Publishing, 1991, 584 pages, $16.95.

A Travel Guide to Jewish Europe by Ben Frank, Pelican, 1992, 400 pages, $15.95.

A Traveler's Key to Sacred England, by John Michell, Alfred A. Knopf, 1988, $18.95.

Virginia Woolf—Life and London, A Biography of Place by Jean Moorcraft Wilson, W.W. Norton, 1988, 256 pages, $18.95.

Walking Switzerland: The Swiss Way, Marcia and Philip Lieberman, The Mountaineers, 1987, 272 pages, $12.95.

Women Travel: Adventures, Advice and Experience, edited by Natania Jansz and Miranda Davies, Prentice Hall, 1992, 532 pages, $12.95.

Organizations

The Festival des Films des Femmes, Maison des Arts, Place Salvador Allende, 94000 Créteil, Paris, France (49-80-38-98).

Frauen Unterwegs (Women on the Move), Potsdamer Strasse 139, 1000 Berline 30, Germany (030/215-1022).

International Feminist Bookfair, Permanent Secretariat c/o Carol Seajay, Feminist Bookstore News, PO Box 882554, San Francisco, CA 94188 (415/626-1556).

Student Travelers

Books

The International Youth Hostel Handbook, by International Youth Hostel Federation, Vol. I—Europe and the Mediterranean, 304 pages, Vol. II—Africa, America, Asia, and Australia, 244 pages, Harper Perennial, 1991, $10.95 each.

Time Out: Taking a Break from School to Travel, Work, and Study in the U.S. and Abroad by Robert Gilpin and Caroline Fitzgibbons, Simon and Schuster, 1992, 333 pages, $12.00.

Organizations

Council on International Educational Exchange (and the CIEE Education Abroad Scholarship Fund for Minority Students), in the U.S.: 205 E. Forty-second Street New York, NY 10017 (212/661-1450); in the U.K.: 28A Poland Street, London W1V 3DB (071/437-7767); in Australia: 222-224 Faraday Street, Carolton, Melbourne, Victoria 3053 (03/347-6911).

International Youth Hostels Association, in the U.S.: American Youth Hostels National Office, PO Box 37613, Washington, DC 20013 (202/783-6161); in Great Britain: Youth Hostels Association of England and Wales, Trevelyan House, 8 St. Stephen's Hill St., Albans, Herts AL1 2DY, England (071/ 836-1036); in Ireland: Irish Youth Hostel Association, An Oige, 39 Mountjoy Square, Dublin 1, Ireland; in Australia: Australian Youth Hostels Association, Level 3, Mallett Street, Camperdown, New South Wales 2050, Australia (61/565-1699); in Canada: Canadian Hostelling Association, 1600 James

Naismith Drive, Suite 608, Gloucester, Ontario K1B 5N4 Canada (613/748-5638).

TravMed—Student Overseas Medical Coverage, (800/732-5309).

Travel Equipment

Cascade Designs, to order the Seal Pak: (800/531-9531).

Magellan's, to order the filtration water purifier cup: (800/962-4943).

Hidden Assets, to order the half-slip with concealed pockets: 1539 First Avenue, Box 20056, New York, NY 10028 (212/439-0693).

Travel with a Child

Books

Adventuring with Children: The Complete Manual for Family Adventure Travel by Nan and Kevin Jeffrey, Avalon House Publishing, 1991, 330 pages, $14.95.

Innocents Abroad: Traveling with Kids in Europe by Valerie Wolf Deutsch and Laura Sutherland, Penguin Books USA, 1991, 500 pages, $15.95.

Kidding Around Books, John Muir Publications, 1990, 63 pages, $9.95 to $12.95.

Take Your Kids to Europe by Cynthia W. Harriman, Mason-Grant Publications, 1991, 222 pages, $12.95.

Travel with Children by Maureen Wheeler, Lonely Planet Publications, 2nd Edition, 1990, 160 pages, $10.95.

Traveling with Children and Enjoying It: A Complete Guide to Family Travel by Car, Plane, and Train, by Arlene Kay Butler, Globe Pequot Press, 1991, 256 pages, $11.95.

Organizations

American Wilderness Experience, PO Box 1486, Boulder, CO 80306, (800/444-0099).

Appalachian Valley Bicycle Touring, PO Box 27079, Baltimore, MD 21230 (410/837-8068).

Grandtravel, c/o The Ticket Counter, 6900 Wisconsin Avenue, No. 706, Chevy Chase, MD 28015 (800/247-7651).

O.A.R.S. Rafting Adventures, Box 67, Angels Camp, CA 95222 (209/736-4677).

Rascals in Paradise, c/o Adventure Express, 185 Berry Street, Suite 5503, San Francisco, CA 94107 (800/443-0799).

Sierra Club Family Outings, 730 Polk Street, San Francisco, CA 94109 (415/776-2211).

Volunteering Abroad

Books

Environmental Vacations: Volunteer Projects to Save the Planet by Stephanie Ocko. John Muir Publications, 2nd Edition, 1992, 248 pages, $16.95.

Vacation Study Abroad, Institute of International Education Books, 1992, 278 pages, $31.95, 809 U.N. Plaza, New York, NY 10017 (212/984-5412).

Volunteer Vacations, A Directory of Short Term Adventures That Will Benefit You...And Others by Bill McMillon, Chicago Review Press, 1991, 399 pages, $11.95.

Organizations

Earthwatch, 680 Mount Auburn St., PO Box 403, Watertown MA 02272 (617/926-8200).

Habitat for Humanity, Habitat and Church Streets, Americus, GA 31709 (912/924-6935).

Operation Crossroads Africa, 150 Fifth Avenue, New York, NY 10011 (212/242-8550).

Smithsonian Research Expedition Program, Smithsonian Institution, 490 L'Enfant Plaza S.W., Rm. 4210, Washington, DC 20560 (202/287-3210).

TERN, the Traveler's Earth Repair Network, Friends of the Trees Society, PO Box 1064, Tonasket, WA 98855.

Youth Service International, 301 North Blount Street, Raleigh, NC, 27601 (800/833-5796).

Women's Travel Writing

Changes in Latitude : An Uncommon Anthropology by Joana McIntyre Varawa, Harper Collins, 1990, 304 pages, $8.95.

Full Tilt : Ireland to India with a Bicycle by Dervla Murphy, Overlook Press, 1987, 288 pages, $9.95.

High Albania by Edith Durham, Virago/Beacon Press, 1987, 352 pages, $10.95.

Klee Wyck, by Emily Carr, Irwin Publishing, 1986, 174 pages.

Muddling Through in Madagascar by Dervla Murphy, The Overlook Press, 1990, 276 pages, $9.95.

My Journey to Lhasa by Alexandra David-Neel, Virago/Beacon, 1988, 300 pages, $12.95.

Nothing to Declare by Mary Morris, Houghton Mifflin, 1988, 250 pages, $17.95.

One Dry Season: In the Footsteps of Mary Kingsley by Caroline Alexander, Random House, 1990, 304 pages, $10.95.

Passionate Quests: Five Modern Women Travelers by Sonia Melchett, Faber & Faber, 1991, 209 pages, $13.95.

A Season of Stones: Living in a Palestinian Village by Helen Winternitz, Atlantic Monthly Press, 1991, 303 pages, $21.95.

Spinsters Abroad: Victorian Lady Explorers by Dea Birkett, Basil Blackwell, 1989, 300 pages, $24.95.

Tracks by Robyn Davidson, Pantheon Books, 1983, 256 pages, $6.95.

A Traveller on Horseback: In Eastern Turkey and Iran by Christina Dodwell, Walker & Co., 1989, 192 pages, $18.95.

Travels in West Africa by Mary Kingsley, C.E. Tuttle, 1976, 270 pages, $7.95.

Two Oregon Schoolma'ams Around the World, 1937, via Trans-Siberian Railroad by Mildred Widmer Marshall, Widdy Publishing, 1985, 120 pages, $6.95.

Two Wheels and a Taxi: A Slightly Daft Adventure in the Andes by Virginia Urrutia, The Mountaineers, 1987, 276 pages, $14.95.

Unbeaten Tracks in Japan by Isabella L. Bird, Virago/Beacon, 1984, 332 pages, $10.95.

Working Abroad

Books and Newsletters

The Almanac of International Jobs and Careers by Ronald and Caryl Krannich, Impact Publications, 1991, 320 pages, $14.95.

The Directory of Jobs and Careers Abroad, by Alex Lepinski, Peterson's Guides, 1991, 342 pages, $14.95.

Directory of Opportunities in International Law by Paul Brinkman, 9th Edition, 1992, $20 ($10 for students), John Bassett Moore Society of International Law, University of Virginia School of Law, Charlottesville, VA 22901.

Directory to Overseas Employment, published annually, PO Box 344, Amherst, MA 01004 (800/562-1973).

Guide to Cruise Ship Jobs by George Reilly, Pilot Books, 1986, 46 pages, $4.95, 103 Cooper Street, Babylon, NY 11702.

How to Get a Job in Europe: The Insider's Guide, edited by Robert Sanborn, Surrey Books, 1991, 550 pages, $15.95.

The International Employment Gazette, published biweekly (800/882-9188).

Opportunities in Foreign Languages Careers by Edwin Arnold, National Textbook Co., 1992, $10.95.

Project Concern's *Options,* PO Box 85333, San Diego, CA 92138.

Overseas Academic Opportunities, a newsletter, 949 East Twenty-ninth Street, Brooklyn, NY 11210.

Teaching English Abroad by Susan Griffith, Peterson's Guides, 1991, 320 pages, $13.95.

Time Out: Taking a Break from School to Travel, Work, and Study in the U.S. and Abroad by Robert Gilpin and Caroline Fitzgibbons, Simon and Schuster, 1992, 333 pages, $12.00.

Transitions Abroad Magazine, published six times a year, PO Box 344, Amherst, MA 01004 (800/562-1973).

Work Your Way Around the World by Susan Griffith, Peterson's Guides, 1991, 432 pages, $16.95.

Organizations

Fulbright Teacher Exchange Program, 301 Fourth Street S.W., Washington, DC 20547.

Project Hope, People to People Health Foundation, Carter Hall, Millwood, VA 22646 (703/837-2100).

Work Abroad program for students: CIEE, 205 East Forty-second Street, New York, NY 10017.

Miscellaneous Topics

Books
How to Find Your Family Roots by Timothy Field Beard, McGraw-Hill, 1977, 1007 pages.

Magazines and Newsletters
Connecting, a newsletter for solo travelers, 1-1866 West Thirteenth Avenue, Vancouver, BC V6J 2H3, Canada (604/737-7791).

Consumer Reports Travel Letter, published monthly, James Davis, Publisher, Consumers Union of the U.S., 256 Washington Street, Mt. Vernon, NY 10553 (914/667-9400). $5 per copy.

ACKNOWLEDGMENTS

A great lesson of my travels is the power of community. A steadfast joy in my life is the community of friends who encircle me with love and support. I wish to express my deepest appreciation to Sarah Ann Cook, Maura Doherty, Karen Harding, Elizabeth Kaufman, Esther Lev, Mimi Maduro, Tom Norton, Sandy Polishuk, Beverly Stein, Ken Walker and Dania Wheeler for encouraging the writer within me.

My heartfelt gratitude goes to many others who provided generous assistance during the writing this book, including Terry Anderson, Nancy Becker, Donna Colvin, Jerry Dahlke, Julie Davis, Kristie Duyckinck, Steven Fulmer, Kathy Hammock, Barbara Head, Mary Heffernan, Burt Lloyd-Jones, Patricia McCaig, Len Norwitz, Kim Osgood and Michael Roach, Jamie Partridge, Susan Paulson, Don Powell and Robin del Rosso, Cathy Siemens and Kip Hard, Rhys Scholes, Ted Sturdevant, Naomia Sweet, Livia Szekely, Lynn Taylor and Peter Thacker, Louise Tippins, Lynn Youngbar, Becky Wilson and Fred Kopatich.

Special thanks to my dear friend and writing coach, Andrea Carlisle, and to the Tuesday Night Writers. Much appreciation to Ellen Shannon and Eleanor Haas for housing, to Harrison Typesetting for office space, and to Nancy Nordhoff and Cottages at Hedgebrook for my stay in the enchanted forest.

I am eternally grateful to Harry Dalgaard for suggesting that I write this book, and to Ruth Gundle for her steadfast support, artful suggestions, and incisive editing in bringing it to publication.

I am indebted to the women named throughout the book who shared their travel stories in personal interviews, to the many readers of the manuscript, to Judy Jewell, Bill McCrae and the staff of Powell's Travel Store and Cris Miller and Sandy Braun of Adventure Associates for research assistance, to Joanie Kirk and Mary Scott for alternative healing therapies, to Jeff Kosokoff and Tony Lafrenz for computer advice and assistance and to Karen Brummel-Smith for medical advice.

Loving thanks to my family, to Connie Dadas for inspiring my journeys, to Doña Tito, Don Victor, Pede, Lia, Mattie, and the families and friends around the globe who took me in and shared their lives.

ABOUT THE AUTHOR

Thalia Zepatos has traveled to twenty-nine countries via plane, train, donkey, camel, oxcart, bicycle, bus, truck, boat, and on foot. She lectures on independent travel for women and is currently at work on a collection of short stories. This is her first book.